Nimitz's Newsman

Waldo Drake and the Navy's Censored War in the Pacific

HAMILTON BEAN

Naval Institute Press
Annapolis, MD

Naval Institute Press
291 Wood Road
Annapolis, MD 21402

Library of Congress Cataloging-in-Publication Data

Names: Bean, Hamilton, author.
Title: Nimitz's newsman : Waldo Drake and the Navy's censored war in the
  Pacific / Hamilton Bean.
Other titles: Waldo Drake and the Navy's censored war in the Pacific
Description: Annapolis, MD : Naval Institute Press, [2024] | Includes
  bibliographical references and index.
Identifiers: LCCN 2024006324 (print) | LCCN 2024006325 (ebook) | ISBN
  9781682477939 (hardcover) | ISBN 9781682470343 (ebook)
Subjects: LCSH: World War, 1939-1945—Pacific Area—Censorship. | World
  War, 1939-1945—Pacific Area. | World War, 1939-1945—Press coverage. |
  Drake, Waldo (William Waldo), 1897-1977. | United States. Office of
  Naval Intelligence—Biography. | Nimitz, Chester W. (Chester William),
  1885-1966—Friends and associates. | United States. Navy—Censorship. |
  World War, 1939-1945—Naval operations, American. | Public relations
  personnel—United States—Biography. | BISAC: HISTORY / Military / Naval
  | HISTORY / Wars & Conflicts / World War II / Pacific Theater
Classification: LCC D799.U6 D733 2024 (print) | LCC D799.U6 (ebook) |
  DDC 940.54/88673—dc23/eng/20240315
LC record available at https://lccn.loc.gov/2024006324
LC ebook record available at https://lccn.loc.gov/2024006325

♾ Print editions meet the requirements of ANSI/NISO z39.48-1992 (Permanence of
Paper).
Printed in the United States of America.

32 31 30 29 28 27 26 25 24   9 8 7 6 5 4 3 2 1
First printing

In memory of Errol

Contents

Foreword

AMERICANS THOUGHT the Pacific War was in good hands because they trusted the U.S. Navy admiral who ran that theater of combat: Chester W. Nimitz.

Nimitz had all the qualities Americans most admire in a leader. He was tall and resolute, yet quiet and unassuming. He had deep roots in America's heartland, hailing as he did from a small town in Texas. He was tough, a fifty-eight-year-old who could whip any young ensign at tennis even after swimming two miles in the morning. He was a man of action who showed up on the front lines to direct combat in his war zone. He was a warrior with a common touch.

Americans accepted this portrait of Admiral Nimitz thanks to the devoted toiling of Nimitz's hot-tempered but very loyal staff aide: Waldo Drake. It was the mercurial Drake, based at the Pacific Fleet's headquarters at Pearl Harbor, who drafted nearly all of Nimitz's speeches, letters, and communiques out of which emerged the indelible image of Nimitz as a "homespun hero." But as Hamilton Bean brings out in this seminal work on Drake, he was far more than Nimitz's "ventriloquist," to use Bean's artful term; he was the Pacific Fleet's first public relations officer (PRO). As such, he played a key role in deciding what Americans would know about the war raging in the Pacific, and what the U.S. Navy was doing to win that war.

Drake seemed a natural for this task. Until he was activated by the U.S. Navy, he had been an admired journalist at the *Los Angeles Times*, where for years he served as maritime editor, covering shipping and the knockabout realm of the Los Angeles–area waterfront. Smart, feisty, a bit profane, pushy when he had to be, Drake not only survived in that rude domain, getting the stories and scoops he wanted, but he flourished, earning the sobriquet "dean of the shipping news reporters." Consummate newsman he may have been, he also wore another hat: officer in the U.S. Naval Reserve. He may have thought he would be doing public relations for the Navy, but in the 1930s and early 1940s the Navy had its own definition of public relations; the Navy put him under the umbrella of the Office of Naval Intelligence (ONI). ONI reshaped Drake's career. Fascinated by ONI's hush-hush world, Drake absorbed the agency's values and emphasis on security, helped it track suspected spies, sometimes using the *Times* to serve ONI ends and, at the same time, promote the Navy. Living in a different era, oblivious to the ethical issues involved, Drake merged his two spheres in a way that would horrify editors today. ONI thought it was fine.

By the time the Imperial Japanese Navy raided Pearl Harbor on December 7, 1941, Drake had already taken a leave of absence from the *Times* and joined the staff of the Pacific Fleet, serving first the luckless Husband Kimmel, and then Chester Nimitz, as a lieutenant commander, the Fleet's first PRO. The job was riddled with contradictions. The Navy had no theory of public relations, just three priorities: publicity for the Navy, censorship, and security (keeping critical information away from the Japanese). As journalists poured into Pearl Harbor to cover the war, Drake charged ahead, working with correspondents in the morning, reviewing their copy, then censoring it in the afternoon. Applying the strictures he had learned at ONI, he put security first, a mindset that led him to use his "red pencil" liberally. Correspondents howled. They griped that Drake was butchering their stories. They also charged that Drake "sat" on stories he didn't like, played favorites, even read their private letters. He was loathed, at times nearly coming to blows with an angry correspondent. The Fleet's press room turned into a mini war zone.

Petty, and predictable, as such incidents may have been, they were symptomatic of what many Navy officials saw as a broader problem: a major breakdown in communication between the Navy and the public. They contended that the larger picture of what the Navy was accomplishing in the Pacific was not getting out. Months into the war the Navy seemed invisible. Many blamed Drake and his overly restrictive approach to censorship. One critic was Frank Knox, Secretary of the Navy and owner of the *Chicago Daily News*, whose Pearl Harbor correspondent kept him apprised of Drake's peccadilloes. When Knox gently suggested to Nimitz he should bring in a new PRO, CINCPAC flatly rejected the idea, stating he was satisfied with the current arrangement; just as Drake protected Nimitz, the admiral shielded his PRO.

Nimitz did so for a reason. He didn't like large organizations; he wanted to keep his public relations staff small, as did the "lone wolf" Drake. CINCPAC could be a puzzle. Much as he benefited from Drake's "folksy" image making, Nimitz didn't like publicity (an attitude reinforced by his cranky boss, Ernest J. King, Chief of Naval Operations and Com-mander-in-Chief, U.S. Navy, who reviled the press). When Drake wanted the Navy to challenge the Army's false claim that its bombers had sunk several Japanese carriers during the Battle of Midway, Nimitz wouldn't let him. The admiral preferred interservice harmony to chest thumping. Knox and his allies in Washington , D.C., faced a problem that went well beyond Drake: the Navy's deep-rooted antipublicity culture.

As Hamilton Bean points out in his study of Drake, that culture began to crack in April 1944, when Knox died suddenly of a heart attack. His successor, James Forrestal, equally concerned about the Navy's low profile in the war, was even more convinced than Knox that Drake had to go. And he was less bashful about taking on Nimitz. A master of organizational maneuver, he contrived to have Drake removed via a time-honored trick: he had him "kicked upstairs," appointed deputy director of the Office of War Information in Washington, D.C. By the summer of 1944, Drake was gone; Forrestal now had his own man at Pearl serving as Nimitz's PRO.

Did the change make any difference? Bean thinks it did. He shows Drake's successor expanding the Fleet's PR staff and beginning to think more strategically about public relations and its long-range goals. Still, he gives Drake some of the credit, noting that his successor's triumphs were built upon foundational pieces laid by Drake. He allows that Drake accrued public relations victories of his own, most notably escorting correspon-dents onto the beaches of three Central Pacific islands, even sustaining a serious head wound on Eniwetok from a Japanese mortar. And, of course, there was Drake's mission to sculpt Nimitz as a "humble hometown hero," an image that endures to this day and that may be, Bean suggests, "Drake's greatest strategic communication legacy." Fine as his loyalty to Nimitz may have been, it wasn't enough; in Bean's judgment, Drake didn't become sufficiently independent of Nimitz to grow and develop as a public relations strategist. The Navy's image suffered as a result.

In this colorful and thoroughly researched work, Bean explores and opens up a crucial area of the Navy's wartime culture that has been slighted, if not altogether overlooked, in most histories of the Pacific War. He brings alive the press battles of the early 1940s, sheds new light on the thinking and the sometimes curious decision making of Admiral Nimitz, and charts the zigzag course that led to the modern public affairs program the Navy has in place today.

Elliot Carlson
July 2023
Silver Spring, MD

Preface

I BEGAN THIS PROJECT in 1994 as a nineteen-year-old undergraduate history major at the University of New Mexico (UNM). Work on the project stopped after I completed a related thesis in 1996 (postgraduation plans awaited), but I took it up again in August 2020 after a conversation with Padraic (Pat) Carlin at the Naval Institute Press. At one point in my life—ages twenty to thirty-five—Waldo Drake was technically my step-grandfather. My father, Reynold Bean, married Waldo's daughter, Errol Drake, in 1995. It was the third marriage for them both. They divorced in 2010. Nine years later Errol died, with Reynold following the year after, in 2020. I never knew Waldo Drake; he died in 1977. But I never forgot about him, and in a strong sense, I owed him, too.

In the early 1990s, Errol told me about Drake: a smart, handsome, and fierce-tempered journalist who worked for the *Los Angeles Times* for forty years. During World War II, he took a hiatus from the *Times* to serve as the U.S. Pacific Fleet's first public relations officer (PRO). After the war, Drake covered many of the twentieth century's most important events, first as the *Times'* Asiatic correspondent and later as its European bureau chief. I once glimpsed three of Drake's passports; nearly every page was black with ink from all the countries he'd visited. A note of condolence written by the *Times'* owner, Otis Chandler, to Drake's widow Mary in 1977 described Drake as a legend in the newsroom.

So when I learned Drake was "literally hated" by correspondents assigned to cover the war against Japan, I couldn't square these two images of him: admired *Times* newsman and despised Navy PRO. In 1996, when I wrote a letter to one of the correspondents who knew Drake during the war, I received a one-sentence letter in reply: "If you can't say something good about a man, shut up."

In fact, I am not the first person to be intrigued enough by stories about Drake to delve into his wartime role. In her 1946 Stanford University master's thesis on wartime Navy public relations in the Pacific, Irma Cunha wrote that while working at the *Honolulu Star-Bulletin* during the war, some of the correspondents she interacted with were "vehement in their criticisms" of Navy censorship.[1] As Fleet PRO, Drake bore the brunt of these criticisms. Cunha resolved after the war to "understand fully just what problems actually existed . . . in order to determine the degree of legitimacy of complaints uttered by correspondents."[2] The picture is complicated. Along with the criticisms, accounts of Drake's loyalty, bravery, kindness, and professional skill are also present in the historical record. Despite his slight snarl, one sees in Drake's eyes the compassion that marked his nature, as depicted in the portrait of him included in this book by noted artist McClelland Barclay. Barclay sketched the portrait of Drake as a thank you to him sometime before July 18, 1943, when Barclay was reported missing in action after the LST 342 landing ship he was on board was torpedoed in the Solomon Islands.

Unlike Drake's assistant PRO, Lt. Cdr. James Bassett, USNR, who kept a diary and wrote a book, *Harm's Way* (later turned into the 1965 movie *In Harm's Way*), Drake left behind few traces of what he thought about his wartime experience. It is a notable coincidence that Drake followed Adm. Chester W. Nimitz, USN, in declining to write an autobiography. As a result, and even though in the mid-1990s I had attempted to understand who Drake was, he remained a mystery to me. I never could shake the feeling I hadn't uncovered the whole story about his interactions with Nimitz.

Nearly all the people mentioned in this book are dead, and while the dead cannot outright disagree with you, they certainly can provoke your self-doubt about what the historical record reveals and conceals concerning their motives and intentions. My formal training in academic history ended upon my graduation from the University of New Mexico in 1996, and I don't pretend this book represents a traditional historical study. It is mostly an interpretation of other people's histories, memoirs, and memories, but it is one I hope will add a new perspective on Navy public relations in the Pacific during World War II. My doctoral training is in organizational communication and gives my investigation of Drake's wartime role a novel twist. In 2014, I earned Accreditation in Public Relations from the Public Relations Society of America, and I have taught undergraduate and graduate courses in strategic communication since 2009. These experiences have helped me better understand the dilemmas Drake confronted. If nothing else, they have taught me how organizational politics can distort U.S. national security decision making.

Both Pat Carlin and Adam Kane at the Naval Institute Press asked me why Drake's relationship with Nimitz was important and worth writing a book about. The answer is simultaneously easy, complicated, and personal. The easy answer is it helps fill in missing pieces of the puzzle concerning why Navy public relations stumbled following the Pearl Harbor attack and why problems persisted until late 1944. The more complicated answer is it helps account for the transformation of Navy public relations in 1945 and in the war's aftermath. Navy public affairs (today's official moniker) has developed in part as a response to the problems Drake and Nimitz's relationship exemplified. The personal answer is I owed this book to the people who helped me back in 1994–1996 and hoped I would one day write it.

Given my connection to the Drake family, some might wonder whether my motive in writing this book was to try to rehabilitate Drake's image. His story has enticed, inspired, and shocked me, and I believe more students of World War II should know about it. But ultimately, as the late communication scholar H. L. Goodall Jr. once taught me, the reason why Drake's relationship with Nimitz is important and worth writing a book about is, like any good story, it can help us better understand our own.

Acknowledgments

T HE PEOPLE WHO FIRST assisted me with this project in the mid-1990s must be thanked at the outset, even though most of them are now gone. Still, I would like to acknowledge the help of Frank Tremaine, United Press; Ann Hassinger and the staff of the U.S. Naval Institute; Patsy Wagstaff; John and Barbara Drake; Helen McDonald; Paula Usery and the staff of the Nimitz Museum; the staff of the Naval Operational Archives; Dan Lewis and the staff of the *Los Angeles Times*; Robert Miller, United Press; Charles Arnot, United Press, later ABC; Alec MacDonald, *Honolulu Advertiser*; Elizabeth McIntosh, *Scripps-Howard Newsletter* and *Honolulu Star-Bulletin*. Rear Adm. Donald Showers, USN (Ret.); Capt. Howell Lamar, USNR (Ret.); Sam Sorrinson; Sunny Paullus; and Karen Gash and the staff of the University of Nevada Archives. In addition to Dr. Ferenc Szasz, University of New Mexico professors who provided helpful advice include Dr. Melissa Bokovoy (who graciously provided it again in 2023), Dr. Charlie Steen, Dr. Timothy Moy, and Dr. Paul Hutton. Dr. Brooke Evans provided vital help with the project in 1994–1996, and our son, Max, has greatly assisted me with this book.

Without the support and patience of Pat Carlin and Adam Kane at the Naval Institute Press, completing this book would have been impossible. Thank you also to the Institute's reviewers: Paul Stillwell provided incredibly detailed feedback and improvements to the manuscript, and Dr. Ryan Wadle provided keen insights, corrections, and suggestions as well.

The COVID-19 pandemic prevented archival research for more than a year and complicated access throughout the project's duration. Several people assisted in more recent research and writing. Dr. Amanda Nell Edgar provided invaluable editing help. Also assisting in research and/or writing were Nathaniel Patch, Paul Cogan, and the staff of the National

Archives at College Park; Laura Waayers and the staff of the Naval History and Heritage Command; the staff of the Library of Congress; Ron Drabkin; Lt. Col. Charles Patterson, USA; Andy and Debbie McKane; Greg Wilsbacher; Glenna Witt Sexton; Chris Russell; Richie Plaisance; Randy Thompson and the staff of the National Archives at Riverside; the staff of the Huntington Library; the staff of the American Heritage Center at the University of Wyoming; Rear Adm. Brent Baker, USN (Ret.); Rear Adm. Tom Jurkowsky, USN (Ret.); Dr. Matthew Seeger; and especially Elliot Carlson, whose volumes on Joe Rochefort and Stanley Johnston inspired my re-engagement with this project and whose contributions convinced me it was viable.

At the University of Colorado, I would like to thank Dr. Bryan Taylor, Dr. Sarah Fields, Dr. Sonja Foss (emerita), James McNeil, Dr. Lisa Keränen, and Dr. Stephen Hartnett (fellow traveler in dusty archives and complex narratives of America's fraught history in Asia). Dr. Lorna Hutchison provided helpful writing suggestions. Portions of the book were completed in spare moments during my summer 2021 visiting professorship at Kyoto University's Disaster Prevention Research Institute (DPRI), and I am thankful for the help of Dr. Ana Maria Cruz, Dr. Mika Shimizu, and Kyoto University's faculty, students, and staff. Some of Drake's grandchildren, whom I'd known before, supported this project and made it possible; thank you to Sarah Colley and Mike Mikula, Leslie Colley, Scott Drake, and Jennifer Drake Schroeder. I received immense help writing this book, but any errors are mine alone.

Finally, I am grateful to my loved ones Lauren, Max, and Sophia for their support and helpful observations. Lauren's frequent insights and encouragement were especially appreciated. I know my father, Reynold, would have been delighted to read this book and talk about it with me. I like to think in some mysterious way, we will get that chance, and I hope Waldo and Errol will be there to join us.

Abbreviations

CHINFO	Chief of Information and the Office of Information
CIA	Central Intelligence Agency
CINCPAC	Commander-in-Chief Pacific Fleet
CINCUS	Commander-in-Chief United States Fleet
CNO	Chief of Naval Operations
COMINCH	Commander-in-Chief United States Fleet
COMSOPAC	Commander, South Pacific Area
CPO	Chief Petty Officer
IJN	Imperial Japanese Navy
I-V(S)	Officers of the Volunteer Reserve appointed for special intelligence duties
LST	Landing Ship, Tank
LVT	Landing Vehicle Tracked
NBC	National Broadcasting Company
ONI	Office of Naval Intelligence
OPI	Office of Public Information
OPR	Office of Public Relations
OWI	Office of War Information
PRO	Public Relations Officer
ROTC	Reserve Officers' Training Corps
SECNAV	Secretary of the Navy
USAFISPA	United States Army Forces in the South Pacific Area
USN	United States Navy
USNPAA	United States Navy Public Affairs Association
USNR	United States Naval Reserve
WAVES	Women Accepted for Volunteer Emergency Service

Introduction

> It is in this nether region of organizational life—the inter-
> section of good intentions, selfishness, power, concern for
> others, survival, retreat, advocacy, and collaboration—that
> decisions about public relations are born.
>
> —Christopher Spicer

For Capt. William Waldo Drake, USNR, February 18, 1944, was a mix of anticipation, exuberance, and pain. At dawn, he'd stood on the signal bridge of the USS *Rocky Mount* (AGC 3), watching Operation Downside transform Eniwetok Island into shades of red, yellow, and black smoke.[1] A half-dozen cruisers and destroyers fired upon the seven hundred Japanese troops huddled in their foxholes and trenches. The subsequent bombing and strafing from Navy Avengers thickened the gray haze above the island. The bombardment dust wafted over the *Rocky Mount*, burning Drake's eyes and desiccating his throat. The 22nd Marines and 106th Infantry Regiment—recruits mostly from Upstate New York—went ashore at 0917 only to find that the Japanese troops had seemingly vanished.

Now Drake scanned the smoky horizon from the brand-new LVT motoring toward the beach a few hundred yards offshore. A squall struck, and the bow of the landing craft plunged under the whitecaps, but it held its position in the line of LVTs and Higgins Boats plodding forward. The third wave of the amphibious assault on the cigar-shaped island had begun at 1000. Drake eagerly led a dozen correspondents toward the fight, presuming

1

that any major resistance the troops encountered near the beach would be mopped up by the time they arrived. There would be just enough danger to scratch the correspondents' itch for action, but not enough for them to accuse Drake of trying to get them killed. As the U.S. Pacific Fleet's public relations officer (PRO), he needed to facilitate press coverage of the assault while not deliberately putting correspondents in harm's way. Nevertheless, some of the newsmen had seen more combat than the troops on Eniwetok, and attempting to keep a correspondent safe could be viewed as an insult.

Drake, forty-six years old, was notorious for his "grim visage" and "brusque" manner when correspondents showed up at the public relations office at CINCPAC headquarters in Pearl Harbor.[2] He believed he needed to control what correspondents were permitted to write or they'd reveal secrets that damaged operational security. Hal O'Flaherty from the *Chicago Daily News* stood near Drake in the damp, shuddering transport, but Drake wasn't friends with O'Flaherty or any of the other correspondents headed toward the beach. He'd interacted with them countless times since the war had begun, but the nature of those interactions kept him from being their friend. As Fleet PRO, Drake facilitated their reporting, but he also censored their stories for security. He even scrutinized their personal mail. Some correspondents found the deletions from Drake's red pencil and his privacy invasions intolerable. Drake professed to have a cooperative relationship with the press, but correspondents often found themselves at "swords' points" with the PRO.[3] Twenty-seven months into the war, Drake still hadn't figured out how to keep irate correspondents from complaining about him to their civilian bosses or to his own bosses in the Navy.

The web of press-military relationships Drake confronted was complicated. O'Flaherty had been managing editor at the *Daily News* in 1940, when his boss at the newspaper, owner Frank Knox, appointed by President Roosevelt to serve as Secretary of the Navy, called on him to join the Navy's new Office of Public Relations (OPR) in Washington, D.C. Knox asked Adm. Chester W. Nimitz, then chief of the Bureau of Navigation (the Navy's personnel bureau), to expedite O'Flaherty's commission but promised his managing editor he could return to the *Daily News* after six months at OPR.[4] Now, four years later, O'Flaherty was covering the war in the Pacific from the front lines. Drake may have thought it wise to keep

O'Flaherty close on the chance he might provide a favorable report about him to Secretary (and *Daily News* owner) Knox. Drake knew that unflattering reports about him reached the secretary. Those reports accused him of indifference, impulsiveness, favoritism, and especially excessive control.[5]

As the cacophonous line of landing craft neared the beach, all that didn't matter: Drake felt glorious. One correspondent would later write that everything about that day had a "fantastic and unexpected quality."[6] The sea spray hitting Drake's face carried him back to his yacht racing days in Southern California. In 1928, he'd participated in a race from Los Angeles to Ensenada, Mexico, and back. His new wife, Mary, and her sister Patsy greeted Drake as he wearily stepped onto the beach at the conclusion of the race, his nose bleeding from a severe sunburn, his lips swollen and cracked. His eyes, however, sparkled with joy. The women asked him how he'd found the race. "Marvelous! Absolutely marvelous!" he exclaimed.[7] He'd come a long way from his traumatic childhood in Yellow Springs, Ohio, where his mentally ill mother had been institutionalized and his father had abandoned the family. As a young man, Drake had moved to Long Beach, California, where the Pacific Ocean had healed and transformed him.

Now, here he was again, cutting across the Pacific, but the stakes were deadly and the prize profound: a victory for the Navy he loved. He was shepherding a group of correspondents who would, he hoped, appreciate him for ensuring they witnessed the battle, landing with the troops on this narrow atoll in the Marshall Islands. The Navy was on its way to knocking the Japanese out of the Central Pacific and sailing triumphantly into Tokyo Bay.

This was Drake's second time riding in a landing craft aimed at an island full of Japanese soldiers, and his confidence showed. Less than a month earlier, he'd joined the troops and correspondents during the capture of Kwajalein atoll. For the first twenty-six months of the war, Drake had sat at a desk in the public relations office at CINCPAC headquarters. But Nimitz had recently promoted him to captain, and with the Central Pacific campaign underway, Drake now proudly sailed with the Fleet. Behind him were the chaotic days following the Pearl Harbor attack when, as lieutenant commander, he'd struggled to control the news that much of the Fleet had been critically damaged. Some Navy officers blamed

Drake for botching the reporting of the Navy's stunning victory at Midway in June 1942 as well as for compromising the security of the cryptographic secrets that had facilitated it.[8] Despite Drake's fumbles, Nimitz had supported and protected his PRO. Drake, in turn, loyally protected his commander-in-chief.

Seemingly behind Drake, too, were the major conflicts with correspondents. He'd butted heads with the *Chicago Daily News'* Robert Casey, who'd accused Drake of assigning "security guards" to spy on him.[9] The United Press' Frank Tremaine had screamed at him over a disputed censorship decision.[10] Tremaine wasn't the only one. The *Daily News'* Barney McQuaid had pushed Drake past his breaking point.[11] Drake's unusually raspy voice led the correspondents to mock him behind his back. They even composed songs about him. One was set to the music of *H.M.S. Pinafore*: "Oh, just stay at home and never go to sea, and you'll be a Captain in old Chet's Navy." ("Old Chet" referred to Nimitz).[12]

But the Battle of Tarawa in November 1943 had been a turning point, and Drake had earned the respect of some of the correspondents who'd previously been critical of him. The stories from Tarawa that Drake and the CINCPAC censors approved for release were brutal, but they sold newspapers. A group of distraught mothers of dead U.S. Marines objected to the coverage, protesting outside the Navy Department, but Drake heard few complaints from the brass in Washington, D.C., about the gory dispatches. In fact, one OPR official would later say that Fleet public relations during the battle had facilitated "the greatest job of coverage in the history of warfare."[13] Drake's earlier reticence in publicizing news that could injure American morale had given way to the realities of war in the Central Pacific. Correspondents, editors, and even some Navy officials had demanded less sanitized press coverage, and Drake had delivered.

When he arrived at the rendezvous point on Eniwetok Island behind the fire trench seventy-five yards up from the beach, Drake learned that the troops had begun moving in groups north and south as the guns from the destroyers cleared the way ahead of them. A half-dozen correspondents, all hungry for news, converged on the rendezvous point. His PRO position officially required him to provide "earnest cooperation with all accredited civilian and combat correspondents," but given the mix of old animosities and new objectives, Drake now had to decide what "earnest cooperation" meant amid the unfolding battle.[14]

※※※※※※※※※※

Waldo Drake served as the first PRO for the U.S. Pacific Fleet. When he began duty in June 1941, he was an admired maritime editor for the *Los Angeles Times* and a Naval Reserve officer appointed to intelligence duties. His tenure as Fleet PRO, however, proved tumultuous. This book delves into the circumstances that led to Drake's appointment as Pacific Fleet's PRO, the struggles that occurred during his time on the CINCPAC staff, and the events that led to his removal. Examining Drake's relationship with Nimitz sheds light on this little-known chapter of naval history.

Drake's absence from most naval history books about World War II in the Pacific is unsurprising; public relations is known for its invisible hand. As Edward Bernays, one of the field's pioneers, wrote in his 1928 book *Propaganda*, "We are governed, our minds are molded, our tastes formed, and our ideas suggested, largely by men we have never heard of . . . [it] is they who pull the wires that control the public mind."[15] Drake's "pull of the wires" cannot be ignored. While Nimitz's innumerable letters, speeches, and communiques during World War II are attributed to him, many were first drafted by Drake, whose duties required it. But Drake's work went well beyond ventriloquizing Nimitz. His approach to public relations influenced Nimitz's decision-making, shaped the Fleet's organizational structure, personnel, and public relations practices, and helped determine what news and publicity reached the American public. Navy officer and historian Etta-Belle Kitchen once remarked that Drake was "as close to Admiral Nimitz as any officer on his staff."[16] For students of World War II in the Pacific, it is essential to understand who Drake was and his role in the rise of Navy public relations. Although often overlooked, his contributions were significant and their implications far-reaching.

Today, Navy public affairs is an established occupational field with strong professional traditions and practices. The establishment of the United States Navy Public Affairs Association (USNPAA) in 1994 is evidence of the field's rich heritage. Of the field's history, the USNPAA's website states, "The U.S. Navy Public Affairs Officer Specialty traces its beginning to World War II when civilian journalists, public relations people and photographers were given naval reserve line officer commissions (1105) and served as Public Relations Officers (PROs) or as Enlisted Naval Correspondents (ENCs). At the end of the war, these reservists were released from active duty and returned to civilian life."[17] Similar to the USNPAA's website, Navy histories acknowledge that World War II was the origin of public affairs' transformation, but the actual *catalyst* of that transformation is seldom identified. The evidence assembled in this book supports the thesis that the relationship that developed between Drake and Nimitz served as that catalyst. Specifically, their relationship permitted the conflation of public relations and censorship activities, stymied the flow of news and publicity from the Pacific theater, and allowed public relations problems to fester until late 1944. The 1945 and postwar transformation of Navy public affairs occurred largely in response to these conditions.

Scholarship investigating Navy public relations during World War II has focused on the dynamics among the leaders of organizations in Washington, D.C.[18] These organizations included OPR, the Office of War Information (OWI), which dealt with military affairs and political propaganda, and the Office of Censorship, which handled all wartime information (civilian or military) developed *inside* the United States. Yet the wartime history of U.S. *military* public relations and censorship has remained, as historian John McCallum has put it, "surprisingly elusive."[19] Over the years, fragments of the history of the Pacific Fleet's role within the larger story of wartime Navy public relations have appeared in books, memoirs, and theses. In perhaps the most thorough account available, Robert Dale Klinkerman's 1972 thesis aimed to "document the changes that occurred in U.S. Navy public relations policies and practices during World War II and, in so doing, to investigate any causal relationships between these changes and basic Navy attitudes toward the public relations function."[20] By contrast, the focus of this book is narrower: it investigates the role Drake played as Pacific Fleet PRO in the Navy's censored war in the Pacific. To do so, it follows Drake into what organizational theorist Christopher Spicer calls the "nether region of organizational life—the intersection of good intentions, selfishness, power, concern for others, survival, retreat, advocacy, and collaboration," the place where "decisions about public relations are born."[21]

This investigation sheds light on lingering questions. Specifically, why did the Navy, which had established a professional and effective public relations capability late in the interwar period, see the Pacific become a hive of public relations problems in the aftermath of the Pearl Harbor attack? (Readers unfamiliar with these problems will find them described in subsequent chapters.) Why did Drake remain on Nimitz's staff despite his role in underpublicizing the Navy's victory at Midway? How was Drake able to survive the related Stanley Johnston fiasco, an event that nearly compromised the Navy's most secret intelligence-gathering program? Johnston, a correspondent for the *Chicago Tribune*, implied in a front-page story that the Navy had cracked Japan's secret code, leading to the victory at Midway (a conclusion a careful reader could derive). Drake "appeared to make the U.S. Navy complicit in an offence that Navy officials regarded as a severe breach of national security."[22] Why did it take nearly three years to adequately address the Fleet's public relations problems? These questions are complex and complicated, but the evidence assembled in this book points to the critical role Drake and Nimitz's relationship played in determining their answers.

Portions of Drake's story have recently been revealed in the volume *The War Beat, Pacific: The American Media at War against Japan*, by Steven Casey, published in 2021.[23] Casey focuses on the Pacific War from the correspondents' perspective, toggling between Nimitz and MacArthur's commands, emphasizing how Drake's overzealousness for security hindered the correspondents' work. Casey focuses intensely on the Central Pacific campaign. Casey's volume shines a spotlight on the correspondents, but this volume keeps the spotlight on Drake. Recent scholarship concerning Nimitz has focused on his leadership abilities. Craig Symonds' 2022 volume, *Nimitz at War: Command Leadership from Pearl Harbor to Tokyo Bay*, shows how Nimitz's combination of experience, interpersonal sensitivity, and calculated risk-taking made him the ideal commander of Pacific forces.[24] Trent Hone's 2022 volume, *Mastering the Art of Command: Admiral Chester W. Nimitz and Victory in the Pacific*, develops and applies concepts from organizational theory to explain how Nimitz's "strategic artistry" characterized his effective leadership style.[25] *Nimitz's Newsman* draws inspiration from both Symonds' and Hone's volumes to ask how Nimitz's leadership intersected with the Fleet public relations. It finds that a web of competing loyalties created "moral mazes" for Nimitz and Drake in dealing with officials in Washington, D.C., and correspondents in Pearl Harbor.[26] To make sense of these mazes, the Navy in World War II can be understood as a patrimonial organization. Despite its commitment to rational-legal bureaucracy (a system characterized by the separation of offices from persons), the Navy—like all large-scale organizations—was marked by factions, alliances, and all varieties of human behavior. Credit and blame were pushed upward or downward to shape perceptions, advance interests, and protect one's promotability. While he was a supremely effective commander, Nimitz was not immune to these organizational forces.

Nimitz once stated that the first six months of the war were the most anxious and uncertain for him.[27] Drake, of course, had no way of knowing in early 1942 which way the winds would blow, so it is important to understand the decisions he made and to assess what influence they might have had if events in the Pacific had unfolded otherwise.[28] Either way, Drake was caught in a vise some contemporary public relations practitioners would find familiar. On one side were the mild-mannered Nimitz and his superior, the short-tempered Adm. Ernest J. King. Both men embodied the Navy's long-standing avoidance of publicity and the press. On the other side were OPR's leaders—Adm. Arthur Hepburn, USN, and later Capt. Leland Lovette, USN—and their superior, Secretary Knox (later Forrestal), who continually pushed Navy officers to be more conscious of the value of publicity. All these officials occasionally displayed inconsistency, contradiction, and confusion in their public relations preferences and activities, yet Drake was caught in the middle of competing impulses and had to walk a fine line. Err too much on the side of Nimitz and King, and he would find himself battling correspondents, their editors, and publicity-conscious OPR officials. Err too much on the side of OPR officials and the Secretary of the Navy, and Drake risked releasing information that might spark Nimitz's displeasure or King's wrath. At the end of the day, Drake was Nimitz's newsman, and he would tilt toward Nimitz's (and thus King's) preferences in performing his public relations duties.

The few accounts of Nimitz's leadership that mention Drake offer competing images of the PRO. Some accounts depict Drake as a hapless newsman hailing from the *Times* who had little public relations experience and was placed in the untenable position of having to assist correspondents despite Nimitz's ambivalence toward the press.[29] Other accounts imbue Drake with more agency; he is depicted as having an agenda, being out in front of Nimitz on censorship decisions and in tight—almost dictatorial—control of press reporting.[30] This latter depiction sees Nimitz occasionally reining in Drake's overzealousness. The historical record supports both depictions because Drake possessed a liminal occupational identity: he was a journalist, a Navy public relations officer, a censor, and a reserve intelligence officer. Drake embodied all these occupational identities at the same time. These competing identities help account for the divergent depictions of Drake's wartime role. He was tasked with joining together a forward-looking Navy public relations organization (OPR) with a censorship apparatus described as "haphazard," "convoluted," and "unusually complicated."[31] Yet if we acknowledge Drake's oscillating behavior, how should historians account for it? Did it stem from his personality and the way he handled his competing occupational identities, or was the structure of Navy public relations itself partly responsible? What role did Nimitz play? This book provides answers.

⚙⚙⚙⚙⚙⚙⚙⚙⚙⚙

This story draws upon scholarship concerning public relations and organizational studies. Today, public relations is defined as "a strategic communication process that builds mutually beneficial relationships between organizations and their publics."[32] This contemporary definition sits alongside an older, more general understanding of public relations as the attempt to control the ideas, attitudes, and behaviors of publics.[33] Enlightened images of "mutually beneficial relationships" were mostly absent in May 1941 when the Navy established the OPR (Office of Public Relations) under the Secretary's auspices in anticipation of war. By that point, public relations for the Navy had become principally about protecting military secrets. A February 8, 1941, Navy communique warned the press, "A sentence spoken or printed might wreck an arsenal, sink a battleship or destroy the lives of many."[34] But the Navy had a much broader concept of public relations just a few years earlier.

Ryan Wadle argues in *Selling Sea Power: Public Relations and the U.S. Navy, 1917–1941* that during the interwar years, the Navy had built an effective Public Relations Branch, skilled at handling crises, supporting journalists, and generating publicity. "When war came in December 1941, there was no need to create a PR organization from scratch because, unlike any other time in the navy's history, navy public relations had long since been mobilized," Wadle writes.[35] But Wadle's account stops in 1941, just on the eve of war and as OPR was being formed. Because Navy public relations seemed well-positioned to handle the looming war, it is vital to understand why accounts from historians, correspondents, and officials depict the period from 1941 to 1944 as rife with problems, especially arbitrary censorship and a lack of news and publicity from the Pacific.

Historian Brayton Harris speculates in *Admiral Nimitz: The Commander of the Pacific Ocean Theater* that problems arose because the Navy had not, in fact, adequately prepared for the public relations crisis caused by the Pearl Harbor attack. Harris claims Drake was given no public relations roadmap and was largely "making it up as he went along; there were no established rules for dealing with reporters."[36] If Harris' account is accurate, then what happened? The answer provided in this book is twofold. First, in 1941, the Navy began to reorganize its public relations function in anticipation of war, but the West Coast and Hawaiian naval districts, and especially the Pacific Fleet itself, were insufficiently prepared. As a measure of the Navy's support for Fleet public relations, officials had put in place precisely one individual to handle everything: Drake. OPR officials grasped how the outbreak of war would require adaptation to ensure a sufficient flow of news and publicity from the Pacific theater, but the Navy's topmost commanders disallowed adequate expansion at the Fleet level. Second, OPR officials in Washington, D.C., tolerated the conflation of public relations and censorship that occurred in the Pacific under Drake, and with Nimitz's approval. This conflation caused bitter, intractable conflicts between Drake and the correspondents. Historians agree the Navy didn't develop truly effective public relations for the Fleet until late 1944.[37]

Censorship is defined here as the suppression or prohibition of information that threatens security.[38] Drake was Nimitz's PRO *and* his press censor, although this latter role Drake performed because the Fleet's intelligence officer, Lt. Cdr. Edwin Layton, USN, delegated those duties to him. Drake's dueling occupational identities were not easily managed. He assisted correspondents in gathering news but then immediately censored their copy for security. While correspondents believed they supported the Navy in not informing the enemy of Allied military capabilities, activities, and intentions, the role of the press in a democratic society cannot always be reconciled with national security strictures. How did Drake manage his competing responsibilities to the Navy, to the correspondents he assisted, and to the country? How did Drake understand the meaning of security in relation to his duties? What can contemporary public relations professionals learn from the choices he made? This book provides answers.

The tension Drake confronted in attempting both to be loyal to Nimitz and to serve the public interest illustrates an enduring ethical dilemma confronting public relations professionals. The Public Relations Society of America's Professional Values state, "We serve the public interest by acting as responsible advocates for those we represent."[39] But assessing how responsible advocacy is performed in wartime is an ideological and political question. Spicer argues, "The organizational public relations function is situated at the fault line where organizational and public interests intersect, sometimes in collusion, often in conflict."[40] Given what we now know about World War II, was Drake a responsible advocate for both the Navy and the public interest? In what ways do his actions reveal an answer to that question? Scrutinizing how Drake performed his duties as Nimitz's newsman helps readers better understand how competing personal, occupational, and patriotic loyalties generate inevitable dilemmas for strategic communicators.[41]

※※※※※※※※※※※

In presenting this story, I draw upon archival material, interviews with those who knew Drake, memoirs, letters, photos, and film.[42] To some extent, however, all historical biographers rely on the fictions of presence, coherence, and continuity in constructing their subjects, and I have taken artistic license in interpreting blank spaces in the historical record.[43] Specifically, I have speculated about Drake's thoughts as well as imagined scenes based on archival or published material. All direct quotations, however, have originated from reporting, letters, memoranda, books, or other documentary sources. The chapters that follow tell the story of Nimitz's newsman to pinpoint the answers it provides to questions concerning the Navy's censored war in the Pacific during World War II.

1

The Dean of the Shipping News Reporters

Should war come tomorrow, the wrath of America against her own leaders would be fearful. For she would find her Navy, as in 1917, as in 1907 and as in 1898, woefully weak.

—Waldo Drake

WALDO DRAKE, twenty-four years old, strode into the offices of the *Los Angeles Times* for his second meeting with assistant managing editor Ralph Trueblood. In 1922, the *Times'* offices were at the bustling corner of First Street and Broadway. Drake had been hired on June 1 as the new waterfront reporter for San Pedro, a neighborhood twenty-five miles south of downtown, taking over that beat from veteran newsman Arthur Pangborn. The *Times'* wealthy owners, Harry Chandler and family, were promoting their newest venture—the Los Angeles Steamship Company—and they needed friendly relations with the businessmen who ran the port. Drake had already been working for a year at San Pedro's *Daily Pilot*, establishing connections with the area's power brokers and the growing list of officers of the U.S. Navy's Battle Fleet, the bulk of which had made San Pedro its home port three years earlier (portions of the Battle Fleet, including it submarines, had remained in San Diego). Trueblood wanted to size up Drake one more time before he hit the docks for the *Times*.[1]

Trueblood's rolltop desk stood behind a low wall on the far side of the open bullpen, where *Times* reporters chain-smoked cigarettes and clacked away on typewriters set upon rows of tables pressed edge-to-edge. Window shades were drawn low to block out the intense southland sunlight. From his desk, which burst with copy, letters, and editions of the *Times*, Trueblood kept one eye on the newsroom. He spied Drake at the door and beckoned him over. Contrasting with his crisp, high-collared shirt and striped tie, Trueblood wore a rumpled beige jacket with deep pockets whose contents mirrored the chaos of his desk. Trueblood pulled up a straight-backed chair for Drake, and after an exchange of pleasantries, he lectured Drake for five minutes without pause. "Well, you're starting out as a green hand here," he warned. "You've got to prove yourself, and we'll give you a few months at it. We're letting you have a free hand, and any mistakes you make are yours alone."[2] Trueblood was a taciturn editor. In a newsroom filled with "old-time, hard-nosed guys," the weight of Trueblood's expectations hung heavy in the air.[3] But Drake, with his six-foot frame, good looks, and can-do attitude, assured Trueblood he'd keep his "nose on the desk and the job of the day."[4]

The meeting with Trueblood marked the start of Drake's forty-year career with the *Times*, paused only to serve the U.S. Navy during World War II, with most of that time spent as the Pacific Fleet's PRO under Nimitz's command. Drake's work for the *Times* led him to become "dean" of the shipping news reporters in San Pedro, enabling his interactions with Nimitz and other top Navy officers in the years leading up to the Pacific War.

William Waldo Drake was born July 19, 1897, in Yellow Springs, Ohio, to Ralph Drake and Bertha Drake (née Hupman). In Drake's early childhood, Ralph left Yellow Springs with another woman, leaving Bertha to care for Waldo, as he was called, his younger sister Doris, and younger brother Eliott. Bertha told little Waldo he descended from Sir Francis Drake, the sixteenth-century English sailor and explorer.[5] Bertha suffered from mental illness and was soon admitted to the State of Ohio Asylum for the Insane, later known as Columbus State Hospital. Her children went to live with her sister, Nellie Hupman, in Springfield, Ohio.[6]

Once, when Waldo was four years old, he accompanied Nellie to Sunday school at the Fourth Lutheran Church in Springfield. Nellie walked home after their classes, which were held in different areas of the church. She assumed Waldo had walked home as well, but he'd gotten locked in the church basement after everyone had left for the day. As reported in the *Akron Times-Democrat*, the pastor's son discovered him by accident when looking for a lost umbrella. Little Waldo was "almost dead from fright."[7] The *Newark Advocate* carried a similar report: "But for the effort to recover the umbrella it might have been days before the boy was found."[8] Both newspapers left unexplained why a thorough search of the church for the missing boy hadn't been conducted earlier. Despite his cries for help and kicks to the church basement door, no one came to his rescue. Being abandoned by those he most trusted left a deep wound. Whether Waldo's screams during his isolation somehow scarred his vocal cords is unknown, but he suffered from an unusually raspy voice his entire life.

The 1910 census lists Waldo and Eliott as living with their father, while Doris is listed as adopted by the Garrisons, a family unrelated to the Drakes or Hupmans. Despite the census, family lore maintains that Waldo assumed responsibility for his younger brother and sister as they entered grade school. He filled his spare time with chores around his aunt Nellie's farm. When he reached his teens, Drake became a lumberman to earn money. Two days before his twentieth birthday, on July 17, 1917, Drake enlisted in the U.S. Army, serving with the 20th Engineers in the American Expeditionary Force in France. A primary function of the 20th Engineers was forestry, producing timber for Allied forces. Drake's lumberman days as a teenager had prepared him for the work. Under the command of Gen. John Pershing, USA, Drake's division participated in the drive toward Saint-Mihiel, the site of a major battle fought September 12–15, 1918.[9] He was wounded from a German gas attack, and it caused him to endure periodic, excruciating headaches for the rest of his life. The Germans were defeated on November 11, 1918, and Drake returned home to Ohio. He was discharged from active service with the grade of corporal on May 29, 1919.

Drake did not stay long in Springfield. Like many young people of the day, he traveled west. He moved in with his uncle's family in Long Beach, California, on East Fourth Street. He hadn't completed high school in Springfield, so once he reached California, he enrolled in the largest high school west of the Mississippi: Long Beach Polytechnic. Although Drake was already twenty-two years old, it was not unusual at the time for veterans to return to high school to earn their diplomas. He served as a captain in ROTC, second in command of his battalion (he would briefly serve in the Army Reserve). Under Drake's leadership, Company B easily won the Rotary Cup for the best drilled company by "displaying a snap and precision seldom found in similar organizations."[10] The war veteran easily bested the other commanders.

Drake also served as advertising manager and editor for *Hi Life*, the high school newspaper.[11] While studying journalism at "Poly," he came under the guidance of a teacher there named Arretta Watts, a former student and instructor at the famed Missouri School of Journalism at the University of Missouri. The rigorous "Missouri method," as it was known, involved classroom instruction along with real-world experience. When Watts' students took over the April 7, 1920, edition of the *Long Beach Daily Telegram*, Drake's headlines included "Enrollment 2,556, Gain of 28 per cent at Local High School" and "Much of Value in Evening School's Classes in L.B. [Long Beach]."[12] Drake's stories covered all manner of serious topics, from teacher pay to bank robberies, but it was his amusing take on the local library that gained him notoriety. According to Drake's account, the library assistants were at their wits' end with the Poly students, who had no idea how to properly request a book. Instead of asking politely, they would barge up to the desk and demand, "Say, gimme, Sutton!" leaving the librarians dumbfounded. Thankfully, Drake offered a solution: with a little coaching, the Poly students could learn to approach the library with a bit more "finesse."[13] His stories appeared regularly that year in the *Daily Telegram*. Drake's journalism displayed markers of his character: respect for institutions, rules, and authority.

Studying journalism at Poly seemed like a safe bet. By 1920, Los Angeles had six daily newspapers in circulation; only New York City could boast more. The famed *Daily News* would open its doors in 1923, and Los Angeles was the fastest growing metropolis in the country. The reputation of the city's journalists was not yet on par with New York or Chicago, but the city's reputation for crime and corruption was already well-established.[14] Area journalists were "a mixed bag of responsible, ethical newsmen and women and fascists, Communists, crooks, thugs, and opportunists."[15] Los Angeles in the 1920s was certainly an exciting time and place for a young man from Ohio seeking to reinvent himself.

Drake demonstrated a flair for combining journalism and public relations. As manager of Poly's production of *H.M.S. Pinafore*, he ensured ticket sales smashed previous records. His knack for publicity is evident in newspaper coverage of the production. A front-page story in the *Daily Telegram* noted that Drake had arranged for twelve members of the "Girls' Glee club" to sing songs from the show at ten area grammar schools for assemblies of children, no doubt a clever attempt to entice parents to purchase a ticket to one of the forthcoming performances.[16] But Drake's public relations skill was self-taught; the first college course on public relations would not be offered until 1923 by Edward Bernays at New York University, and it would be fifty more years before public relations education was firmly established in the United States.[17]

While Drake was developing his public relations skill, the U.S. Navy was developing its own capabilities in Washington, D.C. Following the First World War, trends including the rise of air power, naval arms control, and budget pressures had compelled the Navy to professionalize its public relations function, including crisis management. The year 1921 was "a disaster of epic proportions" from the Navy's perspective.[18] In November, the world's largest naval powers gathered in Washington, D.C., to begin a conference that would lead to a series of treaties reshaping global affairs. U.S. Navy officials lamented that the resulting arms limitations had created a hollowed-out "treaty navy," and they resolved to use public relations to better inform and educate the American public in order to secure future support, resources, and personnel. The Navy League, a civilian organization dedicated to educating citizens about the Navy (founded in 1902 at the suggestion of President Theodore Roosevelt), had proved ineffective in 1921 in protecting the Navy's interests.

Standing in the way of better public relations was a naval culture in which officers viewed themselves as high-minded gentlemen, nearly as members of a priesthood, who looked askance at the workaday world and who would never stoop to seeking publicity. The Navy's insular culture had created mutual distrust between the officer corps and the press.[19] Seen as entitled and effete by a considerable portion of the public, senior officers proposed creating an office of press relations within the Office of Naval Intelligence (ONI) to help reshape public opinion. In February 1922, that office was approved as the Information Section, but it was less well-resourced than its planners envisioned, with only three officers and one civilian assigned to the staff.[20] Appropriate staffing was a problem because experienced press agents, publicists, and public relations "counsels" were rare; all three occupational titles were relatively new and had arisen in tandem with the development of mass media. The separate naval districts spread throughout the United States were not yet keeping pace with needed transformations; for example, the public relations function was not even mentioned in naval district manuals of 1921.[21]

Within this context, and upon his graduation from high school, a small newspaper in San Pedro called the *Daily Pilot* hired Drake to report the news from the port and the surrounding area. From there, he joined the *Times*. In 1922, the waterfront beat provided influence, and Drake realized he'd been given an unusual opportunity for such a young man.[22] His early articles were promotional in tone. Headlines such as "Harbor District Sets Pace for City Growth: Gateway of Southwest Climbs to Lofty Place among Ports of World Renown" were typical.[23] Los Angeles was booming, and the *Times* could claim some of the credit. The *Times'* owner, Harry Chandler, was an entrepreneurial easterner who had come to Southern California seeking a new life and fortune. Drake must have recognized something of himself in Chandler's story. The *Times*, though, was not the largest newspaper in the city, coming in at number three or four by circulation numbers. As the news business consolidated in the years before World War II, the *Times* would endure and prosper, but it never reached the circulation figures of its rivals, especially the William Randolph Hearst–owned publications.[24]

Two days before his twenty-seventh birthday, Drake made the news himself. Three men on board the water taxi *Vampire* were motoring through the harbor when they ran out of gasoline and began drifting into the path of the oncoming Standard Oil tanker *W. S. Miller*. Drake was on board the water taxi *Wa-We-Go II* and saw what was about to happen. He quickly instructed the pilot to pull alongside the *Vampire*, throwing the men a loop of rope and directing them to lasso the bow. The *Vampire* was pulled out of the deadly path of the oncoming tanker just in time, and Drake's heroic deed earned him acclaim throughout the port.[25]

In September 1926, Drake transferred from the Army Reserve to the Naval Reserve as a commissioned lieutenant. He simply loved the Navy. He took every chance to serve, every chance to make new contacts and connections. He did not hesitate; for Drake, the Navy came before all else. He trained on the battleships *Arizona* (BB 39), *Pennsylvania* (BB 38), *West Virginia* (BB 48), *Tennessee* (BB 43), and *Maryland* (BB 46), and on the cruiser *Chicago* (CA 29). Drake's Naval Reserve commission made him unusual among the *Times'* hard-nosed reporters who "learned their news sense from the street, most often with their fists. . . . Beating the competition on a story meant playing dirty. And playing dirty was a fine art among Los Angeles newsmen."[26] Drake likewise earned a reputation for toughness on the rough-and-tumble waterfront, but he also found his commission in the Naval Reserve a ladder to higher social status.

By now, Drake was an excellent reporter. His colleagues considered him a "dashing" young man, and he made connections all over Southern California.[27] Part of the reason for his appeal lay with his social instincts. He tried to fit in on all occasions. He had impeccable manners and took pride in his appearance. He was always well-dressed in the latest fashions. Drake spent much time in the company of men, and he earned a reputation as a "man's man." He was more at ease with men, and they considered him a loyal and honest friend. Colleagues remarked that when Drake told a person something, he or she could count on its truth, and he never hesitated to grant a favor.[28] At parties, he was typically the center of attention, and guests listened closely to his exciting stories. He studied naval craft and technology and read numerous books, including many histories. He taught himself French, the language of diplomacy, and later became adequate in German. He played sports, especially tennis. Drake acquired all these skills while writing constantly for the *Times*. He was scrupulous in his attention to detail, occasionally revising a single story up to five times. He reported the news exceptionally well and was respected for his intelligence and charm.[29]

In 1927, Drake met Mary Ann Ballanfante, an attractive Southern California woman with blond hair and a dignified manner. Mary was living in La Jolla, attending the local junior college. An athletic young woman of twenty-two, Mary was a champion high diver, nearly making the Olympic team. When she met Drake, she was attracted by his good looks, energetic manner, and the sense of security he provided her; her family of five brothers and sisters had been facing financial difficulties. Mary was not shy in a crowd, and she impressed Drake with her natural social graces. Those who knew Mary observed she was "definitely not the silent type who stayed at home."[30] Drake courted Mary for a year. Since she had been dating a naval aviator when she met Drake, she later joked she had married him merely to get away from the persistent young pilot. Mary gave Drake both attention and devotion, something he hadn't experienced during his childhood in Ohio. Drake was, in turn, captivated by Mary, wanting to do everything for her. Her younger sister, Patsy, once remarked that Drake dressed Mary better than she could dress herself. He picked out clothes that made her look "fantastic."[31] One is left to speculate how a farm boy from Ohio acquired such sophisticated tastes.

Together, Drake and Mary made an entertaining, good-looking couple. When Mary agreed to marriage, the small ceremony followed quickly on May 13, 1928. Only a few in Mary's family had not met Drake before their marriage, and Drake was exceptionally polite in their company. He also tried to hide his jealousy when Mary gave them her attention. Whatever the extent of his insecurity, it was noticeable that Drake always sought Mary's attention, and for the most part achieved it. Their first child, William Waldo Drake Jr., was born in 1932. John came soon after in 1933, and Errol, their daughter (named after Mary's father), in 1938.

During this period, Drake's articles for the *Times* dealt mostly with the expansion of the Port of Los Angeles.[32] The increase in international trade caused large-scale development of the marine areas in Los Angeles, San Pedro, and San Diego. His articles appeared under the "Shipping News" section of every other day's newspaper. One could not say Drake's writing was artful or flamboyant; by today's standards, it might even be called dull. His stories were serious and accurate; professionally, he was all business. In 1929, Drake earned his byline at the *Times*, and his articles in the Shipping News were subtitled "by Waldo Drake."

In 1930, the Shipping News began appearing daily. It contained Drake's articles and numerous data charts including passenger schedules, vessels in port, arrivals and departures, sun, moon, and tides, radio reports, ship movements, U.S. Navy crafts in port, naval orders, and the air mail schedule. Drake was able to assemble such extensive information in part because he and Mary lived on the tip of San Pedro peninsula near both the Marine Exchange and the Point Fermin Lighthouse. The Marine Exchange kept close tabs on ship movements in the harbor. Their home on Carolina Street was a mere one hundred yards from where several houses had tumbled into the ocean due to cliffside erosion, but Drake prized the location. From there, he was able to watch ships passing Angels Gate Lighthouse as they entered and exited the port.[33]

Due to his rising professional stature and social acumen, Drake was accepted into the most exclusive of the Southern California fraternities: the yacht racers. In this capacity, he crewed for some of California's wealthiest men, including John Barrymore (the progenitor/forerunner of the acting family) and Tommy Lee. Lee was the son of the wealthy owner of a radio broadcasting network in the region and a regular at the Coconut Grove, the famed nightclub inside the Ambassador Hotel on Wilshire Boulevard in Los Angeles. There, Lee met singer Maxine Gray, a favorite of big band leaders, and the two fell in love. Through acquaintances such as Lee and Gray, Drake flirted with the glamourous lifestyle of the era. In the 1932 Olympic trials in Los Angeles, Drake helped crew Lee's six-meter sloop, *Caprice*. Drake is listed on the official Olympic roster but identified only in his capacity as a member of the press. Nevertheless, Drake crewed the *Caprice* throughout the early 1930s, winning races for Lee up and down the California coast. Sailing became a passion, and Drake was an admired member of this prestigious group.[34]

Drake's inclusion in the fraternity of yacht racers didn't endear him to the labor organizers on the waterfront. Under Chandler, the *Times* was no friend of local unions. In fact, earlier in the century, Chandler's wealthy father-in-law had owned the *Times*, and he so antagonized the unions they bombed his offices, killing twenty-one people. In 1934, the longshoremen were once again united against the shipowners, and the *Times* again supported the latter. During the showdown in late February, Drake was assigned to interview the newly named commander-in-chief of the U.S. Fleet, Adm. Joseph Reeves, USN. Drake traveled to Tucson, Arizona, to join Reeves' train and interview him on his way back to Southern California. After returning to San Pedro, Drake headed up the hill to Point Fermin. There, he found Mary in a "considerably nervous condition."[35] The night before, longshoremen, Drake presumed, had driven up and torn the screens off their home and bombarded the house with brickbats (chunks of brick, concrete, or stone). Drake telephoned L. D. Hotchkiss, who had replaced Trueblood as managing editor of the *Times*, and asked whether their antiunion reporting might be eased back a bit. Drake explained that labor organizers had been harassing him on the waterfront, and now they'd attacked his home. Hotchkiss told Drake he'd talk to Mr. Chandler about it. When he did, Chandler replied, "Well, I sympathize with Mr. Drake, but that is one of the prices for being on the firing line! [Tell Drake] to keep it up!"[36] Drake followed Mr. Chandler's orders even though they threatened his family's safety. Drake's loyalty to the Navy was matched only by his loyalty to Mr. Chandler and the *Times*.

On Friday evening, October 18, 1935, Drake arrived at the Rotary Club in San Pedro to give a speech: "Our National Defenses."[37] Rear Adm. Wat Cluverius, USN, introduced Drake to the audience, praising the newsman for his extensive knowledge of naval affairs, the merchant marine, and general maritime conditions. Drake approached the lectern and unveiled a dramatic chart of the coastal area. He argued that the center of gravity for the U.S. Navy had shifted from the North Atlantic to the Pacific. "Let me remind you," he intoned, "on the 17th of July, 1919 . . . the vanguard of the newly-organized United States Pacific fleet, flying the flag of Admiral Hugh Rodman, sailed from Hampton Roads to California . . . today more than 90 per cent of the navy's combatant strength is concentrated here."

In a striking departure from his passionless prose, Drake implored the audience to pressure Congress to reinvigorate the moribund U.S. merchant marine. "Sea power is composed of three major factors," he argued, "fighting ships, bases to serve them and the merchant marine." He called the state of the merchant marine "pathetic," and he excoriated Congress for its "treasonable" inaction. Drake identified Japan as America's nemesis, and maintained that building up the merchant marine as an auxiliary force would help deal with any future conflict. He left the audience a warning: "We must in this advantageous moment which has been accorded us either determine to restore our estate on the high seas or else be prepared to pay a penalty beside which in comparison the exactions being now thrust upon China [by Japan] will be a mere *bagatelle*."

Drake was a *Times* newsman, but he was also among the most active and effective promoters of the Navy in Southern California. In the many hundreds of articles Drake wrote for the *Times*, it is nearly impossible to find a critical word about the Navy. In the early 1930s, Drake was promoted to maritime editor, and he began writing more features and editorials, but these too supported the Navy's interests. The Rotary Club audience could be forgiven for wondering whether the Navy had provided Drake his talking points. His promotional tone was no coincidence, because he was working for the Office of Naval Intelligence (ONI), an inevitable role for him given his extensive knowledge of the world's naval and commercial vessels plus his connections with naval, press, and civilian officials.

In April 1931, Drake was called to Washington, D.C., for a six-month active-duty assignment with ONI. He had been "selected for this assignment in competition with scores of other officers in the United States naval reserve" to "assist the naval intelligence office in developing a course of study to fit reserve officers for wartime duties."[38] In July, he and Mary drove from Washington, D.C., to Ohio. The visit was unusual because, according to Drake's sister-in-law, he never spoke about his family, nor did she recall him ever returning to Ohio to visit them.[39]

Drake and Mary's return to Washington, D.C., took a sudden turn at a Hagerstown, Maryland, intersection. Out of nowhere, a stolen truck driven by desperate men fleeing the law careened into their Model A Ford. The impact knocked Drake unconsciousness. Mary fared only slightly better; her body was bruised from the violent collision. The incident was reported in a San Pedro *News-Pilot* story on July 6, "Waldo Drake Hurt in East." The *Times*' headline the same day declared, "Times' Employee Injured in Crash." A July 7 follow-up story in the *News-Pilot* clarified that Drake's injuries were not so serious after all. The articles emphasized his duties with naval intelligence. The *News-Pilot* admiringly referred to Drake as "the 'dean' of shipping news reporters at San Pedro," although he was just thirty-three years old.[40] Foreign intelligence agents residing on the West Coast in the summer of 1931 likely could have guessed Drake's ONI affiliation, but any agent reading the local newspapers would now have known it with certainty.

Drake's promotion of the Navy may have been heartfelt and sincere, but it was also strategic, designed to advance the Navy's overall aims and interests and to secure the means of achieving them. By journalism standards of the 1930s, reporters' ONI affiliations were acceptable to newspaper publishers and editors, even if most readers were unaware of or did not understand the possible conflicts of interest. The Navy understood the dangers, however, and the Bureau of Navigation (the Navy's personnel department) issued a memorandum in 1937 warning District commandants to keep such affiliations secret.[41]

Drake's Rotary Club speech exemplifies the Navy's objective of full expansion within peacetime limits. Increases in and improvements of ships, bases, equipment, and auxiliaries were sought as well as greater recruitment of personnel, both officers and enlisted.[42] Drake had been promoting those increases and improvements for years. His April 9, 1933, feature in the *Times* Sunday Magazine, "Why Uncle Sam Is Worried about His Navy," declared, "Should war come tomorrow, the wrath of America against her own leaders would be fearful. For she would find her Navy, as in 1917, as in 1907 and as in 1898, woefully weak."[43] One commentator declared Drake's feature a "brilliant analysis, by the man who knows as much about the Navy as the Navy does itself."[44]

Drake's June 6, 1937, article featuring the Battle Force demonstrates his fondness for the Navy. Headlined "Fleet Back from Cruise," the front-page article included the subheadline, "Spectacular Entrance Made by Warships after War Game."[45] Readers were invited to imagine the majestic scene: "The backbone of the United States Fleet was back on San Pedro Bay yesterday, as the battleship, cruiser and aircraft carrier squadrons returned from the Hawaiian war games, after tarrying a week at San Francisco for the Golden Gate Bridge celebration. The ships made a spectacular entry to the roadstead just before noon. They swept down channel in column on the wings of a fresh westerly breeze, passing the San Pedro fairway and entering the anchorage through the Long Beach fairway."[46] Drake did not report the details of the war game, which involved a dawn attack on Pearl Harbor. Carriers moved in and delivered a surprise raid on the Army and Navy installations, backed up by battleships and cruisers steaming in under the cover of aircraft.[47] An April 24, 1937, Associated Press report of the war game included in the *Times* noted, "Defending Army planes located the main body of the United States Fleet as it moved toward Honolulu for a long-awaited war game attack."[48] The Fleet, of course, was masquerading as America's presumed enemy: Japan.

Japan was seen as a major threat following its victory in the Russo-Japanese War of 1904–1905. The war had left Japan the most dominant force in Asia and the Pacific. This situation prompted the Navy to develop War Plan Orange in 1911, a contingency plan against possible Japanese aggression toward the United States. Japanese occupation of Manchuria and northern China during the early 1930s contributed to the deteriorating climate of U.S.-Japan relations. Most Navy officers presumed that a war between the United States and Japan was inevitable, and Drake's Shipping News and features amplified the Japanese threat. For example, his May 20, 1934, *Times* Sunday Magazine feature, "The Fleet's Gone, Now Where's Our Coast Defense," warned readers that the U.S. Fleet's months-long sojourns left the Pacific Coast "helpless" against overseas attack, "or even invasion."[49] Likewise, Drake's March 21, 1937, article "Cotton Export Trade Periled" relied on alarming statements from an exporter: "The Japanese today control the destiny of the world cotton industry . . . not only because of their cheap labor in the mills, but chiefly because of their splendid, modern merchant marine."[50] Similar headlines such as "Japanese Oil Imports Soar" and "Japan Move Confirmed: Action Taken toward Direct Government Control of Shipping" confirmed the Navy's suspicions and stoked public anxieties.[51] Some Navy officials had also become distrustful of Japanese Americans living and working near military installations and defense plants in Southern California. ONI regarded most Japanese, whether visitors, immigrants, or native-born, as potentially subversive, and the large Japanese American community on Terminal Island next to the Port of Los Angeles in San Pedro was under surveillance.[52]

Drake's reporting for the *Times* contained few overt traces of the racism and xenophobia found in the area's Hearst-owned newspapers,[53] but Drake was still a product of his time. Once in the early 1930s, he had been invited on board a Japanese vessel docked at the port. He invited Mary, her sister Patsy, and some friends to join him on the tour. The group made their way around the vessel, stopping in front of a circular hole in one of the decks. Drake became excited and tried his best to explain with a straight face that the Japanese didn't have regular toilets and the hole in the deck was what they used. The women marveled at Drake's sense of humor, as he couldn't help himself from laughing to tears, joking, "Do you think you could manage, Patsy?"[54]

In sum, Drake's unfortunate childhood did much to shape his character and relationships. The institutionalization of his mother and abandonment by his father required Drake to become self-reliant and responsible for his younger siblings. When he finally could, he ventured far from his ill-fated home, first to the battlefields of France and then to Southern California. His early traumas, travels, and service provided Drake a level of maturity that convinced *Times* editors to hand over the waterfront beat to a twenty-four-year-old cub reporter. He overcame considerable obstacles to develop his "dashing" persona, hone his professional skill, and win his superiors' confidence. But his gender, race, and good looks in the hothouse of image-conscious Los Angeles must be acknowledged for the privileges and opportunities they gave him. Despite his outgoing personality, popularity, and confidence, Drake carried a deep-seated insecurity that plagued him. His parental abandonment caused him to struggle to form deep, meaningful connections. Though he knew countless people in the Navy, he never let anyone get close, maintaining a wide but shallow network of relationships that left him isolated. While he loved his family, he was frequently absent, leaving Mary to shoulder the burden of raising their children.

But Drake's struggles went beyond emotional distance. He could lash out with a fury that left those around him trembling. In an apologetic letter to Mary in 1938 he wrote, "If you will come back with the children I will promise herewith not to trouble you again with remarks about the bills."[55] Their daughter, Errol, later explained that "trouble" meant rage. Although he tried to hide it, the truth was that "trouble"—about the bills or any other matter—could light Drake's short fuse at any moment. In Mary's close-knit family, Drake was often uncomfortable, feeling like an outsider. Yet he tried to develop closer bonds. In the letter to Mary, he mentioned taking her sisters, Lois and Patsy, who were visiting San Pedro while awaiting the return of Patsy's husband, Ruben, from Honolulu, to a screening of *The Wizard of Oz* at the Fox Cabrillo Theater. "[T]ell mother that Patsy looks splendid . . . and is in excellent spirits," Drake wrote. Yet he signed the letter to his wife "sincerely" rather than "love," displaying either a lack of intimate feeling or an odd formalness. Either way, comparing Mary's close family bonds to his own fractured connections must have been painful. Drake instead found belonging and purpose in his other family: the Navy.

☙☙☙☙☙☙☙☙☙☙

At the time of Drake's Rotary Club speech in 1935, Capt. Chester William Nimitz, USN, had just begun serving as assistant chief of the Navy's Bureau of Navigation in Washington, D.C.. The "cotton-haired," fifty-year-old Texan had recently returned to the United States from the Far East, where he'd commanded the heavy cruiser USS *Augusta* (CA 31), the flagship of the Asiatic Fleet. Despite its name, the Bureau of Navigation was charged with personnel management, and a rotation through the bureau was a stepping stone to further promotion in the Navy. Leaders of the bureau memorized the service records and capabilities of the Navy's topmost officers, enabling well-informed and strategic command assignments.[56] Captain Nimitz was so well-suited to the job that after serving a three-year rotation as assistant chief, he'd been given only a one-year sea command before returning to the bureau as its chief. Brief sea commands were typical at the time to give officers more experience before direct Navy involvement in the war in Europe and the presumed outbreak of war in the Pacific.

Nimitz was born February 24, 1885, in Fredericksburg, Texas. In addition to sharing the name "William," Drake and Nimitz shared childhood misfortune. Nimitz's father died of a rheumatic heart condition before Nimitz was born. Nimitz's uncle married the widowed Anna, and the family moved to Kerrville, Texas, when Nimitz was five years old. Like Drake, Nimitz was an eldest child, a half-brother to siblings Otto and Dora. Drake and Nimitz also shared the experience of having grown up far from the sea; yet each man would spend most of his adult life plying the Pacific Ocean. Both men grew up without their biological fathers, although in each case, extended family members shaped the trajectory of their lives, a supportive uncle in Drake's case and a seafaring grandfather who became a Texas hotelier in Nimitz's. Both men left home without earning a high school diploma, although Nimitz left to attend the Naval Academy, an honor Drake lamented he never achieved.[57] Drake's status as a Naval Reserve officer did not trouble Nimitz, however. Throughout his career, Nimitz would insist regular officers and reservists wear the same uniform and be shown the same level of respect. Both sets of officers performed similar duties, and Nimitz often worked to reduce or eliminate status differences to promote unity and effectiveness.[58]

Both Drake and Nimitz excelled at sports. Yachting and tennis were Drake's favorite pastimes. Nimitz was a strong tennis player, and he enjoyed swimming, hiking, and horseshoes. Both men possessed lively social circles and charmed dinner guests with their exciting stories, which often contained a humorous or risqué edge. Twelve years older than Drake, Nimitz had already achieved a notable naval career by the time Drake began working for the *Times* in 1922. By then, Nimitz had served on board the USS *Ohio* (BB 12) in San Francisco, cruising the Far East. As a commissioned ensign in 1907, he'd commanded the gunboat USS *Panay* in the Philippines. He'd then commanded the USS *Decatur* (DD 5) and was mildly reprimanded for grounding her. Upon his return to the United States, he was ordered to submarine duty, commanding a succession of vessels and then the entire Atlantic Submarine Flotilla. In 1913, he'd begun a series of appointments overseeing the development of marine diesel engines. In 1917, he was assigned as aide and chief of staff to the Commander, Submarine Force Atlantic, serving in that role during World War I. After the war, in 1919, he'd served one year's duty as executive officer of the battleship USS *South Carolina* (BB 26), and in 1920 he'd overseen the construction of the submarine base at Pearl Harbor.

In 1923, Commander Nimitz became aide and assistant chief of staff to the Commander, Battle Fleet, bringing him, his wife, Catherine, and their three young children (Catherine, "Chet," and "Nancy") to reside in Southern California (another daughter, Mary, would be born in 1931). Over the next eighteen years, Drake and Nimitz routinely crossed paths as Nimitz's duties brought him to San Diego, San Pedro, and Berkeley (where he established the first ROTC unit for Naval Reserve personnel at the University of California). Press coverage of Nimitz at this time, however, focused mostly on the salons, luncheons, and dances hosted for Navy officers, their wives, or their families. A September 29, 1925, *Times* front-page story (doubtlessly written by Drake before he'd earned his byline) noted that Commander Nimitz was serving as assistant chief of staff to the newly named commander-in-chief of the U.S. Fleet, Adm. Samuel Robison, USN. Later, the front page of the September 18, 1938, edition of the *Times* included a huge photograph of Nimitz taking command of Battleship Division One.[59] As a veteran member of the press, Drake was on board the USS *Arizona* to witness the traditional ceremony. Drake also attended the dinner-dance farewell that weekend for the officers and crew of the USS *Pennsylvania*, which was headed for a three-month overhaul at the shipyard in Bremerton, Washington.[60] The related *Times* article noted that Nimitz was one of three honored guests at the event, which was held at the California Yacht Club where Drake was a regular presence.

Their ages and career trajectories aside, a difference between the men was their attitude toward the press. Drake was a respected maritime editor, while Nimitz was wary of reporters. Drake promoted the Navy in his *Times* editorials and civic engagements, while Nimitz dutifully permitted press coverage of the command changes, celebrations, and other newsworthy happenings falling within his responsibility, while trying to avoid the spotlight himself. Nimitz was conservative by nature, and as a submarine officer, he shared that community's "silent service" ethos. Moreover, a controversy that occurred when Nimitz was a midshipman at the Naval Academy stuck with him throughout his career. The case involved a dispute arising between Adm. William Sampson, USN, and Adm. Winfield Scott Schley, USN, over the actions the commanders had taken during the Spanish American War. The Academy's midshipmen observed firsthand how negative publicity could destroy interpersonal relationships, degrade interservice cooperation, and tarnish the Navy's reputation. Nimitz's ambivalence toward the press had deep roots.

Another difference between the two men was their relationship to ONI. As chief of the Bureau of Navigation, Nimitz was involved in the Navy's effort to counter spies and saboteurs. In a July 22, 1941, memorandum issued to "All Ships and Stations," Nimitz warned, "Recently an employee of an important Naval shore facility, who possessed vital defense secrets, was approached by a neighbor with whom he had had no previous relations. This neighbor was fully informed as to the nature of the naval employee's duties, and extended considerable hospitality of an expensive nature. The employee reported the matter directly to the Office of Naval Intelligence, which identified the neighbor as an agent of a foreign government."[61] Nimitz and Drake were aligned on the Navy's need to protect security, but Nimitz's rotation through the Navy bureaucracy never included a tour in ONI, which at times was considered a dead end for ambitious officers seeking rapid promotion.[62] Drake, on the other hand, became steeped in ONI's intelligence dilemma in ways Nimitz never experienced. Drake was ONI's newsman before he was Nimitz's.

2

An Intelligence Dilemma

I think the value to Japan of those vessels is the information
they give.

—Waldo Drake

O N TUESDAY MORNING, April 22, 1941, Adm. Husband Kimmel, USN,
commander-in-chief of the U.S. Fleet (CINCUS), sat down at his desk
in his office on the second floor of the submarine base at Pearl Harbor
to read his mail. Kimmel, fifty-nine-years-old and a Kentuckian, had only
been on the job for about two months and had recently transferred his staff
from his flagship, the USS *Pennsylvania*, to the submarine base to allow
them more room to operate. At the suggestion of Navy Secretary Frank
Knox, President Roosevelt had appointed Kimmel to relieve Adm. James
Richardson, USN, as commander-in-chief of the U.S. Fleet. Richardson had
repeatedly objected to the Battle Force's basing at Pearl Harbor instead of
San Pedro. As Richardson's replacement, Kimmel had also been given the
title of commander-in-chief of the reconstituted Pacific Fleet (CINCPAC).
Although he was designated CINCUS, that title had become mostly symbolic by 1941 as the commands of the Asiatic, Atlantic, and Pacific Fleets
operated separately in practice.[1]

As usual, Kimmel began the day's work with the most recent letters
from his boss, Adm. Harold Stark, USN, who served in Washington, D.C.,
as Chief of Naval Operations (CNO). At sixty-one years old, Stark was
the top uniformed official in the Navy, and he was known for his genial

demeanor and administrative skill. The two admirals frequently exchanged letters. In fact, the brief one Kimmel held in his hand that morning didn't even include the date. CNO Stark wrote,

> Dear Kimmel: As the days grow more critical, I am wondering whether or not you have considered the advisability of attaching a public relations officer to your staff. A study of the British system reveals that a reserve officer especially assigned to handle such details from the Fleet unloads a great deal of responsibility from the fighting staff members and assures a good documentary and propaganda liaison. It might be helpful to have such an officer—as for example, someone like Waldo Drake whom you probably remember from the *Los Angeles Times*—to take care of details of correspondents, photographers, and artists, plus the other ever-pressing requests of press and radio agencies. What do you think? Keep cheerful.[2]

ONI's Public Relations Branch began preparing in early 1941 to become a separate, larger office reporting directly to the Secretary of the Navy (ONI's Information Section had been renamed the Public Relations Branch in 1931), and it is likely that Drake's name surfaced for the role of Pacific Fleet PRO then. By 1941, the war in Europe had been escalating for two years. Japan had invaded China four years earlier. After he'd been appointed Navy Secretary in 1940, Knox carried out President Roosevelt's plan (aided by Representative Carl Vinson (D-GA) and approved by Congress eight days prior to Knox's appointment) to create a two-ocean Navy capable of fighting presumed enemies in the Atlantic (Germany) and the Pacific (Japan). President Roosevelt, one historian noted, "respected Knox's public speaking and public relations ability,"[3] and Knox immediately began exercising personal stewardship over Navy public relations.

Kimmel replied to Stark,

> So far I have not felt the need for a Public Relations Officer on my staff. Situated as we are, the majority of this work has been very successfully handled by the District under Admiral Bloch. We have been in perfect accord as to what should and should not be released. From the

standpoint of the newspaper and publicity men the situation may not be as satisfactory as it is from my standpoint. I can see where the services of a man like Waldo Drake could be of great value to the Service. So my answer is that if you can send Waldo Drake out here to serve on my Staff, I will be very glad to have him. An individual with less expertise might do more harm than good.[4]

On April 26, 1941, Drake learned that his nearly two decades of hard work for the *Times* and ONI had culminated in a remarkable turn of events. Almost forty-four years old, he'd reached an unexpected personal and professional milestone: he was headed to Pearl Harbor to serve as the first PRO for the Pacific Fleet.

ÆÆÆÆÆÆÆÆÆÆ

Drake's affiliation with ONI began with his transfer from the Army Reserve to the Naval Reserve in 1926. He was the perfect contact for ONI, a respected maritime reporter who had carte blanche access to ships in Southern California. As an officer in the Naval Reserve, he knew most of the officers in the U.S. Battle Force (renamed the Battle Fleet in 1930), and he knew the captains of the commercial ships that regularly traveled in and out of San Pedro. Drake's brother-in-law, Ruben Wagstaff, graduated from the Naval Academy in 1933, giving Drake an even better view of the inner workings of the Navy.

A May 28, 1932, memorandum from the commandant of the Eleventh Naval District lists Drake among more than two dozen I-V(S) officers, the prewar Naval Reserve designation for commissioned intelligence officers qualified for specialist duties.[5] The District's I-V(S) network in the region included other maritime reporters and editors as well as police officers, investment bankers, real estate developers, postmasters, and even a local art instructor. By 1935, these I-V(S) officers were routinely assisting ONI with counterintelligence activities.[6]

For example, eight months before Drake's Rotary Club speech in 1935, Lt. Cdr. Arthur McCollum, USN, arrived in San Pedro as a new staff member of the branch Hydrographic Office.[7] But the position was simply a cover for McCollum's real duties as assistant to the District intelligence officer in San Diego. McCollum's office in San Pedro allowed him to serve more easily as ONI's liaison to the commander-in-chief of the U.S. Fleet, Admiral Reeves. Reeves had recently been in Washington, D.C., to discuss his concerns about Japanese espionage aimed at the Fleet in San Pedro. Lt. Cdr. Joe Rochefort, USN, who served on Reeves' staff as Fleet intelligence officer, convinced Reeves to ask the director of ONI to send McCollum out to San Pedro to help address the problem. Rochefort and McCollum had served together in Japan and in Washington, D.C., and were friends. It had come to Reeves' attention that documents related to Fleet gunnery exercises were being stolen from officials' offices and sold to an unknown Japanese intelligence agent in the area. McCollum's job was to locate this agent.

ONI enjoyed friendly relations with both the Los Angeles sheriff's office and the Los Angeles municipal police department, and McCollum arranged for one of the local I-V(S) officers, a former Long Beach police detective, to work with him on the case. McCollum had been born in Japan and had spent a considerable portion of his youth there. He was ambivalent about how the Navy viewed the Japanese American community on the West Coast. "There was a feeling of mistrust of these people, whether they were American citizens or not, some it justified, most of it, of course, not."[8] McCollum's attention, however, was soon drawn to a Japanese tuna clipper captain in San Pedro, "Mr. Tani," who'd befriended a former yeoman in the Coast Guard, Harry Thompson. McCollum and the detective soon unraveled the conspiracy, learning "Mr. Tani" was not a tuna clipper captain at all but instead Lieutenant Commander Toshio Miyazaki, a Japanese naval intelligence officer then serving as a language student at Stanford University. Through Thompson, McCollum began feeding Miyazaki doctored information about the Fleet. As McCollum later explained, "The last thing it is desirable to do is to make an arrest, because then you have the whole thing to do over again. As long as you are in a position to control what information is fed out, you have obtained your objective pretty much."[9] McCollum and ONI officials identified similar intelligence networks in San Francisco and Seattle before he returned to sea duty in 1936. Eventually, the Americans were arrested and the Japanese intelligence agents were deported.

Regarding I-V(S) officers like Drake, McCollum later remarked, "I think one of the most stimulating things I had was the selfless devotion of these Reserve Intelligence Officers. . . . The usual unit consisted of maybe half a dozen of these fellows, and they would drop whatever they were doing and come running when the call went out. The trouble, of course, was that they were all people who had to make a living. They weren't paid anything by the Navy. It was all volunteer. . . . I mean they were a dedicated bunch of people, but they had the faults of all amateurs. They were overly enthusiastic, sometimes."[10] McCollum continued: "Later on, we organized each Naval District into what we called Zone Intelligence Areas . . . the three West Coast districts, the 11th, 12th, and 13th, the intelligence set-ups there were organized on this zone basis, so you would take a town or a center of population and you would pick out and talk to a fellow who was willing to do this part time. For instance, in Santa Barbara we had a zone. The zone there was headed by the editor of one of the local papers, and that sort of thing."[11] The zone intelligence officer whom McCollum refers to is almost certainly Drake.[12]

Drake's ONI affiliation raises the question of whether he was involved in counterintelligence activities while working at the *Times*. We cannot eliminate that possibility because ONI's organizational structure commingled public relations and counterintelligence. ONI's primary function was to collect, synthesize, and distribute information about foreign naval and maritime technology, yet a secondary aspect of ONI was to provide security "to the nation against foreign or foreign-inspired espionage, sabotage, and subversion."[13] As Drake's colleague at the *Times*, Lt. Cdr. James Bassett, USNR, later put it, "The Navy had a rather silly idea that public relations and censorship and intelligence were all one ball of wax, so we were all bracketed into ONI . . . which was an impossible and schizophrenic idea."[14]

By the time President Franklin Roosevelt took office in 1933, there was a genuine public fear about the danger of war with Japan. In 1934, Japan signaled it would no longer abide by the 1922 Washington Naval Treaty, sparking an arms buildup.[15] As McCollum's investigation in 1935 revealed, of particular concern to some officers in the Navy were the Japanese and Japanese American fishing boats that had become a major part of Southern California's fishing industry. It was difficult for the Navy to monitor the movements of this fishing fleet, which was suspected of conveying information about both California's ports and the movements of the Navy's ships to Japan's intelligence services. Some officers asserted that the fishing fleet followed the Battle Force on its maneuvers, took pictures, and conducted radio surveillance.[16] Direct evidence of espionage was elusive, but the Navy's local allies in California lobbied Congress to restrict the fishing fleet's composition and movements.

Drake's coverage of maritime issues led to his testimony before the Committee on Merchant Marine and Fisheries of the U.S. House of Representatives in 1937.[17] Rep. Charles Colden (D-CA) introduced Drake to the committee: "Mr. Chairman. I want to say this man Drake, who is a very modest man, has probably done more investigating personally of this question and knows more about the Navy situation than anyone I know of."[18] Rep. Colden asked Drake directly about the fishing fleet threat, "Do you think that the alien ownership of fishing vessels on the California coast is a menace in time of war?"[19]

Drake responded, "I do not think, Mr. Colden, it is a menace from any tactical value or power that those vessels might have, but it is a distinct menace from the standpoint of information—if you get what I mean. San Pedro Bay is the only major operating base of the naval fleet on the face of the earth where alien vessels of all types are allowed to circulate freely among our battleships, cruisers, and aircraft carriers."[20]

Rep. Colden pressed the matter: "Is it not a fact that in nearly every instance with the Pacific Fleet cruising off the coast of California, either incidentally or planned, a Japanese tanker or some other vessel is meandering along with that Pacific Fleet?"[21]

Drake replied, "Yes; and that proves the point of their naval intelligence. The boys know it is going on. I mean, we make every effort to keep the dates and times of those operations from the public, but they get it. I mean, I cannot subscribe to the statements of people that those Japanese or Yugoslavs, or what have you, fishing vessels operating out of San Pedro Bay, could blow up our battleships or wreck our navy yards, or anything of the sort. I think the value to Japan of those vessels is the information they give."[22] Drake's congressional testimony depicted the fishing fleet as a significant source of intelligence, but historians have downplayed its value.[23]

Nevertheless, Drake's testimony helped secure a half-billion-dollar congressional appropriation for the Navy.[24]

Drake's *Times* articles tended to avoid the fishing fleet and instead focused on the movements of Japan's merchant ships. His articles described itineraries and cargo, noting Japan's rush to stockpile oil, chemicals, cotton, and scrap metal. He would have passed any knowledge of Japanese activities along to ONI, and he likely knew many of the Japanese naval officers and commercial ship captains who were under ONI's surveillance. ONI regarded Japan's overt intelligence gathering efforts as espionage but was unable to take preventive measures unless officers were found to be actively engaged in clandestine activities.[25] Incongruously, Drake's Shipping News supplied general readers—including Japanese naval officers and intelligence agents—with a remarkable amount of highly detailed information about the Navy.

Regarding those Japanese naval officers and agents, in 1939 ONI officials were closely tracking the movements of Commodore Tokiji Taira, a high-ranking Imperial Japanese Navy (IJN) officer who routinely visited Southern California. In fact, Drake printed Taira's movements in his Shipping News column. An August 31, 1939, article under Drake's byline with the subtitle "Japan Navy Mission" announced, "On undisclosed mission except that they are 'on inspection,' two Japanese naval officers and a clerk disembarked from the Nippon Yusen Kaisya liner Taiyo Maru, in yesterday from the Orient. They are Commodore Tokiji Taira, Comdr. Arito Yatugi and Mr. G. Isimaru. They will pass two days at the Miyako Hotel and take a train to New York."[26] The story ran the same day in the *Wilmington Daily Press Journal* with the more nefarious sounding headline, "Nippon Navy Men on Secret Tour." The *Press Journal* included an additional subsection, "May Bar Diplomats," noting, "According to diplomatic usage, every country has the right of refusing to accept a particular diplomatic agent sent to it on any ground whatsoever."[27] With their movements disclosed in local newspapers along with thinly veiled threats, Japanese naval officers visiting Southern California could have no doubt they were under ONI's surveillance.

Drake's disclosure in the *Times* of the itinerary of visiting Japanese naval officers raises the question of whether such coverage was incidental to ONI's interests or instead part of a counterintelligence operation. With

Drake—the dean of the shipping news reporters—assisting them, ONI officials could place messages in local newspapers meant for the eyes of specific readers, including actual or would-be intelligence agents. ONI officials presumed that Japanese intelligence officers and agents were reading local newspapers because that is precisely what U.S. naval attachés working in Japan did as part of their efforts to gather information.[28] In this way, articles such as "Nippon Navy Men on Secret Tour" can be seen as a strategic attempt by ONI—with Drake's assistance—to undermine Japan's establishment of intelligence networks in Southern California.

In late 1939, Washington's concerns about both Japan and Germany intensified. Proclamation No. 2352, issued by President Roosevelt on September 8, established a "national emergency" in response to Germany's invasion of Poland, requiring Navy officials to strengthen defenses within the limits of peacetime authorizations. ONI likewise expanded its counterintelligence activities across Southern California (and into Mexico), and the Eleventh Naval District mobilized for an increasingly probable war with Japan. Drake's April 1, 1940, article, "Fleet Ready for Maneuvers," described the Battle Force's preparations for the possible confrontation: "Under the cloak of midnight, nearly a hundred ships of the United States Fleet will sail from San Pedro Bay tonight, bound for Hawaii and the middle-Pacific war games of Fleet Problem XXI."[29] Drake's article began, "Complete secrecy enshrouds the war-game missions," yet he proceeded to divulge in detail that "A total of 140 vessels, 500 planes and 45,000 men will participate," noting that the expected composition of the force included exactly "11 battleships, the aircraft carriers Saratoga, Lexington and Yorktown, 12 cruisers, 47 destroyers, 8 submarines and 15 auxiliary craft." Drake further reported on April 15 that the Fleet would "be engaged for the next fortnight on the Fleet problem; which is a campaign between the invading Maroon fleet, led by Vice Admiral Adolphus Andrews, and the defending Purple armada, under Admiral Snyder [Commander Battle Force]. With the great defense installation on the island of Oahu as expected prize of the final 'battle' of the operation about April 26, the Army's Hawaiian air wing also is to participate."

Since Drake and his ONI superiors assumed that Japanese intelligence agents were reading the *Times* and other local newspapers, the article's assertion that "complete secrecy enshrouds the war-game missions" can be seen as a lure to catch readers' attention and to supply them preferred information about the Fleet. After the Battle Force sailed out of San Pedro for the war game, President Roosevelt ordered the armada to remain in Pearl Harbor as a deterrent to Japanese advancement elsewhere in the Pacific. The signal was clear: the U.S. Fleet was ready to counter Japan's aggression. But the pleas of Admiral Richardson, commander-in-chief of the U.S. Fleet, to President Roosevelt to return the ships to San Pedro led only to his eventual replacement by Kimmel.[30] Meanwhile, the Eleventh Naval District modified its organizational structure to handle its rapid development under the June 14, 1940, Naval Expansion Act.

///////////

Just five days after the act went into effect, on June 19, 1940, Capt. Richard Coffman, USN, assumed duties as the newly created assistant commandant for the San Pedro–Los Angeles–Long Beach area. A Virginian twelve years older than Drake, Coffman served as the local representative for the commandant of the Eleventh Naval District based in San Diego. In July, Coffman's staff consisted of just two commissioned officers and three chief petty officers.[31] Toward the end of August, however, Drake was called to active duty as part of the Navy's mobilization under the president's national emergency declaration. Drake took a leave of absence from the *Times* and joined Coffman's staff as PRO.[32] Drake's last set of articles for the *Times* foreshadowed his future in the Navy. "Alien Seamen Plans Revealed" noted that federal agencies had started surveilling foreign nationals entering U.S. ports via merchant vessels.[33] In the same Shipping News column, Drake also observed the giant Japanese tanker *Kyokuyo Maru* was in port: "Under charter to Mitsui interests, she will sail for Osaka tomorrow with a cargo of 130,000 barrels of fuel and Diesel from the General Petroleum Corp. docks."[34] The U.S. oil embargo of Japan in 1941 halted such transfers.

An exchange of memoranda illustrates the frenzied atmosphere within the new assistant commandant's office.[35] On July 26, 1940, Coffman requested from the commandant in San Diego a copy of the "Training Instructions for Public Relations Personnel of the Naval Intelligence

Service. ONI T-15 Restricted." The commandant declined Coffman's request, explaining that "the District Intelligence Officer has only enough of the subject manuals in stock for the essential training of reserve officers under his direction."[36] The commandant then suggested that Coffman "arrange to use a copy of the manual either in possession of or one available to Lt. Comdr. Waldo Drake, USNR, recently assigned to duty in the Office of the Assistant Commandant."[37] The commandant further explained that Drake could, if needed, obtain a copy from the assistant District intelligence officer, San Pedro. The assistant District intelligence officer worked close to Coffman's office. Why a telephone call among the parties could not suffice to clarify such a mundane matter is unclear, but it illustrates the chaotic environment and how any intelligence officer on the commandant's staff was considered "ONI's man" and was not necessarily engaged in the routine activities of the District.[38]

In his new role, Drake wrote near daily press releases to publicize the Navy, promote its expansion, affirm its readiness, and encourage volunteerism. Generally, these releases were mailed to fifty newspapers in the region with the hope that editors would print them or use them to develop their own stories. The veteran *Times* editor was a boon to the Navy; large portions of Drake's releases were often printed verbatim.[39] One of the first releases Drake wrote, on August 13, 1940, described the upcoming training of new Naval Reserve ensigns from the Los Angeles area, noting their scheduled cruises "on the battleships *New York, Texas,* and *Wyoming.*"[40] Drake highlighted their ports of call in Cuba, Panama, Virginia, and New York before listing the requirements for prospective applicants. The story ran in more than a dozen outlets from Los Angeles' *Daily News* to the tiny *Plumas Independent.*[41] The next day's press release spotlighted an upcoming training cruise for local officers and enlisted men of the Naval Reserve. The detailed release provided the names of various commanders and vessels as well as details about the types of tactical exercises that would be conducted. Related coverage appeared in outlets from the *San Francisco Examiner* to the *Chula Vista Star.*

Drake's publicity and recruitment push had to contend with growing security concerns, including the Secretary of the Navy's September 30, 1940, memorandum on "Subversive Activities." In that memorandum,

Secretary Knox warned of subversion and sabotage on ships and shore stations, and he required commanders to take "utmost precautions" to ensure "subversive elements and saboteurs" did not join the Navy "at this time of great expansion."[42] In response to Secretary Knox, Coffman issued a memorandum on October 18, 1940, clarifying press controls in the Los Angeles–San Pedro–Long Beach area.[43] Coffman noted that increased demand for news from local reporters required better centralization and coordination to protect security. He referred all district activities to contact Lt. Cdr. Kenneth Ringle, USN, who had been named assistant District intelligence officer just a month before Drake had joined Coffman's staff. If Ringle was unavailable, personnel were instructed to contact Drake, whom Coffman described as "the liaison officer between the Assistant Commandant and the Assistant District Intelligence Officer of this area." Personnel were encouraged to supply Ringle and Drake "news-worthy information" and were reminded not to distribute material to the press that hadn't been cleared, especially "photographs of naval subjects." One day later, the U.S. Fleet's Admiral Richardson affirmed Coffman's public relations drive, issuing a memorandum to the Commandant of the Eleventh Naval District that stated, "The Commander-in-Chief is convinced that unless some news of the U.S. Fleet is released to the press that much rumor and speculation concerning it will appear in print or over the radio."[44] Richardson authorized Ringle (and therefore Drake) to release Fleet information related to ships in port, arrival of task groups, casualties, changes in command, and photographs.

A Kansan three years younger than Drake, Ringle served as ONI's point person for surveillance of Japanese and Japanese Americans on the West Coast. He was one of the few Navy officers possessing Japanese-language skills, having served as naval attaché at the U.S. embassy in Tokyo from 1928 to 1931. From July 1936 to July 1937, he served as assistant District intelligence officer for the Fourteenth Naval District in Honolulu. Ringle was aware that at the end of 1940, Japanese officials had shifted their propaganda strategy in the United States from "cultural enlightenment" to "political propaganda."[45] Special attention was paid to the American Communist Party as well as to the economic and social activities of the Soviet Union within the United States and in Central and South

America.[46] Given his expertise, Ringle led counterintelligence efforts against the Japanese, while Drake focused more on anticommunism and German propaganda, although their work overlapped. Drake also served as the duo's press liaison.

To aid Ringle, in January 1941, Drake opened the Los Angeles District Naval Intelligence Office. The office was "created for the convenience of the public in reporting matters inimical to the Navy and its efficient operation in the National Defense."[47] As the officer-in-charge, Drake tracked down unauthorized photos of Navy ships, collected and filed reports of "untrustworthy" naval personnel, and investigated suspected cases of espionage and subversion. Drake also kept tabs on new technologies, especially cameras, that might be used for espionage.[48] For example, Drake helped ensure that officers were aware of the new "Minox" camera, which was advertised as being able to be "tucked unnoticingly into your vest pocket ready to swing into action the moment some interesting subject matter presents itself." He spent time equipping ONI's frequently changing branch offices with furniture and supplies, along with safes and burglar-proof screens. In one case, Drake requested that he be allowed to use his personal property—a battleship-type, four-tumbler, York safe—until an official Navy safe could be purchased. The safe was soon bursting with secret documents, prompting Drake to plea for a bigger one. Adding to an air of intrigue surrounding his activities, Drake was provided an "official automobile" that bore "no markings or license plates to indicate that it is Navy property."[49]

A January 2, 1941, confidential memorandum Drake wrote to Capt. Bruce Canaga, USN, the District intelligence officer in San Diego, illuminates the type of work Drake performed (Canaga was a lifelong friend of Nimitz, the two men having graduated together from the Naval Academy). A colleague reported to Drake that the U.S. Treasury Department believed "67,000 packages per month" of pro-German propaganda materials were arriving in Los Angeles via Japanese cargo vessels. The materials were bound for distribution across the United States and were addressed to German American consulates, organizations, and individuals.[50] Treasury Department personnel had attempted to record and categorize the addressees but were overwhelmed. The FBI declined to help because the materials did not violate any U.S. laws. Drake proposed to Canaga that up to fifty reservists be organized into shifts to assist the Treasury Department in its recording and categorization efforts.

A March 18, 1941, confidential memorandum Drake wrote to the FBI office in Los Angeles further illustrates the type of counterintelligence work he performed.[51] That memorandum began with Drake claiming the information came from a "confidential and thoroughly reliable source." The unnamed source had, in turn, relied extensively on wiretaps and home surveillance. The memorandum outlined the pro-union activities of Mae Huettig, then a graduate student at the University of California–Los Angeles writing a dissertation on the history and industrial development of the U.S. motion picture industry. Huettig's husband worked as an engineer for North American Aviation, and they both became involved in an aircraft labor relations dispute in 1940. Drake documented telephone calls and meetings between Mae Huettig and her family members, officials in Washington, D.C., and labor organizers, concluding that her activities "might provide some light on Communistic activities in the National Defense program." Drake reported that the informant believed Huettig and her husband "have been planted in the War Department Mediator Group for subversive reasons."[52]

Drake's work reflected and reinforced ONI's intelligence dilemma, that is, its use of antidemocratic methods to protect democratic values and the Navy's interests.[53] Notably, while the U.S. Supreme Court in 1939 had placed strict limits on the use of evidence derived from wiretapping, on May 21, 1940, President Roosevelt issued a confidential memorandum to his attorney general reiterating that wiretapping for national defense was still authorized and approved.[54] The lines of appropriateness were ill-defined, however. A May 10, 1941, confidential memorandum from the Chief of Naval Operations' office to the commandant of the Eleventh Naval District informed the latter that the FBI had opened an investigation of "alleged interception of telephone conversations by tapping wires to a private residence in Los Angeles." The memorandum requested, "Please inform this office of the particulars of this case in the event that the intelligence department of your organization has been involved in this activity."[55] Whether the FBI's investigation was related to the Huettig case is unclear, but Drake issued his memorandum concerning Huettig to the FBI eight days later.

Drake's relentless counterintelligence and administrative duties consumed so much of his time that on March 10, 1941, the commandant announced that Lt. (jg) James Bassett, USNR, had been brought on board to direct all press and public relations of Navy activities in the area, under supervision of the assistant District intelligence officer (Ringle).[56] As with Drake, District personnel were instructed to advise Bassett of newsworthy matters coming to their attention and assign a liaison to work with him. Bassett, fifteen years Drake's junior, had been his colleague and mentee at the *Times*.[57]

A week later, the commandant issued another order clarifying that Ringle was the assistant District intelligence officer, Los Angeles Area, while branch offices had been established in San Pedro and Los Angeles, with the latter being under Drake's control.[58] District personnel might have been confused because both Ringle and Drake's offices were located in the same downtown Los Angeles Federal Building on separate floors. The commandant's order noted, however, "Lt. Comdr. Drake may be addressed directly in his collateral duty as supervisor of public relations matters for the Los Angeles area."[59] Even with Bassett on board, Drake continued to oversee public relations.

A public relations crisis for the Navy affected both Drake and Nimitz in early March. An article in the March 5, 1941, edition of the *Times* reported that Lt. Joseph Shaw, USN (Ret.), the brother of the mayor of Los Angeles, had been working in an unofficial capacity for the Navy in Washington, D.C.[60] Shaw had recently been convicted of illegally selling civil service jobs during his brother's administration and had been booked into county jail. Shaw's case was under appeal, and he claimed in the *Times* article he was expecting a commission in the Navy once the conviction was overturned. The *Times* article reached the Secretary of the Navy, who inquired of Nimitz in the Bureau of Navigation as to the status of Lieutenant Shaw. The Navy wanted to avoid being tainted by Shaw's aura of political corruption. On March 14, Nimitz wrote a terse memorandum to the commandant of the Eleventh Naval District, stating "the subject officer is not on active duty nor is he employed in any unofficial capacity in the Navy Department."[61] Moreover, Nimitz stated that if Shaw's conviction was upheld, the Navy would immediately drop him from the retired list.

He urged the commandant to "refute" Shaw's claims. The commandant directed his District intelligence officer (Canaga) to assign the matter to the Navy's newsman: Drake.[62] Nimitz and other Navy officials were pleased to see the results of Drake's handiwork on April 3, when the *Times* ran the headline "Joe Shaw Declared Not Serving Navy."[63] The article asserted that the Department "had no intention of employing him in any capacity." Drake's connection to the *Times* had proven useful in dispatching Shaw's threat to the Navy's image.

Among the flurry of press releases Drake and Bassett wrote in March, one was particularly noteworthy: an announcement of a March 18, 1941, invitation to more than fifty local, second-generation ("Nisei") Japanese American civic leaders to meet with the Eleventh Naval District's top intelligence officers during an "informal dinner-forum" at the University Club on March 21.[64] The release explained that the "host" of the dinner-forum was the recently promoted Commander Ringle, and he'd invited Coffman, Canaga, Col. Allen Kimberley, USA, the commanding officer at nearby Fort MacArthur, and Los Angeles County sheriff Eugene Biscailuz. Drake and Bassett would also attend. The officials and invited guests were brought together for "a friendly opportunity for discussion of community and citizenship problems of the Southland's many Nisei." The dinner-forum was a bold move. According to historian Pedro Loureiro, none of the District intelligence officers at the time had received formal counterintelligence training,[65] yet the overt nature of the event appeared to pay off. Japanese intelligence agents reading about the dinner-forum in local newspapers would have feared its consequences. The event had been organized, in part, to entice participants to come forward with information about possible cases of espionage, sabotage, or disloyalty.[66]

Based on the information Drake had been receiving from members of the public at the time, Ringle had good reason to think someone might do so. On March 25, 1941, Mr. Al Blake contacted the Los Angeles District Intelligence Office with a tip. Whether he initially spoke to Drake or Ringle is unclear, but Blake explained an old acquaintance, Mr. Toraichi Kono (who had served for many years as a valet and secretary for Charlie Chaplin), had remarked to him it was a pity Blake was no longer in the Navy because a Japanese naval officer living in the area was willing to pay generously for information about the Pacific Fleet.[67] Sensing something awry, Blake concocted a story about a friend still in the Navy who might be willing to provide such information. Either Drake, Ringle, or both encouraged Blake to keep up the façade to help uncover the identity of the local Japanese naval officer. ONI placed Mr. Kono's house under surveillance, soon learning that a young Japanese naval and language officer, Itaru Tachibana, already known to ONI, routinely visited the house. ONI had been tipped off to the most high-profile case of prewar espionage in Southern California: the Tachibana spy ring. Tachibana and Kono would be arrested on June 7, 1941, and charged with espionage, but the charges would later be dropped due to diplomatic concerns. Underscoring the Navy's desire to ensure that publicity did not inadvertently disclose sensitive information, the FBI noted in its arrest report that "about 70% of the national defense information [in Kono and Tachibana's possession] was compiled from public reading material," especially local newspapers.[68]

The District's counterintelligence activities were reaching new levels of intensity in the spring of 1941. On April 3, Coffman took over direct administration of the Port of Los Angeles for all naval affairs, and Drake was instructed to report to him directly on intelligence matters.[69] Ringle ordered Drake and his ONI counterpart in San Pedro to "report promptly and fully to the Assistant Commandant any matters which may arise or come of their knowledge which will assist him."[70] Additionally, ONI issued new censorship regulations on April 4, 1941, and Drake had to ensure that his and Bassett's publicity efforts conformed to the new rules.[71]

Drake and Bassett performed censorship duties for Coffman in addition to their other roles because the District *Manual* indicated such duties fell to intelligence officers. Notably, the April 4, 1941, regulations specified that all private postal correspondence of Navy personnel would now be reviewed and censored before being sealed. Any mention of military forces, personnel, locations, weaponry, or disposition would be removed. The regulations also applied to radio, cable, and telegram messages. Correspondents assigned to cover the Navy would now have to always carry with them a license signed by the chief censor of the force or base concerned, and their stories had to be submitted for censorship. The censors' level of control was stunning, as they were able to "suppress, delete parts, or delay the correspondence that passes through their hands as the circumstance appear to them to warrant" and, moreover, were not required to "notify the senders of any correspondence, of any class or kind, as to the action taken by them in any case."[72] The April 4, 1941, censorship regulations exacerbated the contradictions in Drake's competing roles, hindering his ability to tell the Navy's story while simultaneously intensifying ONI's intelligence dilemma. But Drake's dedication to the Navy ensured that he did not complain.

Nevertheless, the extreme pressure of his counterintelligence, public relations, and censorship duties probably contributed to Drake's inability to ward off a case of the mumps, which earned him a playful jab in the *Times* on April 18, 1941. The article, "Mumps Down Navy Officer," teased,

> Somebody's sabotaging the Navy. In other words mumps is no respecter of persons, even lieutenant commanders. Lieut. Comdr. Waldo Drake, long marine editor of The Times, is puffed up like a pouter pigeon and domiciled at his Miraleste home for no telling how long. Apprised that his sons were down with mumps, he moved away to Los Angeles but the germs still pursued him, smote him on both cheeks. Navy Intelligence is investigating.[73]

CNO Stark's letter reached Kimmel in Pearl Harbor while Drake was still recuperating. The news that he'd been tapped to serve as the Pacific Fleet's first PRO must have re-energized Drake. He needed the boost because the weeks before his departure were draining. On May 1, the Navy formally replaced the Public Relations Branch with the Office of Public Relations (OPR). No longer would ONI manage the Navy's public relations function. OPR reported directly to the Secretary of the Navy. Stark's May 9, 1941, memorandum directed the commandants of the naval districts to likewise transfer public relations duties from ONI to "a separate status directly under the respective Commandants."[74] Stark also indicated that the Bureau of Navigation (where Nimitz was then serving as chief) would supply reserve officers for the new public relations work. It cannot be ruled out that Nimitz—having been pleased with Drake's work during the Joseph Shaw affair—endorsed him for promotion to Fleet PRO. On

May 14, Drake received his orders to report to OPR's inaugural director, Admiral Hepburn.

Just before departing for Washington, D.C., Drake requested an ONI investigation to "determine the background, character, reliability, and loyalty" of a reservist of German ancestry.[75] Drake and Bassett also wrapped up a few more press releases, with items including a recruitment push for the Merchant Marine and publicity for the construction of a new base on Terminal Island (with no mention of the area's displaced Japanese American residents). Drake also worked to harmonize the publicity of keel laying that put local facilities at a disadvantage with their competitors in other naval districts. The Eleventh Naval District's security restrictions prevented local newspapers from carrying the types of stories and photos published elsewhere in the country.

Drake's final press releases for Coffman involved a series of stories related to a May 15 visit of a delegation of naval officers from eleven Latin American republics. This last set of press releases once again supported ONI's counterintelligence activities. Knowing Japan had turned its attention to Central and South America, Drake's publicizing of the Latin American naval officers' visit may have been aimed less at American readers and more at Japanese ones. The highly detailed press releases (portions of which were printed verbatim in the *Times* and other local newspapers) gave readers the impression of close ties between the United States and the Latin American republics: "Homes of leading Los Angeles citizens will be open to the visiting Chiefs of Naval general Staffs of 11 Latin American republics next Sunday evening (May 18) during the southern hemisphere's Admiralty visit to the West Coast. As part of the elaborate program designed to strengthen ties of friendship and cooperation between the two Americas, the high-ranking Naval officers will dine in private homes that night."[76] The message would be clear to any Japanese intelligence agent: The U.S. Navy was aware of Japan's ambitions in Central and South America and would thwart them.

Drake departed for Washington, D.C., just before another wave of District reorganization and security restrictions commenced. Additional clampdowns occurred less than a month after OPR had been established. The first ten months of his leave of absence from the *Times* had thus been a whirlwind for the dual-hatted newsman. Within that hectic time frame, there had been four directors of ONI.[77] Press releases written for Coffman in August 1940 would have earned the censor's rejection stamp (perhaps Drake or Bassett's own) just eight months later under the Navy's ever-tightening security restrictions. The Navy's PROs confronted seemingly contradictory demands: maximize publicity *and* security. Drake had demonstrated through his work for Coffman an ability to maximize both in the ways the Navy desired.

After serving a brief tour of duty in Washington, D.C., meeting officials and learning about his new role (described in the next chapter), Drake departed San Francisco for Honolulu on board the USS *Saint Louis* (CL 49). Standing on the signal bridge, the June wind whipping through his short, thinning hair, Drake didn't look back. The light cruiser passed through the submarine nets and under the Golden Gate Bridge. Like the proverbial cat that ate the canary, Drake couldn't stop grinning. He was taking responsibility for the public relations of his beloved Pacific Fleet; he'd become its first PRO.

3

Mustafa's Misfortune

I do not wish to build up a large organization for publicity purposes in this area.

—Adm. Husband Kimmel, USN

ACCORDING TO ITS West Coast editor, Jean Herrick, the November 18, 1941, issue of *Look* magazine had "one of the finest covers we have had in a long time."[1] The issue was on track to be "a complete sell-out," he gushed in a letter to Drake. On the cover, Kimmel stood alone on the deck of his gleaming flagship, his flawless white uniform set off by the endless Pacific sky behind him.[2] Under the ship's massive 14-inch guns, binoculars at the ready, Kimmel gazed assuredly at the horizon. A more confident pose could scarcely be imagined. Commanded by the regal Kimmel, whom CNO Stark had dubbed "Mustafa" on account of his surname sounding like Mustafa *Kemal* Atatürk (the first president of Turkey), the Navy appeared supremely ready to fight Japan. Drake had landed "Mustafa" on the cover of America's second most popular magazine (*Life* being the first), impressing his superiors at OPR and earning him half-hearted thanks from the publicity-shy Kimmel.

The *Look* magazine cover almost never happened. Less than two months on the job as Fleet PRO, Drake had nearly been relieved of duty. Drake's liaison at OPR, Lt. Cdr. James Stahlman, USNR, rebuked him in a July 26, 1941, letter: "Admiral Hepburn has directed me to say to you that he is 'damned peevish' about the condition into which the Public

50

Relations Unit of the Pacific Fleet finds itself of this date. He is holding you responsible for that condition, and unless the situation shows considerable improvement, there will be another public relations officer at the head of the Pacific Fleet Unit."[3] Stahlman and Hepburn were incensed that Drake appeared to have sabotaged the appointment of a photographic officer to the Fleet, suggesting to Kimmel that OPR's candidate for the job was unqualified. Stahlman accused Drake of also failing to inform Kimmel about OPR's plans to increase the size of the Fleet's public relations staff. Stahlman scolded Drake, "You have been yelling your head off for officer personnel for your Unit." He warned him, "Please let me impress upon you the necessity for your handling yourself with more discretion than you have exhibited to date." Stahlman continued, "Admiral Blakely, Captain Ravenscroft, and Captain Canaga were considerably peeved at some of your actions in the Eleventh Naval District before your summary departure for the Fleet." He then repeated that Hepburn "is literally sore as Hell," and he instructed Drake, "Get yourself squared away in good shape and hold that course." Drake's position as Fleet PRO hung by a thread.

The second reason the *Look* magazine cover almost never happened was that Kimmel had gotten cold feet. Drake had started working with Herrick on the *Look* piece in July and had passed negatives of the photoshoot to Ringle in Los Angeles with instructions to review and release them there. But in an August 16 letter to Herrick, Drake apologized for the delay: "After the negatives were in Lt. Ringle's hands someone here raised doubt in the Admiral's mind about the purpose of the pictures, with the result that he instructed me to have the pictures returned for his inspection. I will try to secure the Admiral's approval and air mail you a set of negatives after he sees them here."[4] Kimmel decided he did not want a profile of himself written in the magazine after all, so the *Look* cover ran without an accompanying article.

Instead, Herrick invited *New York Times* journalist Hallett Abend to contribute his piece, "How the U.S. Navy Will Fight Japan." Drake could hardly object to Abend's contribution; the two men had worked together at the *Los Angeles Times* from 1922 to 1924 when Abend had been city editor and Drake had been a new cub reporter.[5] Abend's article correctly anticipated the primacy of naval aviation and submarines, but it uncritically repeated the flawed assumption that battles in the Pacific would be fought in Far Eastern waters, predicting, "When the clash comes, the Japanese fleet will have to stay in home waters, to guard the islands of the Empire against naval raids. Our own fleet will cruise somewhere west of Hawaii, with scout planes far over the sea day and night to prevent surprise raids on the Pearl Harbor naval base or on our own West Coast cities."[6]

Unfortunately, toward the end of 1941, scout planes were *not* flying far over the sea day and night north of Oahu to prevent a surprise raid on Pearl Harbor. Kimmel's reasons for not conducting the scouting flights included lack of aircraft and trained personnel, the perceived ineffectiveness of scouting flights, poor organizational communication and coordination, concerns about frightening Honolulu residents with dawn air patrols, and above all, the mistaken belief among Kimmel and his staff that Japan would not open the war with a direct assault on U.S. forces in Hawaii.[7]

❧❧❧❧❧❧❧❧❧❧

The May 16, 1941, edition of the *Times* saluted Drake with the article, "Waldo Drake, 'Times' Man, Gets Assignment with Fleet."[8] Based on a press release Drake wrote himself, the article began, "It's anchors aweigh for Lieut. Comdr. Waldo Drake, former marine editor of The Times, who recently went on active service in the Naval Reserve. Comdr. Drake yesterday received orders to report to Rear Admiral Arthur Jay Hepburn, director of naval public relations in Washington, D. C., on May 26 for duty at the national capital." Drake's return to Washington, D.C., was like the family reunion he'd never had. He'd passed through the doors of Main Navy on Constitution Avenue a dozen times over the past decade, and he connected with old colleagues and new acquaintances including McCollum, Stahlman, and Lt. Cdr. Robert Berry, USN.

McCollum served as director of ONI's Far East Asia section. Back in San Pedro in the mid-1930s, sharing a drink with McCollum at the local watering hole supplied Drake the type of amusing stories that served as currency among Navy officers. It also tempered any imprudent comments Drake might have written about the Japanese in the Shipping News.

McCollum viewed the Japanese as a capable adversary, and he bemoaned the attitude of some high-ranking Navy officers—made worse by commentary from prominent journalists—that the Japanese were incapable of mounting a serious challenge to U.S. power in the Pacific.[9] Drake likely agreed with McCollum it would take a Japanese attack on U.S. interests somewhere in the Pacific to shift American public opinion toward supporting a declaration of war. McCollum had documented this opinion in an October 7, 1940, memorandum to the director of ONI.[10]

Also likely agreeing with McCollum's sentiments were Stahlman and Berry. Stahlman, forty-eight years old, had volunteered for active duty in February 1941. He was the owner and publisher of the *Nashville Banner*. As head of OPR's naval district section, he also acted as liaison to the Atlantic Fleet PRO and Pacific Fleet PRO.[11] Berry had continued to head OPR's press section after it absorbed ONI's Public Relations Branch in May 1941. A New Yorker one year younger than Drake, Berry had been a submariner for most of his naval career. When he learned in early 1940 he'd been assigned to support ONI's Public Relations Branch, Berry was "shocked and horrified," believing the assignment would torpedo his prospects for further advancement.[12] All Berry knew about public relations was that anyone in the Navy "who had become affiliated in the least way with The Great Fourth Estate—or press—usually wound up with a general court martial on their record or at the minimum, a poor fitness report upon which all promotion in the Navy is based."[13] Berry soon discovered, however, that his role was more enjoyable than he'd predicted. He befriended Washington-area journalists who sponsored his membership to the National Press Club (Drake was a member as well).

Under OPR's organizational structure, Drake liaised with Stahlman, who in turn reported to Hepburn. Drake and Hepburn had crossed paths in San Pedro when Hepburn commanded the U.S. Fleet from 1936 to 1938. The choice of Hepburn—sixty-four years old with reclusive tendencies and a scholarly demeanor—to lead OPR was not intuitive but stemmed from the publicity he'd earned in connection with the 1938 "Hepburn Board Report," a set of recommendations that had helped secure shore establishment expansion for the Navy. In remarks to the Overseas Press Club soon after Drake departed for Oahu, Hepburn told the assembled correspondents that "men trained in the Navy are more desirable for the press relations work than are veteran newspapermen."[14] He acknowledged, "I know that sounds unusual . . . but newspapermen often are licked by a bit of red tape, and it takes a Navy man to learn how to repair a type-writer." Hepburn's remarks may have been tongue-in-cheek—meant to tease Drake—but Drake, in fact, preferred to see himself as a Navy man. After arriving in Honolulu, he told a reporter, "I didn't mind leaving civil-ian life . . . because my heart has always been in the navy. It's an entirely dif-ferent life from newspapers, but the sea is just about second home to me."[15]

During his tour in Washington, D.C., Drake likely met the two admi-rals who would most influence his public relations activities for the Pacific Fleet: King and Nimitz. At the time, King was serving as commander-in-chief of the Atlantic Fleet, having been rescued from the General Board a year earlier by his friend, CNO Stark. Nineteen years older than Drake, King's reputation for ill-temper and unwillingness to engage with the press were well established; in fact, he hated even the "concept" of public rela-tions.[16] In the mid-1930s, King served as Commander, Aircraft, Base Force. Drake's December 11, 1936, *Times* article, "Naval Air Base Extension Seen," described a "surprise survey" on Terminal Island for the project. King, true to form, skipped attendance of the public event, sending his chief of staff instead.[17] Although King avoided the press, Drake attempted to boost his image anyway; a November 6, 1938, *Times* article described the Fleet's planning exercises and "secret maneuvers" in preparation for a possible war in the Pacific, with Drake writing, "Most spectacular will be the roles played by the air forces, particularly the carrier-based squadrons under Vice Admiral Ernest J. King."[18] Throughout the war, King would defer to Nimitz regarding the Fleet's public relations activities, especially because Nimitz himself preferred to minimize the staff; yet King flew into a rage when press reports that breached security crossed his desk.[19]

At the time of Drake's visit to Washington, D.C., Nimitz was serving as chief of the Bureau of Navigation, and he and King probably discussed how Drake's promotion of the Pacific Fleet could benefit the bureau's broader recruiting strategy. In his reply letter accepting CNO Stark's offer to send Drake to Pearl Harbor, Kimmel asked Stark to speak to Nimitz about ensuring that officers and enlisted men stationed in Pearl Harbor stayed put for longer periods of time.[20] Kimmel explained that the Pacific Fleet was expending too much effort constantly training ever-rotating personnel. Even if they had not met in Washington, D.C., Drake would have been aware of some of Nimitz's concerns, since he had received copies of Bureau of Navigation memoranda when he was a member of Coffman's staff in the Eleventh Naval District. Those memoranda showed that Nimitz faced questions about the status of naval aviation and whether a separate Air Force should be established (Nimitz was not in favor of a separate service). With an "unlimited national emergency" having gone into effect in May 1941, Nimitz was also concerned about subversive activities. A Bureau of Navigation memorandum warned that foreign agents were seeking contacts with "individuals possessing information of value to an enemy."[21] Security had become a top concern.

During his visit to Washington, D.C., Drake certainly met with Secretary Knox. President Roosevelt had appointed Knox Secretary of the Navy in July 1940. Sixty-seven years old and a Republican, Knox well understood the value of publicity. It was Knox's view that the Public Relations Branch should be moved out of ONI, placed under the secretary's auspices, and given expanded and improved resources. In 1940, Drake had met Knox briefly during the secretary's inspection trip to the West Coast, but he did not know him well.[22] CNO Stark, on the other hand, knew Drake from when the *Times*' reporter covered Stark's duties with the Battle Force in the early 1930s.[23] Drake would have wanted to thank Stark for the opportunity he'd been given.[24]

Drake likely also met with James Forrestal. A civilian five years older than Drake, Forrestal had been appointed by President Roosevelt in August 1940 to the newly created position of Undersecretary of the Navy. To Berry, Forrestal "was a tough looking individual who seemed to need a shave all the time."[25] Like Drake, Forrestal had worked for a newspaper after high school, the *Matteawan Journal*. He'd also been the editor of his college newspaper, the *Daily Princetonian*. In World War I, he'd earned his wings as a naval aviator. He subsequently became a successful Wall Street trader, which accounted for his status as "one of the country's best dressed men."[26] But his true talent was bureaucratic administration. Like Knox, Forrestal believed the Navy could benefit from increased and improved publicity, but Knox kept public relations under his own purview, tasking Forrestal with the oversight of procurement.[27]

The *Honolulu Advertiser*'s August 1, 1941, edition hinted at what would later become a tense relationship between Forrestal and Drake. That edition contained an article by Lee Van Atta congratulating Drake on his new assignment, "L.A. Ship News Reporter Now Official Eyes, Ears of U.S. Fleet." The article described Drake's remarkable level of influence, noting, "His title is fleet public relations officer, and his job is to coordinate the vast amount of publicity the Navy must daily send out; to censor and release stories to the American Press on activities of the fleet, and to plan pictures and stories to 'humanize' the U.S. Navy."[28] A column inch away in the same edition, however, a United Press story was headlined, "Forrestal Lands in San Diego." Forrestal, along with Rear Adm. John Towers, USN, an advocate for the primacy of naval aviation, had just returned to the West Coast from Pearl Harbor, where they'd toured the Navy's facilities and interacted with the members of Kimmel's staff, including Drake. Now in Southern California, they were inspecting aircraft manufacturing plants in the region.

Given Forrestal's interest in publicity, he may have inquired about the Eleventh Naval District's public relations activities. Had he done so, he would have found the situation disheartening. Bassett, who'd taken over Drake's duties in late May, had written troubling memoranda to the District PRO in San Diego. In one memorandum dated June 24, 1941, with the subject line "Public Relations Problems," Bassett explained, "[T]he primary need, from our point of view here, appears to be for a definitive directive outlining the scope of Public Relations in the field, and its relation to Naval activities such as shipbuilding, inshore patrols, ships of the Fleet, recruiting, and the like. In other words, to what extent will all naval activities in an area be required to co-operate with Public Relations? And will Public Relations be given direct authority for the release of news of such activities?"[29] If Forrestal had uncovered Bassett's concerns or spoken to District leaders about public relations, he may have concluded that Drake had not built effective relationships with naval activities after all and had instead left the District's Los Angeles public relations office in some disarray.

The June 5, 1941, *Honolulu Star-Bulletin* article "Waldo Drake Is Coming as Press Man for Fleet" announced Drake's arrival on Oahu. The article noted, "Cmdr. Drake is well known here. He has made several naval cruises to the islands. He is an experienced and authoritative writer of the U.S. merchant marine and navy."[30] Drake had first visited Honolulu in 1926 while crewing John Barrymore's *Mariner* during a transpacific yacht race.[31] He explained to reporters why he'd returned to Pearl Harbor as the Fleet's first PRO: "The commander in chief wants to give the United States people as much information as he can about what's happening to the money they are spending on their first line of defense, without menacing Navy security. We're going to work more and more with the press too."[32] When Drake appeared at CINCPAC headquarters, however, he found Kimmel a reluctant interlocuter with the press.

Kimmel's cool reception could have been predicted from his reply letter to CNO Stark, which acknowledged the need for public relations improvements but warned that such activities could "do more harm than good." Under the circumstances, Drake did his best to provide reporters with interviews and answers to questions, but Kimmel possessed the Navy's shy attitude toward publicity. Drake later claimed Kimmel was one of the few top officers in the Navy he'd never met while serving as a reporter and editor for the *Times*.[33] Kimmel's reply letter to CNO Stark, however, suggested he was familiar with Drake. If the two men had previously met, it would likely have been when Kimmel commanded the cruisers of the Battle Force in San Pedro in the summer of 1939.

CINCPAC, the acronym for the commander-in-chief of the Pacific Fleet, also served as the name of the building where the Fleet's administrative staff worked in Pearl Harbor. CINCPAC headquarters occupied a two-story building at the submarine base Nimitz had helped design and construct more than a decade earlier. The public relations office was on the second floor. The office was large enough at the time for other members of the CINCPAC staff to also have desks there. The commander-in-chief's office was also on the second floor, with the flag secretary's desk just outside. The headquarters had an excellent view of the naval facilities around Pearl

Harbor and Ford Island.[34] Exiting the submarine base, Drake could often
spy gunmetal gray rainclouds obscuring the tops of the Koʻolau Range.

Upon arrival in Hawaii, Drake began establishing ties with local offi-
cials, reporters, and editors as well as developing processes for distributing
Fleet news and publicity back to the mainland. Drake's counterpart at the
Army's Fort Shafter, Capt. Harry Albright, USAR, with whom Drake would
later coordinate, was also a former reporter. Drake met Frank Tremaine, the
United Press' Pacific bureau manager; Eugene Burns, the Associated Press'
bureau chief; and local reporters and editors for Honolulu's two major
English newspapers, the *Star-Bulletin* and *Advertiser*. He also met visiting correspondents passing through Pearl Harbor on their way to or from
the West Coast. One of them was Al Brick, the fifty-one-year-old newsreel
cameraman for Fox Movietone News. Brick and his "sound man," Warren
McGrath, had been on special assignment with the Fleet shooting short
pictures for the Navy. After they completed their project, Movietone News
had ordered the two men to remain in Honolulu to "await developments,"
but Drake sought clarification on their status. In a July 24, 1941, letter to
Stahlman, he wrote, "If trouble in the Pacific arose, the use of Brick and
McGrath would provide us with an excellent record, but I do not believe
the Admiral concurs, judging from past comments. I also feel that he will
not grant them permission to take news reels of any hostilities unless it was
approved by Washington."[35] McGrath soon departed for the West Coast,
but Drake continued to wait for information about Brick.

In his new role, Drake served as the main link between the Pacific
Fleet and the American press. Lee Van Atta's *Advertiser* profile of him
explained that Drake told the American people what was transpiring on
board the battlewagons, submarines, destroyers, and other fighting units
of the Fleet. In addition to distributing press releases, he reviewed correspondents' stories for security and planned pictures and articles to promote the Navy. Drake generated favorable press coverage so the public
would continue to support lawmakers and officials in Washington, D.C.,
in allocating funds for the Navy's expansion. Since he knew more about
the Navy than many naval officers and more about the press than most
reporters, no one was in a better position to improve the Fleet's public relations activities. At least, that's what Drake thought; the PRO for

the Fourteenth Naval District in Honolulu, Lt. Samuel Riddick, USNR, thought otherwise. Riddick had deep ties to Hawaii (his mother had lived on the island of Maui since the 1920s), and he did not think much of the Fleet's shiny new PRO from Los Angeles.[36]

Drake's effort to promote the Fleet also met resistance from Navy officials in Pearl Harbor. On August 5, 1941, he issued a memorandum to units of the Fleet asking for help in identifying "the typical enlisted man."[37] Drake explained he hoped "to secure a cross-section of personnel in the Fleet in order to identify one man who most closely typifies the average enlisted man. It is proposed to use this information for publicity and other purposes. Accordingly, it is desired that each ship nominate one man believed to fulfill the above requirements and to return completed questionnaire, with photograph of subject man via channels." On August 10, the commander of the battleships in Pearl Harbor, Rear Adm. Walter Anderson, USN, wrote to Kimmel, "I am wondering whether your Public Relations Officer has consulted you before putting out the enclosed memorandum. To me the proposition seems somewhat dubious for various reasons and I am venturing to refer the question to you before doing anything about it."[38] Anderson explained, "I don't believe it is practicable to pick out the most typical average enlisted man in any command and I believe the attempt to do so with a probable high percentage of failures will probably have a certain amount of unfortunate reaction. Should a successful choice be made, I don't see what positive good it will do the Navy." Anderson tried to soften the blow: "I have an excellent opinion of Waldo Drake but do question the desirability of this particular scheme." In this case, however, Kimmel felt sorry for his PRO and endorsed the idea, replying to Anderson, "I have turned him down on so many things that I feel he should have his chance on this scheme."[39] Kimmel's support for his PRO was difficult to predict. Drake later issued a press release and photographs of the typical enlisted man, "Henry Harlan Blake," which earned nationwide publicity.[40]

Drake realized a single PRO for the Fleet was not enough, so he asked Kimmel and OPR to allow Bassett to join him. Sensing Kimmel's lack of enthusiasm for expanding the staff, he asked Stahlman to have Hepburn persuade Kimmel of the need for more personnel. But OPR issued orders for Bassett and a photographic officer, Fritz Herman, to join Drake at

CINCPAC without informing Kimmel. When he found out, Kimmel hit the roof. The July 26, 1941, letter from Stahlman to Drake declaring that "Admiral Hepburn [was] 'damned peevish' about the condition into which the Public Relations Unit of the Pacific Fleet finds itself" was the last straw.

On August 8, Kimmel wrote to Hepburn, "I consider [Stahlman's] letter a serious breach of discipline and I will appreciate it if you will see that no such letters are addressed hereafter to any member of my staff. I wish to cooperate in every practicable way with your Publicity Bureau but I do not believe that such cooperation is enhanced by letters of this character."[41] Kimmel then stated, "If it can be avoided, I do not wish to build up a large organization for publicity purposes in this area." The reason why was clear enough, "Space is at a premium and I have found that merely increasing the number of people in an activity is by no means the best answer to efficient operation."

Kimmel's true objection, however, was OPR's encroachment upon his authority: "When it is planned to order personnel to my staff, I would of course appreciate it if the usual procedure of consulting me regarding their acceptability were followed in advance of issuing them orders." Drake had shared Stahlman's July 26 letter with Kimmel. The next passage of Kimmel's letter likely so humiliated Hepburn—who'd held Kimmel's position as commander-in-chief of the U.S. Fleet from 1936 to 1938—it ensured he'd think twice about commenting on Drake's performance as Fleet PRO ever again:

> I note that you are quoted in the attached letter as having directed Stahlman to say that "he is damned peevish about the condition into which the Public Relations Unit of the Pacific Fleet finds itself in this date". I prefer to consider this a statement of a subordinate who is speaking out of turn, but I cannot fail to invite your attention to the fact that I am responsible for the Public Relations Unit of the Pacific Fleet. If there is to be any criticism of the condition of that unit, or the personnel attached thereto, I will appreciate your addressing a letter direct to me giving the facts as you see them, rather than using the personal correspondence of subordinates to voice such criticism.[42]

Kimmel didn't have to point out that Hepburn's behavior was inappropriate for a former CINCUS; the message would have been understood. Kimmel drew a bright line: "Drake cannot serve two masters, and so long as I am in this job I will not permit him to take orders from anybody except me. I consider myself fully qualified to judge the discretion he displays in carrying out his job." He contradicted Hepburn: "From my observations I believe Drake is getting off to a very good start."

Kimmel wasn't done. The next day, he wrote a letter to Nimitz at the Bureau of Navigation, attaching copies of his letter to Hepburn and Stahlman's letter to Drake. "The Public Relations Unit in the Pacific Fleet is coming along satisfactorily but as you can very well understand I do not want my staff cluttered up with newsmen, nor do I wish to make publicity the primary objective of the Fleet," he wrote.[43] Kimmel wanted Nimitz to know he thought the Bureau of Navigation bore some responsibility for the flap. "When Herman was ordered to my staff I learned of it quite through accident as I had not been included as an addressee in the original message and I had never heard of Herman until informed that it was the Bureau's intention to order him here." Nimitz's response to Kimmel is unknown, but Herman's orders were cancelled.

Kimmel's letter to Hepburn would suffice for Drake's response to Stahlman. In a draft letter dated August 7 but marked "not sent," Drake apologized: "I deeply regret that, through an apparent misunderstanding, Admiral Hepburn and you believe me remiss in my duties and guilty of indiscretion. Please believe that I have kept the Commander-in-Chief informed of every development; likewise that my duty to Admiral Kimmel, Admiral Hepburn and you has been my only consideration throughout."[44] But Drake rejected the blame for the Herman mix-up and attributed the fumble to OPR's hastiness:

> As soon as I arrived here, I looked for him and found that he was on the mainland—and checked with Lt. Sam Riddick and Lt. Van Cleave, ADIO [assistant District intelligence officer] here. I found that he is a fine gentleman but experienced only in business administration. On July 2, I received news from you that Admiral Hepburn had approved him for the Fleet photographic job and on July 14, in reply to your

query about whether we were requesting orders for him, I air mailed you that we had not requested orders for Herman because (1) I did not believe that Admiral Kimmel would give us a photographic officer and (2) I did not consider Herman qualified. I heard nothing further until the DIO [District intelligence officer] informed us of Herman's dispatch orders and that the Commander-in-Chief had not been made information addressee. This aroused the Admiral, as he felt he had not been consulted, and he sent his dispatch.[45]

Whether Drake's draft letter to Stahlman remained unsent due to Kimmel's intervention or Drake's reconsideration is uncertain. Either way, Kimmel's rhetorical wallop of Hepburn reverberated for months; but it was less about protecting Drake and more about reasserting his own authority. Nevertheless, it changed Drake's fortunes. No more critical letters from Stahlman were received. In fact, Kimmel's rebuke shielded Drake from criticism from OPR officials even after Kimmel's own removal in December 1941 and retirement in early 1942. Drake had learned the value of loyalty to the commander-in-chief because, in addition to being shielded from OPR's criticism, Drake learned that Brick would be allowed to stay in Pearl Harbor to go out filming with the Fleet if hostilities commenced. Moreover, Bassett's assignment to CINCPAC headquarters was approved, and he arrived in mid-August as assistant PRO with his wife Wilma ("Willie") joining him. They arrived on Matson Line's *Matsonia* along with Drake's own family; Mary and the children had decided to relocate to Hawaii after all, despite claiming earlier they'd remain in Miraleste. The *Advertiser* stated in its September 21, 1941, feature story on Bassett that he was a "noted aviation writer," but when asked why he'd joined the Navy, Bassett remarked, "I would rather work with Waldo than some air corps guy I'd never seen."[46] The story explained that "Waldo" was Drake. Drake warned Bassett they'd soon be "busier than a brace of bird dogs" because, as Drake told Stahlman, "the two of us will have to circulate through the whole Fleet, selling a brand new product to people with lots of sales resistance."[47]

During the men's meager free time, the families joined in Hawaiian traditions. The luau, Bassett once remarked, was a "Hawaiian feast, complete with hula girls and music and a little tropical rain at times to make it all seem true."[48] But the traditional food unnerved him: "It seems that poi is an integral luau dish. And poi resembles nothing more nor less than sour paperhangers paste. You can have it." He likewise found the kalua pig "very fine if you didn't watch them prepare it. They raked it out of the mud, uncovered its pore [sic], quiverin' carcass which had been wrapped in palm fronds, and ripped it piecemeal with their hands." Drake and Bassett agreed they'd much prefer a ham sandwich from Stowell's Cash Grocery in San Pedro. While unfamiliar cooking smells filled Honolulu's streets, the men deemed the nutty Kona coffee superb (when they could get it), although Bassett lamented that some of his colleagues brewed it "strong enough to snap open your eyelids like twobit windowshades."

Throughout the fall of 1941, Drake and Bassett tried to increase Fleet publicity despite Kimmel's lukewarm support. They promoted the "Moon Festival" gala, a fundraising drive for China relief hosted by Doris Duke Cromwell, the millionaire tobacco heiress.[49] The gala introduced Drake to some of the wealthiest and most influential people in Hawaii, especially Earl Thacker, a self-made millionaire in real estate and travel. Thacker would become a key figure in the Pacific Fleet's public relations activities, eventually serving as the Office of War Information's (OWI) liaison in Hawaii until mid-1944. Thacker would also become one of the Fleet's biggest promoters, even nominating Nimitz for *Time* magazine's Man of the Year in 1942 (the Soviet Union's Joseph Stalin was selected instead). The organizing committee for the Moon Festival included Thacker, Drake, the noted illustrator McClelland Barclay (who sketched promotional posters for the event), and Cdr. Leland Lovette, USN.[50]

Lovette, who'd headed ONI's Public Relations Branch from 1937 to 1940, had arrived in Pearl Harbor in August for required sea duty as commander of Destroyer Division Five. A 1918 Naval Academy graduate one year younger than Drake, Lovette had written celebrated books about U.S. Navy traditions and the Naval Academy. He was known as a seafaring officer who had commanded gunboats in the old "China Fleet."[51] If Drake was recognized for his vast maritime knowledge and exciting stories, Lovette was doubly so. He was made for public relations. U.S. radio network executives swooned at Lovette's sonorous voice. Despite his shipboard accommodations, Lovette had a clear view of Drake's public relations efforts, and unlike Hepburn, Lovette liked what he saw. Drake's promotion of the Moon Festival gala prompted a letter from Henry Luce, publisher of *Life* and *Time* magazines, who promised prominent coverage of the event. Drake also coordinated mainland radio hookup of Kimmel's Navy Day speech, providing the Fleet's commander-in-chief a national audience. Drake wisely arranged for the *Advertiser*'s October 26, 1941, Navy Day coverage to feature Lovette.

As he'd done in the Eleventh Naval District, Drake also attempted to neutralize nascent public relations crises. In late October 1941, a threat arose in connection with reporting by Hallett Abend, who'd later share the spotlight with Kimmel in the November 18 issue of *Look* magazine. Abend had recently toured Southeast Asia for *Reader's Digest*, and he'd lunched with Kimmel in Pearl Harbor on October 29. That same day, Kimmel wrote to Stark, "He [Abend] gave us some very interesting information."[52] The information included word from officials in Australia and New Zealand that if Japan attacked Russia, Britain would declare war on Japan, and the Dutch East Indies would follow suit." Kimmel surmised, "At the present writing it appears that the most probable direction for Japanese adventures is to the Northward." He asked Stark, "If they do embark on such an adventure and Britain and the Dutch East Indies declare war on Japan, what will we do?" Kimmel acknowledged the information given to Abend could have been offered "as a propaganda measure," so he asked Stark to "run it down."

The crisis arose after Abend returned to New York and published an article in the *New York Times* describing how Pacific Fleet forces had observed Japanese submarines operating around the Hawaiian Islands. Portions of Abend's reporting were reprinted in newspaper articles throughout the United States. Drake handed one of the articles to Kimmel on November 7, 1941, and in a letter dashed off to Stark the same day, Kimmel was hotter than the hinges. "This story is manufactured from whole cloth," he wrote, "and is based upon nothing that could have been received by Abend from any reliable source."[53] Kimmel declared, "We have no evidence that there has been any Japanese submarine anywhere in this vicinity or near the outlying islands. If this is a sample of Abend's work, I am forced to question the reliability of anything he may write about the Dutch East Indies." In his November 14 reply to Kimmel, Stark agreed:

"The way the yarn was written, one could easily spot it as 'phoney' [*sic*]."[54] An OPR official, however, had handed Berry a profile of Abend backing the correspondent's credibility. Berry gave the profile to Stark, who shared it with Kimmel.[55] Unlike the Joseph Shaw affair, Drake found there was little he could do to counteract Abend's reporting. Kimmel's enthusiasm for interacting with the press faded further. Kimmel would later acknowledge submarine contacts around Hawaii had, in fact, been reported in February and March of 1941 and in the months that followed.[56] Abend's story had been accurate.

Drake's zeal for security didn't keep him out of trouble. He inadvertently landed his former boss in Los Angeles, Ringle, in hot water. Specifically, in late September 1941, Drake mailed Ringle a personal letter, along with a request to develop, censor, and release accompanying film. The photos of naval subjects were to be given to the photographer who'd taken them, *Time* magazine's Peter Stackpole, who'd returned to the West Coast. Drake presumed it would be quicker to mail the film to Los Angeles for development, where Stackpole now resided, than to process, censor, and release the materials in Pearl Harbor. Ringle asked Canaga, the District intelligence officer, for guidance, but receiving no reply after six days called Coffman by telephone, who agreed that Ringle, as assistant District intelligence officer, should censor the photos himself and give them to Stackpole. Doing so would meet Drake's objective of timely release. Six days after Ringle had given the photos to Stackpole, Canaga ordered the photos *not* to be released, thereby rendering Ringle's action a violation of Navy censorship directives, since Canaga had ultimate authority within the District. In a memorandum to the commandant, Ringle tried to explain what had happened.[57] On October 13, Canaga ordered Ringle "in all future cases, to follow the directives issued."[58] The incident passed without broader consequence, but Drake learned he needed to navigate the Navy's censorship gauntlet more carefully.

While Drake struggled to develop Fleet public relations throughout the summer and fall of 1941, the political situation between the United States and Japan reached new lows. As E. B. Potter explained in his biography of Nimitz, the United States, Britain, and the Dutch East Indies froze Japanese assets in July, thereby threatening to cut off Japan's oil purchases.

In August, the United States embargoed oil exports to Japan. Thus, by late fall, according to Potter the Japanese had a choice of three courses of action:

> (1) induce the United States to unfreeze their assets and provide them with oil; (2) terminate their aggression and pull back their forces to the homeland; (3) assure themselves a steady supply of oil by seizing the petroleum-rich East Indies. Because neither the United States nor Japan was willing to change course, informed observers expected Japan to execute the third option.[59]

In early December 1941, newspapers across the United States reported an assemblage of "many Japanese ships in Camranh Bay, on the southeast coast of Indochina," indicating the force was "rounding the southern tip of Indochina and entering the Gulf of Siam," likely "headed for the Malay Peninsula to launch an attack toward Singapore."[60] Unknown to Navy officials, however, Japan's carrier force—the Kidō Butai—had departed Japanese home waters on November 26, headed eastward toward Pearl Harbor to knock out the U.S. Pacific Fleet.

Kimmel called a staff meeting for Saturday morning, December 6, 1941, at CINCPAC headquarters. Toward the end of the staff meeting at eight o'clock, Drake reminded Kimmel that Joseph Harsch, the thirty-six-year-old correspondent for the *Christian Science Monitor*, was scheduled to interview him. An Ohioan like Drake, Harsch had traveled to Hawaii by steamship with his wife Anne, and they'd been staying in the Halekulani Hotel on Waikiki Beach. Harsch's search for war news had led him to Berlin and then to various cities around the Mediterranean. On returning to the United States, he'd covered the Army's training maneuvers in Louisiana. Most officials believed war with Japan was inching closer, and Harsch had traveled to Pearl Harbor to report on the situation firsthand. Drake had arranged for Harsch to interview Kimmel the day before. "Sure, have him come out," Kimmel had said, a response that surprised Drake since, in the aftermath of the Abend incident, he'd spent a lot of time turning down correspondents' requests.[61]

Drake spotted Harsch in the CINCPAC lobby and invited him to join Kimmel and the staff members, who began bombarding him with questions about wartime Germany. They sat in a circle with a large, low coffee table in the middle. Kimmel sat with his white buckskin shoes perched casually on the table. After a half an hour of being subjected to questioning, Harsch wondered who was to be the interviewed, he or Kimmel. Finally, he protested. "Admiral," he interrupted, "it's my turn to now ask the questions."[62]

"All right, go ahead," said Kimmel.

Harsch noted the relaxed atmosphere in the room, a feeling at odds with the headlines in the *Star-Bulletin* over the last few days. Harsch wasted no time in asking the question that was on everyone's mind: "Admiral, now that the Japanese have moved into Indochina and occupied the Camranh Bay area, what do you think they'll do next . . . do you think they're going to attack us?"[63]

Kimmel replied with a surprising and confident "No."[64] Harsch asked the admiral to explain his position. Kimmel presumed Harsch must have missed some news during his cruise out from the West Coast. Kimmel said, "Moscow is not going to fall this winter. That means that the Russians will be in the war this spring. That means the Japanese cannot attack us in the Pacific without running the risk of a two-front war. The Japanese are too smart to run that risk."[65] Then Kimmel declared, "No, young man, I don't think they'd be such damned fools."[66] Even if their personal opinions diverged from Kimmel's, none of the staff members present voiced any disagreement about the immediate prospects for war. Kimmel rose to indicate the interview was over. He later called Drake into his office, told him he'd enjoyed the interview, and asked Drake to show Harsch around Wheeler Field and the Army area north of Pearl Harbor. That Saturday evening, December 6, Harsch and Anne enjoyed a pleasant dinner at their hotel with Navy officers dressed in their white "choker" uniforms and their wives in summer frocks.

4

Pearl Harbor

No, John, there won't be a war.

—Waldo Drake

THE MORNING OF December 7, 1941, dawned peacefully over Haleiwa, Hawaii. Roosters and Japanese hill robins announced the sun as it inched above Oahu's southeastern horizon. The soft trade winds lofted clouds over the Koʻolau Range, and the temperature climbed upward from seventy degrees. Young Bill (ten) and John (eight) got out of bed to play with a rusty old pinball machine that sat in their yard.[1] When Mary and the children followed Drake to Hawaii in August 1941, humid Honolulu was already flooded with a torrent of military personnel, vehicles, and equipment arriving from the mainland. Noxious diesel fumes mixed poorly with the island's sweet fragrances of plumeria and pikake, so the family soon moved into a white, single-story home near Haleiwa auxiliary airstrip on Oahu's North Shore. From their yard they had a wonderful view of what Drake called "the back country of Oahu,"[2] a remote area abundant in coconut palms, sugar cane fields, and pineapple plantations. Haleiwa offered tranquility in contrast to Kimmel's headquarters at the submarine base. Mary spent most of her time caring for the children, glad to be far from cramped and congested Honolulu. Errol (three) was still too little to leave her mother's side. Bill and John spent most of their time after school and on weekends fishing near Rainbow Bridge or playing at the beach. One Sunday afternoon, sitting together on the warm sand, John asked his father, "Is there going to be a war?"

Drake paused for a moment. He turned and looked soberly at his son. "No, John, there won't be a war," he said.[3] John was confused; his father had said it in such a way that he wasn't sure if he was supposed to believe him.[4] Beyond that incident, however, there was little talk about Drake's duties; he was a lieutenant commander on Kimmel's staff, and loose talk was inappropriate, even within his own family.

On the morning of December 7, the boys wore themselves out playing with the pinball machine. They then entered the house, cautiously turning on the Philco radio, being careful not to awaken Errol and their parents, who were enjoying a late slumber on Sunday morning. KGMB's spine-chilling special announcement pierced the airwaves: "All Army, Navy, and Marine personnel report for duty!" Bill and John ran to their parents' bedroom. Roused, Drake followed the boys down the hallway and sat next to the radio in silence. His face showed no shock, no disbelief. Drake got dressed and began making phone calls while waiting for a colleague to pick him up and take him to Pearl Harbor, an excruciating twenty-five miles and forty minutes away. He gave instructions to Mary to take the children and hide in the nearby cane fields if Japanese troops invaded the island. Over the next few days, rumors of Japanese soldiers landing on Oahu were rampant, sending Mary into a frenzy as she was left isolated and alone to protect the children. She later cursed Drake under her breath for abandoning them.[5] For Drake, there was no hesitation: his country, his Navy, was at war.

When the Buick pulled up outside, Drake gave a quick goodbye, telling his family he didn't know when he'd return. John watched him leave. His father was now responsible for managing the Pacific Fleet's *wartime* public relations.

❦❦❦❦❦❦❦❦❦❦❦

As news of the attack was reaching Drake in Haleiwa, Kimmel, at CINCPAC headquarters, radioed the first communique of the war to the Fleet and to the Navy Department at 0812: "Hostilities with Japan commenced with air raid on Pearl Harbor."[6] Shortly after Kimmel issued his communique,

United Press' Frank Tremaine, watching the unfolding attack from the panoramic windows of his hillside home, attempted to call Drake at his office, but no one answered the phone.[7] Drake was still barreling toward Pearl Harbor, the scattered clouds and sunshine obscuring his view to the south, when the second wave of the Japanese attack reached Kahuku Point and deployed over Oahu at 0840. The Japanese planes kept coming in waves that lasted another hour. Drake became caught in the traffic jam that developed along the route close to Pearl Harbor as vehicles and personnel from the north streamed past Aiea cemetery and into the Navy Yard.[8]

When he finally arrived at the submarine base, the view of the wreckage from his second-floor window staggered him. The battleships *Arizona* and *Oklahoma* were destroyed, the latter turned turtle in her berth. The *Pennsylvania* and *Tennessee* were badly damaged, and the *California* rested on the shallow harbor bottom. Drake would eventually learn that the *Nevada*, *West Virginia*, and eighteen other ships had been hit, military hangars and buildings throughout Oahu had been bombed, and nearly two hundred airplanes had been lost.[9] Fortunately, the Fleet's aircraft carriers—USS *Enterprise* (CV 6) and USS *Lexington* (CV 2)—had not been in port. The USS *Saratoga* (CV 3) was entering San Diego Bay at the time of the attack.

Drake was still learning about the enormity of the attack when Al Brick, the newsreel cameraman for Fox Movietone News, appeared at the threshold of the public relations office. Brick had raced to CINCPAC headquarters earlier looking for Drake, and now that he'd found him, they agreed Brick needed to immediately start filming from the harbor.[10] They exited the submarine base and boarded a motor launch. Once steady, they navigated toward Battleship Row, engulfed in smoke and flames. Drake piloted the launch as Brick filmed the devastation: seared and blistered sailors silenced with pain; shocked, oil-soaked men with shattered bones and lacerated flesh were pulled on board rescue boats; burnt corpses floated in the water.[11]

The half-sunk, smoldering battleships transformed Drake's role from promoting the Fleet to concealing the extent of its destruction at the hands of the Japanese forces. Security became his singular, unwavering concern. The Navy Department in Washington, D.C., immediately issued orders,

"Place naval censorship in effect."[12] Just before 1100 in Hawaii, officials banned all civilian communication to and from the mainland, cutting off the few wire service reporters and newspaper correspondents who'd managed to contact their home offices to share news of the air raid. A communication blackout descended upon Oahu for four days, buying Drake time to contemplate his new responsibilities.[13]

At some point during those four days—smoke and fuel oil vapors still wafting from his skin, hair, and clothing—Drake reflected upon what had happened. "Mere bagatelle," he'd remarked during his Rotary Club speech in San Pedro in 1935 when comparing the destruction the Japanese had wrought in China to what their forces might one day do to the U.S. Fleet. That night in 1935, the battleships *Arizona, California, Maryland, Nevada, Tennessee, Pennsylvania,* and *West Virginia* had been moored less than a mile from where he'd given his speech, and all of them were now either damaged or destroyed in the harbor beside him at CINCPAC headquarters, with hundreds of their crewmen dead or wounded. In 1928, Drake had cruised to Hawaii on board the *Arizona* as part of his training;[14] now, more than a thousand of her crew had perished in a single, hellish blast.

Had Drake oversold the Fleet's preparedness? The headline of Lee Van Atta's feature article in the October 5, 1941, edition of the *Honolulu Advertiser*'s Sunday Magazine had confidently declared, "Uncle Sam's Bluejackets Are Ready!"[15] The Navy, Van Atta had written, "must be ever ready for an ever-nearing struggle." Ready they were, he asserted: "Honoluluans would feel even more confident in the power of the Navy that protects their isles and the Continental United States—if they knew the superior type bluejackets who man the battlewagons of today's first line of defense." In a sidebar, Van Atta expressed his indebtedness to Drake and Fleet's public relations staff for the material used in the article.

Drake had facilitated reporting of Navy social events, such as the Moon Festival gala, in part to "humanize" the service and connect Kimmel and senior officers more closely to the community. Had the glowing depiction of the Fleet he'd promoted somehow helped lull Kimmel and others on the staff into a false sense of security? Kimmel's cover of *Look* magazine now seemed tragically misleading, if not outright enraging. But Drake wasn't alone in reassuring the public of the Fleet's preparedness. The *Advertiser*'s

front-page headline the previous Monday had announced, "Navy Is Ready,
Knox Declares."[16] In fact, an article on the morning of December 7 in the
Advertiser's print run just a few hours before the attack described Secretary
Knox's report to Congress, wherein he'd claimed that "there will be no large
fleet problem this year because the nation's warships are situated strategically
to meet any emergency."[17] Drake's depiction of the readiness of the Fleet had
been consistent with the secretary's. Kimmel himself had declared during
his Navy Day address on October 27, 1941, "The Navy, fully mindful of its
grave responsibilities, is bending every effort toward having personnel and
material fit to fight whenever, wherever, or however protection of American
interests may require."[18] But "bending every effort" also meant arguing with
officials in Washington, D.C., about repeated demands to redeploy Pearl
Harbor–based assets to the Atlantic and the Western Pacific.[19]

Drake's ONI colleague, McCollum, would later claim there had been
no hard intelligence that Pearl Harbor was going to be the target of Japan's
opening attack, but he added, "It should have been understood."[20] Although
Drake would not necessarily have known the details at the time, McCollum later explained, "Admiral Kimmel and Admiral Hart [Commander-
in-Chief, U.S. Asiatic Fleet] had been warned at least on three occasions
throughout the summer of 1941 it was the Japanese and the German cus-
tom to attack without warning, frequently on a holiday, and so on and so
on."[21] But if Drake believed Japan was poised to attack Pearl Harbor, he
never said so. Nevertheless, now that Japan's blow had come, he knew it
would galvanize American public opinion.

The Navy needed to establish a public relations narrative for the Fleet
that could simultaneously accomplish four tasks: account for the surprise
of the Japanese attack; downplay its success; reaffirm the Fleet's readiness;
and reassure Americans of the Navy's capability to fight the new war in the
Pacific. The narrative could not be that the Navy had oversold its preparedness or that its leaders had failed. Such a narrative would do nothing for the
Navy or an American public now facing a two-front war, which President
Roosevelt had declared on December 8 (Japan) and December 11 (Germany). The narrative that seemed to work amplified Japan's treachery, its
"sneak attack" on peaceful Americans still hoping to negotiate to avoid war.
Blame for the attack's success needed to be placed solely on the Japanese.

Without Drake's prompting, local reporters provided this preferred framing. "War! Oahu Bombed by Japanese Planes," the *Star-Bulletin's* 1st Extra had declared the afternoon of December 7.[22] The attackers had "flung their missiles on a city resting in peaceful Sabbath calm," but "the defenders of the islands went into quick action," it reported. That framing—a treacherous foe attacking by surprise the peaceful populace—was exactly the one Drake, the Fleet, and the Navy needed. There was not a single word questioning whether the Fleet had been adequately prepared for the assault. Newspapers across the United States soon mirrored the *Star-Bulletin's* framing. Under Oahu's communication blackout, however, Drake gained only a limited sense of how mainland coverage of the attack was unfolding. The Navy's official communication was centered in Washington, D.C., and the nine correspondents in Honolulu were prohibited from disclosing any information the Navy did not approve.[23]

On the night of December 12, Drake received a panicked phone call from L. D. Waldron, the Paramount Newsreel correspondent in Honolulu. Waldron's Washington, DC, manager had told him that Fox Movietone News had received Al Brick's footage of the December 7 attack and was planning to release it the next day.[24] Waldron threatened that he was "pooling his 'power' with M-G-M and PATHE men ... to stop Brick at all costs."[25] After calming Waldron, Drake convinced him that no photographs or film of the attack had left Oahu and that the footage in question was Brick's pre-December 7 film for the Navy. No leaks from the Fleet challenged the surprise attack framing, but Drake's odds of keeping a tight lid on the damage were unfavorable at best. He warned CINCPAC's assistant chief of staff, "In addition to the nine people already at Pearl Harbor, thirteen others are enroute here, by SECNAV's authorization, whether we like it or not."[26]

Not everyone accepted the emerging surprise attack narrative. The commander of the Atlantic Fleet's Cruiser Division 2, Rear Adm. Jonas Ingram, USN, wrote to King on December 13, 1941: "I have wondered what your reaction is to the Oahu fumble. Knowing the situation out there so well it was no total surprise, however shocking. My opinion for the past year, regardless of the political situation, has been that Pearl was the *last place* for the Fleet in the Eastern Pacific."[27] Ingram had once served as the officer-in-charge of ONI's Public Relations Branch in the early 1930s.

Rejecting the "surprise" framing, he continued, "I can figure no possible excuse for the surprise factor and am confident it would not have happened to either you or myself." Nevertheless, he accepted the situation: "However, it's over the dam, and costly as it's been it may be the means of national unification and revitalization of the Navy." Drake would have agreed with Ingram's conclusion. His immediate job was to encourage national unification while keeping secret the brutal losses the Fleet had incurred. After the communication blackout lifted, he permitted reporting of only what could be observed from the hills surrounding Pearl Harbor.[28]

Shortly after the attack, Knox flew to Pearl Harbor for three days of meetings. His friend, Theodore Roosevelt Jr., commended him in a hand-written note on December 11. "I've just heard you've flown to Hawaii. 'Stout feller,' you've struck the right note."[29] Knox waited until his return to Washington, D.C., on December 16 to hold a press conference. For residents of Oahu, Knox's characterization of the losses at Pearl Harbor was shockingly misleading.[30] The secretary's comments about the role that "fifth columnists" played during the attack bolstered the War Department's effort to incarcerate Japanese Americans living on the West Coast, ostensibly to prevent sabotage and subversion.[31] In Pearl Harbor, Knox may have been influenced by remarks like those of Lovette, who claimed in press reports that "Japanese living in Hawaii did everything in their power to create confusion during the attack," and that "Japanese living in the hills obtained by photographs all the information they needed regarding ship movements."[32] More than two thousand people of Japanese ancestry in Hawaii were detained because of suspected disloyalty—mostly without evidence—and Executive Order 9066 issued by President Roosevelt on February 19, 1942, led to the removal and incarceration of more than 120,000 Americans of Japanese descent from the West Coast.[33] There was no mention of the Navy's public relations function in Knox's secret report of his trip to Pearl Harbor provided to the president. Drake's letters to OPR officials likewise made no mention of him having spoken to the secretary nor the fifth columnist accusations.

On December 16, the same day Knox held his press conference in Washington, D.C., Drake finally returned home to his family. He had not seen them since the attack, but even after the long absence, he quickly returned again to the submarine base. Elizabeth McIntosh, a stringer for the Scripps-Howard news service, showed up at CINCPAC headquarters that afternoon.[34] McIntosh had been a familiar sight in Drake's office before the attack. When Drake wasn't looking, she peeked through the piles of paper that covered the top of his desk looking for news. He once caught her snooping and soon began hiding his papers, stuffing them into drawers and into his York safe to conceal them from the curious McIntosh.[35] That day, McIntosh was standing in the office when Drake's phone rang. His phone was special, filled with buttons and lights that connected him with important officials. Rumor had it that Drake even had a line to the White House.[36] McIntosh noticed the biggest red button was flashing, and when Drake answered the phone, he exclaimed, "What? Kimmel and Short? The both of them?"[37] McIntosh tiptoed toward the door, hoping to clear the threshold, leave Drake behind, and run to the Scripps-Howard offices with the news that both Kimmel and the Army's Gen. Walter Short, USA, were being relieved of command because of the Pearl Harbor disaster. McIntosh was almost to the exit. "Young lady, come back here and sit down!" Drake ordered her in his raspy voice.[38] The story would be released Drake's way or not at all.

Under the Navy's wartime censorship directive, Drake and Riddick became responsible for censoring press copy transmitted to the United States from Honolulu, Drake for the Fleet and Riddick for the District. Because transmission facilities were in downtown Honolulu, Riddick's office was the last chance to review correspondents' material before it left Oahu. The stories approved by the Fleet censors at CINCPAC underwent secondary censorship in Riddick's office. Correspondents were soon howling in protest, complaining that the Navy's censorship process (as well as the Army's) was uncoordinated and arbitrary.[39] Drake criticized the process as well, writing in a memorandum, "Press copy filed . . . at 1315 today was so delayed unnecessarily, by the District Censor that it was not cleared to the mainland until 1807. This copy did not reach New York copy desks until after midnight, so that it could not be published until Monday."[40] Drake bemoaned press copy "made valueless by excessive delays in transmission" and urged the District commandant to ensure timely release.[41]

In fact, naval regulations stated that the Fleet intelligence officer was to take responsibility for press censorship duties. At the time of the attack, that officer was Lt. Cdr. Edwin Layton, USN. Layton's intelligence work prevented him from fulfilling his press censorship duties, and they were left for Drake, Bassett, and the handful of staff members they'd arranged to help them. The regulations did not anticipate how District control over commercial radio transmission created a "loophole" (according to Drake) that stymied timely distribution.[42] The Navy also did not yet realize the problem it had created in allowing PROs to censor press copy. New to their wartime censorship roles, Drake and Riddick could not always make the best decisions. Censorship rules were based on uncertain principles: how much the enemy knows or doesn't know, and how much Americans know or should know. Censorship rules were constantly subject to interpretation, modification, and deletion. Drake classified information into four categories—top secret, secret, confidential, and restricted—and he determined which category press copy belonged to, downgrading and releasing information as soon as possible.

Correspondents protested the absence of information about the Fleet. Aside from a few updates about the defense of Wake Island, the Navy's official communiques in Washington, D.C., from December 7, 1941, onward were bereft of news.[43] On December 18, of the Pacific areas, the Navy stated, "There are no new developments to report." The same held true for December 19, although the Navy also mentioned there had been two additional air attacks on Wake Island. "No new developments" were reported in the Pacific on December 20. On December 29, there was "nothing to report." The lack of news raised the temperature of correspondents in Honolulu, who "fretted and fussed,"[44] but the news was uniformly bad, and Drake refused to share it. He enforced strict security.

The *Chicago Times* correspondent Keith Wheeler had arrived in Honolulu shortly after the Japanese attack. He later recalled, "About the time it began to look as though we would spend the rest of the war forlornly sifting the debris of December 7 we were summoned to Pearl Harbor. Lieutenant Commander Waldo Drake, once on the staff of the Los Angeles Times and now fleet public relations officer, spoke mysteriously. He hinted that, contrary to the loud claims of the Japanese and the suspicions of America, some of the fleet was still afloat. A task force would be sailing shortly and it might have 'some fun' before it returned."[45] Most of the correspondents in

Honolulu were soon out with the Fleet. Nevertheless, tensions were about to increase: The Matson Line's *Lurline*, *Monterey*, *Mariposa*, and *Matsonia* arrived in Honolulu escorted by a dozen U.S. cruisers and destroyers. The ships carried an entire Army division to reinforce Oahu. With them came many more war correspondents, all clamoring for news and seeking passage with Fleet task forces.[46]

Given the danger of further Japanese air raids, or even invasion, Drake arranged for Mary and the children to return with the Matson Line's transport convoy to the United States. The family boarded the USS *Harris* (AP 8) on January 10. Willie Bassett returned to the mainland as well, along with the families of other naval officers. Escorting the returning ships home were the destroyers. They zigzagged to avoid enemy submarines rumored to be prowling the waters between Hawaii and the West Coast. Young John later recalled seeing a torpedo pass just to the side of the *Harris*' hull.[47] The Drake family's arrival in San Pedro was announced in the *Times* on January 30, 1942, under the title "Naval Officer's Wife Returns."[48] The family first went to live with Mary's sister, Patsy, in Big Pine, California, where they purchased a 150-acre ranch. Eventually, however, Mary and the children went to live with her mother in Columbia, Tennessee. As the physical distance grew between Drake and his family, so too did the emotional rift, the heavy toll of separation soon threatening to become permanent.[49]

☙☙☙☙☙☙☙☙☙☙☙

By 1941, the occupational field of public relations had existed for roughly two decades, although publicity and press agentry were older forms of similar work. The language used to describe public relations in the May 27, 1941, update to the Eleventh Naval District *Manual* emphasized dissemination activities including "news releases, press, radio, newsreel, photography, motion picture and public addresses [including events and ceremonies]."[50] Control of information to protect security was paramount, with PROs directed to review and restrict information as they "may specify." Yet the PRO's job was also to "further the cordial relationships between the district activities and the public" under the guidance of OPR's directives from Washington, D.C. Nevertheless, how such cordial relationships could be identified, developed, or measured in the context of strict security was not discussed. Drake's public relations activities for the Fleet emphasized one-way communication techniques designed to persuade audiences to support the Navy's interests and protect and improve its image. These techniques involved generating and distributing stories via newspaper, magazine, radio, and film. As CNO Stark had explained in his letter to Kimmel, Drake's role was to take care of the "details of correspondents, photographers, and artists, plus the other ever-pressing requests of press and radio agencies."[51]

Drake had tried to develop Fleet public relations on his own but hadn't gotten far before December 7. In a July 9, 1941, letter to OPR's Stahlman, he explained how he'd written a memorandum outlining a plan for the expansion and improvement of the Fleet's efforts:

> As soon as I was able to form an opinion of the general press situation in the Fleet, I wrote a comprehensive memorandum for the Chief of Staff, recommending what seemed to me a holeproof plan. This comprised: (1) Ordering Jim Bassett here as assistant PRO; (2) A directive to the Fleet by the Commander-in-Chief, providing for expanded output of news and photographic material and through the CinC and with the aid of public relations officers to be appointed by subordinate commands; (3) Services of several V-6 photographers and yeomen (with civilian newspaper experience) and a Fleet Photographic Officer; (4) Textual and photographic coverage of Fleet operations, with proper censorship, as an essential adjunct of an effective publicity campaign; (5) Automobile transportation, for liaison with the press and expeditious coverage of the Fleet in this area.[52]

But under the press-avoidant Kimmel and his staff, Drake explained, "The entire proposal was killed, with the proviso that nothing be done until I have opportunity for further observation in the Fleet."[53] While he would rack up public relations accomplishments, both large and small, Drake's comprehensive Fleet public relations plan never earned approval. He lacked the authority to implement the changes he sought.

To add to the confusion, the Navy permitted the conflation of journalism and public relations. Drake was a capable journalist, skilled in writing ability, news sense, expertise in photography and equipment, and knowledge of publishing practices. As an editor, he understood how to produce a newsworthy press release and photograph, and he maintained a useful network of journalists, photographers, and editors. Drake's journalism experience gave him immense knowledge of maritime affairs and the news business. What it did not give him was expertise in strategic planning for public relations.[54] But in 1941, Drake—the veteran *Times* newsman— was selected to be the Pacific Fleet's first PRO precisely because Navy officials presumed "one hippopotamus can talk to another hippopotamus."[55]

Placing a journalist in the role of Fleet PRO appeared to have little downside prior to the Pearl Harbor attack, but it created immediate challenges once the war began. Critically, the practices Drake used to publicize the Fleet were not the same ones he needed to respond to the Pearl Harbor catastrophe. Crisis communication is most effective when it is part of the decision process itself, but Kimmel and the CINCPAC staff marginalized Drake.[56] Public relations, they deemed, was merely a staff implementation function. As a result, the meaning of the Pearl Harbor attack was left for others to shape. The lack of public relations planning ensured that Drake would be forced to play defense with reporters rather than offense. Aside from wartime censorship policies, the Navy did not develop communication strategies from pre-event to post-event regarding the outbreak of war. Moreover, the Navy's security strictures and censorship directives prevented the development of honesty, candor, and openness, attributes that are needed to build credibility and trust with the public.[57] Some members of the press became suspicious of Drake's motives. By concealing information to protect security, Drake assumed he was operating in the best interest of the public, yet by doing so he ultimately eroded the trust of the journalists he needed to help him tell the Navy's story.

During the interwar period, the Navy had developed considerable skill in handling public relations crises.[58] But OPR officials had no strategic plan to immediately scale up Fleet public relations after the outbreak of war. Drake explained in a July 9, 1941, letter to Stahlman, "Higher authority throughout the Fleet has not been given clear appreciation of the Navy Department's public relations policy. Recommendation: Issue a basic directive, with specific indication of type and scope of news and photographic material essential to success of the mission."[59] But Drake confused policy with strategy. On August 22, 1941, Hepburn issued a memorandum to the District commandants and commanders-in-chief of the Atlantic and Pacific Fleets, with Secretary Knox's endorsement, titled "Public Relations Offices, Organization and functions of," that included three enclosures: (a) "Organization Plan for Establishment of Public Relations Offices Afloat and Ashore"; (b) "Functions of a Public Relations Office Afloat and Ashore"; and (c) "Summary of Ready Clearance Topics for Public Relations Officers Afloat and Ashore."[60] Together, the documents provided a public relations road map for PROs and their supervisors. The primary function of PROs was to facilitate "co-operation with the press, radio and photographic agencies engaged in disseminating public information." At the top of the list of responsibilities was "security of information, disclosure of which might be detrimental to the Naval Service and the national defense." The specific tasks assigned to PROs were immense:

(a) Create favorable opinion for the Navy and its personnel. (b) Correctly state facts concerning casualties and thereby prevent unfavorable treatment of regrettable situations by publication of erroneous matter. (c) Protect Naval secrets and confidential information from publication through a merited confidence of news-disseminating agencies. (d) Simplify release of public information to proper news-disseminating agencies as a coordinating factor for the Naval Service. (e) Plan and develop public events such as visits of distinguished persons to Naval commands. (f) Arrange for and control photographic activities of news agencies within Naval commands in accordance with the provisions of General Order No. 96. (g) Prepare and edit public addresses. (h) Prepare and edit motion picture and radio script. (i) Arrange for public speakers on Naval topics.

The guidance contained in Hepburn's memoranda did not fully address censorship, although security and protection of information could be construed as close cousins. Even with the new guidance in place, however, Drake and OPR officials hadn't developed anything resembling a strategic communication plan. Instead, the Navy's approach to public relations exemplified the "public information model."[61] Drake was a journalist-in-residence who disseminated information about the Fleet but who did not volunteer negative information. He granted reporters access and facilitated coverage, but he did not seek information about key stakeholders or audiences ("publics") through research. He would not have been expected to: public opinion research and strategic planning were conducted under OPR's auspices in Washington, D.C.. Nevertheless, the public information model shaped how Drake and others understood his role, leading to problems that might have been avoided had Fleet officials held a more strategic view of public relations.

Drake's experience as a maritime reporter and editor, coupled with his work as a Naval Reserve intelligence officer, made him well-suited to serve as the first PRO for the Pacific Fleet under prewar conditions. Drake understood how the press worked, and he'd demonstrated an ability to earn publicity while protecting security. But as a journalist-in-residence, Drake was not trained in public relations. Drake's soon-to-be principal contact at OPR, Berry, was a self-confessed public relations neophyte. OPR's first director, Hepburn, likewise possessed no formal background in public relations. They could hardly have been expected to; the occupational field of public relations had barely been established, and it would be years before anything approaching a body of academic literature guided practice. The American Council on Public Relations had been established only in 1939, and the Public Relations Society of America did not yet exist.

In sum, Drake's public relations work, first for Coffman and the Eleventh Naval District, and then for Kimmel and the Fleet, reveals that he conceived of public relations primarily as media relations, a widespread and intuitive conflation that persists today. It is therefore unsurprising his ill-fated prewar memorandum for the Fleet did not propose any basic, fundamental strategic communication planning activities: research, audience analysis, objective setting, message development, or outcomes measurement.[62] Armed chiefly with his expertise in journalism, Drake attempted to manage his overlapping and conflicting duties: security, censorship, public relations, and publicity. But changes were coming: the Pacific Fleet's new commander-in-chief was about to arrive.

5

Bad Manor

There once was a man so handsome and tall, ran Public
Relations with NO VOICE AT ALL.

—Anonymous

PRESIDENT ROOSEVELT and Secretary Knox quickly agreed on who
should relieve Kimmel. Knox informed Nimitz on December 16,
1941, that he'd been appointed the new commander-in-chief of the Pacific
Fleet. Nimitz identified a replacement for his position as chief of the
Bureau of Navigation and three days later departed Washington, D.C., on
the B. & O.'s Capitol Limited. Train travel to the West Coast allowed him
more time to prepare for his coming duties. Accompanying Nimitz was his
flag secretary, Lt. (jg) Arthur "Hal" Lamar, USNR, who carried top secret
photos showing that much of the Pacific Fleet's once glorious Battle Line
lay in ruins at Pearl Harbor, a fact Drake had been trying to conceal from
the Japanese by making sure they didn't read about it in the American
press. After a delayed departure from San Diego, the Catalina Flying Boat
carrying Nimitz touched down in Pearl Harbor late on Christmas Eve.[1]

The next morning, Drake was in his office at the submarine base awaiting Nimitz's arrival. Since December 7, he'd done his best to conceal the
success of the Japanese attack, releasing just enough information about
the Fleet (through OPR officials in Washington, D.C.) to reassure Americans of the Navy's ability to fight in the Pacific. Earlier, during the Joseph
Shaw affair, Drake had proven to Nimitz he could handle public relations

crises, but like other CINCPAC staff members, Drake assumed the new commander-in-chief would replace most of Kimmel's staff with his own personnel. It was just a matter of time before Drake would be reassigned elsewhere in the labyrinth of the Navy, he presumed. Until that day arrived, Drake vowed to support Nimitz.

When he arrived at CINCPAC headquarters, Nimitz called the entire staff into Kimmel's old office. With his blue-gray eyes, fine white hair, and the bearing of an "elder statesman," he spoke softly and to the point. His quiet confidence soon convinced the staff of his ability to pull the Fleet out of the low state in which he'd found it. He described the meetings in Washington, D.C., that had led to his appointment.[2] He'd urged the selection of Vice Adm. W. S. Pye, USN, as permanent commander-in-chief (Pye had temporarily relieved Kimmel), but such a decision was not to be. Looking at the thirty-two men assembled in the office, he said, "I know most of you here, and I have complete confidence in your ability and judgment. We've taken a whale of a wallop, but I have no doubt of the ultimate outcome."[3] The entire staff was transferred intact to Nimitz; there would be no immediate and traumatic changes. Drake breathed a sigh of relief and found renewed purpose, later remarking that "when Admiral Nimitz came, he lost no time in reviving the spirits of all hands. He did it quietly, almost without you realizing it. But the spirit began to come up, day by day."[4]

Drake and Bassett were tasked with publicizing the change-of-command ceremony, a scaled-down affair with none of the traditional pomp or pageantry. The ceremony occurred at 1000 on December 31, 1941. Photographers took pictures of Nimitz with officers and enlisted men on the deck of the submarine *Grayling* (SS 209), but the actual ceremony itself took place on the submarine base ramp. A quadruple line of officers stood at attention to listen to Nimitz read his orders. Bassett was later unnerved when he examined photos of the ceremony; the one person who wasn't respectfully staring straight ahead was an officer in the last row who had his head turned: himself. "I was looking up to be sure that the darned photographers were where they were supposed to be," he lamented.[5] The photo of Nimitz on board the *Grayling* offered a more compelling image. It scarcely mattered; no photographs of the ceremony were published at the time due to security.

Nimitz knew Drake from their interactions in Southern California when Nimitz served as Commander Battleship Division 1 and earlier served as chief of staff to the Battle Force commander. He also remembered Drake from the Joseph Shaw affair as well as from Kimmel's scathing letter to the Bureau of Navigation concerning OPR's overreach. Having the Fleet's PRO already known to him probably eased Nimitz's apprehensiveness. While externally he projected confidence, internally Nimitz was less assured. He was unable to sleep through the night and soon developed symptoms of nervous tension.[6]

Like other naval officers, Nimitz sought to delegate authority and decision making as much as possible. Doing so empowered subordinates to take individual initiative and creatively solve problems. "Pushing authority down to the point where new information was emerging" was Nimitz's managerial style, and it worked.[7] Public relations was an area where Nimitz likewise hoped he could delegate authority and decision making, but Drake needed to prove he could handle his wartime duties. Fortunately, the admiral and his PRO were well-matched. "Drake was a conscientious and extremely loyal man, inclined to hot temper and sometimes injudicious use of language," one historian put it, "but he knew precisely how Nimitz wanted the press handled, and he did as he was told."[8]

☆☆☆☆☆☆☆☆☆☆

After he took command, Nimitz learned about the structure and processes of Fleet public relations. Layton, the Fleet's intelligence officer (and official Fleet censor), continued to delegate press censorship duties to Drake and Bassett, an arrangement codified in a February 12, 1942, Fleet staff memorandum stating, "Effective this date, the Public Relations Officer will assume responsibility for the proper censorship and release of all Public Relations' matter concerning the U.S. Pacific Fleet."[9] Drake reported to Nimitz's assistant chief of staff for administration, Capt. Harold Train, USN (later Capt. Lloyd Wiltse, USN), but he also approached Nimitz through his flag secretary, Lt. Cdr. Paul Crosley, USN. Drake's tasks required him to interact frequently with Nimitz, although this usually took the form of drafting memoranda and letters for the admiral's review and signature.

He didn't always attend Nimitz's daily staff meetings, but he joined often enough to keep abreast of the Fleet's plans.[10] Drake nevertheless realized he was shorthanded. He requested additional personnel, but Nimitz penned his response, "I do not think the time is yet ripe for [public relations] to expand."[11] On January 4, 1942, Drake lobbied Nimitz to allow correspondents to take passage with the Fleet (assigned to ships by lot) as "a measure of basic policy."[12] Nimitz approved Drake's recommendation.

The Fourteenth Naval District's intelligence officer and official censor, Capt. Irving Mayfield, USN, and members of his staff were so overwhelmed with their new duties that Mayfield asked Drake and Riddick to help with radio and cable censorship.[13] The District covered the Hawaiian Islands and outlying islands to the west. Nimitz did not object to Mayfield's request. At the time, only about a dozen correspondents were in Honolulu, so Drake believed he could handle the extra duty. Military operations were covered by the two major Honolulu newspapers, the *Star-Bulletin* and the *Advertiser*, and also by the small staffs of the United Press, Associated Press, and International News Service. Most correspondents interviewed Navy personnel whom Drake or Riddick made available; otherwise, they wrote cheerleading stories or rewrote Navy Department communiques, passing them off as fresh news.[14] Complicating matters, the Navy did not use its own transmission facilities for press copy. Getting the news out of Hawaii was accomplished through commercial companies—RCA, Mackay Radio, Globe Wireless, and the Commercial Cable Company—as well as through the telephone and the U.S. mail. These organizations were forbidden to send back to the United States any news that did not bear Drake or Riddick's stamp of approval.[15]

All correspondents operated under military jurisdiction and were required to submit their material to Drake (for the Fleet) or Riddick (for the District) for review and approval. A January 9, 1942, memorandum Drake drafted provided the basis for his censorship decisions, which were based on Navy Department policy. It stated, "In general, correspondents' copy will be passed if it is: accurate in statement and implications; does not supply military information, aid or comfort to the enemy; does not injure the morale of our forces, the people at home, or our Allies; does not embarrass the United States, its Allies or neutral countries."[16] Drake scrutinized any references to military operations or morale. He ran a red pencil over anything he believed might possibly benefit the enemy, weaken the resolve of U.S. forces or allies, or dampen the morale of Americans back home.

For example, Drake stamped "Released by CINC PACFLT for publication. W. W. Drake" on United States Pacific Fleet Press Release No. 13. The release contained the remarks of Capt. Ellis Zacharias, USN, to his ship's company upon her return to patrol duty after a visit to Pearl Harbor.[17] Drake ran his red pencil over references to the crew's low morale after seeing the destruction at Pearl Harbor. The marks cover these lines: "I am really sorry that the ship had to go into Pearl Harbor the other day and observe what had taken place there, because I think it served to give you all an entirely wrong impression," and, "Therefore, do not let the things you have seen depress you."[18] Protecting morale deeply concerned Drake, but some correspondents did not share his belief that American morale was so fragile.

Drake was the first U.S. Navy official nearly all war correspondents met upon arrival in Honolulu and adjacent Pearl Harbor. Since he stood over six feet tall and often had a severe look on his long, stern face, he proved intimidating to some of the men, a few of whom were barely half his age. When meeting arriving correspondents, Drake could strike terror into the more faint-hearted. One correspondent told his editor that Drake was "the meanest *hombre* in Pearl Harbor."[19] Photographer W. Eugene Smith later recalled his first meeting with Drake, which quickly deteriorated into a fight over censorship, even though Smith had yet to take a single photograph.[20] Whether Nimitz was fully aware of Drake's menacing reputation is unclear, but Drake once observed that the admiral "had a tremendous ability to pick the right man and leave him alone."[21] Nimitz needed to trust his PRO to handle the press, and Drake delivered.

There was actually some good news to report. While the Pacific Fleet, for the most part, played defense in the early months of 1942, the submarines, under the command of Rear Adm. Robert English, USN, went on the offensive, aggressively attacking Japan's merchant fleet. English's successes made him popular, and the correspondents in Honolulu desperately wanted an interview. They needed something substantial to send back to their offices on the mainland. Somehow, behind Drake's back, the correspondents arranged to interview English one morning at the Royal Hawaiian Hotel, several miles away from CINCPAC headquarters. Drake found out about the meeting at the last minute. He rushed southward toward Waikiki where English was already talking to the newsmen. Drake located the group in the Coronet lounge. He let the correspondents finish their interview, uncrossed his arms, then said, "Boys, you cooked this thing up without getting Admiral Nimitz's permission or mine. All these notes have to be turned over to me and we've got to get Admiral Nimitz's approval."[22] The correspondents realized they'd been busted and reluctantly handed Drake their notes.

Nimitz found out about the interview that afternoon and called Drake into his office. The normally calm and steady admiral looked agitated. Before Drake had a chance to speak, Nimitz lashed out, "I know these fellows have been after English. You know the trouble we've had with the submarines and torpedo exploders. This wasn't supposed to get adrift. Now, I find out it has, and I'm not going to put up with it."[23] Drake looked him in the eye and said, "Admiral, they did this behind your back, but I've got all their notes."[24] Nimitz grinned. Drake had proven he could keep the Fleet's secrets out of America's newspapers by himself, and that's exactly how Nimitz wanted it.

It wasn't an easy job. Correspondents in Honolulu befriended military personnel who offered "scuttlebutt" about the Fleet that, according to one journalist, "would make Waldo's ears ring."[25] Said another correspondent, "Scuttlebutt was perpetual and loquacious . . . about everything under the sun—and a surprising amount of it was accurate, originating from 'sources.'"[26] The loose talk prompted Secretary Knox to issue a stern memorandum to all ships and stations: "This irresponsible juggling of vital information is unworthy of the uniform, and a violation of the oath of allegiance."[27] Drake wouldn't confirm any of it, and correspondents were forbidden to print any of it. It was a game of cat and mouse.

During spare moments, the admiral walked around the submarine base, chitchatting with his officers. He might wander over to the public relations unit, where he usually stopped at the threshold, "as if he were waiting for an invitation to come in," before he started talking.[28] Drake and Bassett were at their desks one afternoon when the admiral stopped by. They began discussing the code names that were used when talking about places and objectives in the Pacific. "Take Truk," Nimitz said. "That should be called *cojones*." Nimitz explained that's what he hoped to have the Japanese by in the future.[29] Drake appreciated Nimitz's confidence, bluntness, and humor.

At times, a correspondent might ask Drake if Nimitz would agree to an interview. Nimitz would oblige if there was nothing pressing. He might tell a few of his colorful stories or brag about some of his officers. The correspondent went away pleased, glad to have spoken with the admiral. But as soon as he sat down to write his story, he realized Nimitz had actually told him little. Correspondents hoping for newsworthy information "soon learned to their dismay that the stolid white-haired Texan was determined to give them nothing interesting or quotable."[30] Hounding Nimitz was not an option, however. Bassett explained that Nimitz was "very kindly but nobody took any liberties with him."[31] If a little intimidation underscored this point with visiting correspondents, Drake certainly didn't mind providing it. He'd gained a reputation for toughness while covering the Port of Los Angeles in the 1920s and 1930s, and compared to the fists, brickbats, and knives of striking longshoremen, a tongue-lashing from an irate correspondent hardly registered.

One correspondent noted that some of the more inventive newsmen vented their frustrations over Drake by composing songs about him. To understand these ditties, one must appreciate Drake's raspy voice, a cross between a husky baritone and a gruff whisper. Many correspondents remarked he sounded like a scratchy record. One song went like this, "There once was a man so handsome and tall, ran Public Relations with NO VOICE AT ALL."[32] But correspondents had to ensure that Drake did not catch wind of their antipathy; they needed to get their stories past his red pencil. Correspondents who risked offending Drake might find themselves wandering the streets of Honolulu without much hope of finding news, while those who maintained cordial relations with the PRO could receive orders from Nimitz directing them to board a task force vessel. Drake might call a newsman out of the blue and say, "Don't make any plans for the week end," followed a few days later by, "Be up here by noon today—going fishing."[33] Sailing with the Fleet to an unknown location, however, could be dubious. Foster Hailey of the *New York Times* once clashed with

Drake and found himself assigned to a tanker that eventually ended up in Fiji, a fate worse than death for a correspondent in the Pacific.

✶✶✶✶✶✶✶✶✶✶

Drake's courtesy and care occasionally outshined his steely reputation. A month after the Pearl Harbor attack, he gave United Press' London bureau manager Wallace Carroll and Honolulu bureau manager Frank Tremaine an up-close look at what the Japanese had done.[34] He hoped the tour would give the two men a better understanding of the difficult situation the Navy faced but could not publicly reveal. Drake had received a telephone call from Tremaine, who said Carroll had sailed from Shanghai on the passenger liner *President Coolidge* a day before the Japanese attacked Pearl Harbor. The Japanese offensive had forced the *President Coolidge* to leave her normal route. She had taken a circuitous course far to the south, finally arriving in Honolulu in early January. Drake invited Carroll and Tremaine to come out to CINCPAC headquarters.

Tremaine, twenty-eight years old, had arrived in Hawaii in 1940. Deeply tanned from his year on Oahu and enjoying an extended honeymoon with his new wife, Kay, he'd been one of the first eyewitnesses to file a dispatch of the Pearl Harbor attack. He thought Drake was going to give them a quick briefing, maybe introduce them to some staff members, and let it go at that. Instead, Drake arranged for the three of them to tour the entire yard by launch, getting a water-level look at the devastated Battleship Row. From their position they could also see the destruction at the naval air station on Ford Island. Carroll and Tremaine could not print what they had seen, but the tour enabled Carroll to brief the United Press president, managing editor, and other top people at their New York headquarters, giving them a better picture of the situation than they could get from any other source. Tremaine was appreciative of Drake's transparency and kindness, but also a little confused. He and Wallace were likely the first civilians to have seen the damage up close. "Back at the Sub Base, when we stepped off the launch I thanked Waldo for giving us such an extraordinary view of the condition of the fleet. I didn't think it politic just then to ask why he had done it but I couldn't understand it, grateful as I was."[35] It was in Drake's interest to show influential correspondents and editors that the Fleet's security concerns and censorship were justified.

Whether his usual intimidating behavior was all an act or not, Drake was confronted with some correspondents who didn't fear him. One of them was the *Chicago Daily News'* Robert Casey. Both Casey and Drake had served in the Army in World War I, with Casey discharged at the rank of captain and Drake at the rank of corporal. Portly, pugnacious, and seven years Drake's senior, Casey was a respected, veteran correspondent who'd covered the blitz in London in 1940.[36] The day after the Pearl Harbor attack, Casey had flown to Washington, D.C., to obtain his Pacific Fleet accreditation from Hepburn himself at OPR; having the Secretary of the Navy as one's boss conveyed certain privileges. Accreditation in hand, he rushed back to Chicago and then traveled by train to San Francisco, boarding a Navy supply vessel bound for Honolulu. Also on board were Universal newsreel cameraman Norman Alley, Paramount newsreel cameraman Joe Rucker, and International News Services' Ralph Jordan. The men arrived in Pearl Harbor on December 19 without ever encountering the Japanese vessels presumed to be prowling the waters between Hawaii and the West Coast.

Casey was unimpressed with Drake's *Times* credentials, although he conceded the Fleet PRO "presumably knew something about the newspaper business."[37] For Casey, "That put him one up on everybody in the neighborhood." After a few weeks in Honolulu cataloguing a list of what he believed were the Navy's public relations shortcomings, Casey wrote a complaining letter to his publisher, Secretary Knox. To make sure his letter was brought to Knox's personal attention, Casey included a story about being shadowed by "security guards."[38] Censors intercepted the letter and showed it to Drake, who showed it to Nimitz, who let it pass, trusting Knox's good sense to discredit the claim. Knox, however, was concerned enough to fire off a dispatch to Nimitz. "Bob Casey, *Chicago Daily News*, now in Honolulu, will call on you. Please listen to him on Navy censorship question. You can rely on whatever he tells you. Hope you can correct present conditions that are complained of."[39] Knox's request irritated Nimitz, who considered declining to let Casey privately tell him how to run his command; always the diplomat, though, Nimitz scheduled the meeting.[40]

The meeting was held on January 15, 1942. Present with Nimitz and Drake were Rear Adm. Claude Bloch, USN, the commandant of the Fourteenth Naval District in Hawaii (and the commander-in-chief of the U.S. Fleet from 1938 to 1940), Mayfield, Layton, and Crosley. Facing the intimidating group of brass hats, Casey's only ally in the meeting was the renowned correspondent Hubert Knickerbocker of the *Chicago Sun-Times*. Despite the lopsided affair, Nimitz put Casey at ease, agreeing with him that correspondents should be shown censors' deletions from their stories and allowed to "dress up" missing text.[41] The meeting compelled the Navy to better clarify the distinctions between Fleet and District domains as well as promise to avoid dual censorship. Casey's mollification didn't last long; he continued to feed Secretary Knox reports about the unsatisfactory state of public relations in the Pacific. Only three weeks into his new job as commander-in-chief, Nimitz didn't need to tell Drake that hosting meetings with disgruntled correspondents wasn't to his liking. Drake intuited the admiral's wishes and was eager to ship Casey out of Pearl Harbor. He arranged for Casey's assignment to a task force sailing westward for a raid on the Marshall Islands.

Joseph Harsch, whose wife, Anne, had returned to the West Coast at the same time as Mary and the children, realized, as did Casey, that the news was no longer in Pearl Harbor.[42] While the Navy held position, supporting President Roosevelt's "Europe first" policy, Japan had racked up victories from the Philippines to the Indian Ocean. Harsch asked Drake to get him to Singapore, closer to the action. Drake laughed at Harsch but promised he would see what he could do. Drake had a way of getting things done that left many people with the suspicion he knew everyone in the Navy. A few days later he sent for Harsch and asked him, "Would you like a ride?"[43]

"To where?" Harsch asked.

Drake said, "I can't tell you, but if you want a ride, report to the *Enterprise* tomorrow morning at 0800."

"Waldo, you know I want to go to Singapore. You wouldn't send me on a wild goose chase would you?" Harsch asked.

Drake grinned and said, "If you want a ride, be at the gangplank of the *Enterprise* at 0800 tomorrow morning, and by the way, don't say anything to your editor."[44]

Drake, of course, would have known if Harsch had mentioned anything to his editor because District censors were monitoring correspondents' personal communication for breaches of security and passing along
infractions to Drake to handle.[45] Accustomed to eavesdropping practices
from his work with ONI, Drake had no misgivings about reading correspondents' mail. Censors soon intercepted a letter from the *Chicago Times'*
Keith Wheeler to his editor that contained confidential information,
resulting in Wheeler's temporary deaccreditation. Observing Wheeler's
fate, Harsch got the message. He didn't say anything to his editor, but he
still had a dilemma: his orders were to get to Singapore. He didn't know
whether it would be better to wait for some ship he knew was going to the
Far East or take a chance on what might turn out to be a cruise to nowhere.
Drake offered the same choice to Knickerbocker of the *Chicago Sun-Times.*
Harsch and Knickerbocker talked it over. Knickerbocker was fairly sure
Drake wouldn't deliberately send them on a voyage that would bring them
right back to Pearl Harbor. They packed and arrived at the gangplank of
the massive aircraft carrier USS *Enterprise* at 0800. The flattop would participate in a raid on the Marshall Islands. The two correspondents eventually reached their destinations, "mentally" thanking Drake for having their
assignments in mind when he'd arranged for them to travel on board the
Enterprise.[46] It had been a great favor, for correspondents were not officially
allowed to hitch rides with the Fleet until mid-March.

Drake's menacing reputation tended to overshadow such acts of goodwill. He knew many of the correspondents who'd come to Oahu to cover
the war, but as time went on, it became clear that his familiarity with these
men was not a benefit to the Navy. Personalities often entered the disputes.
If Drake was unfriendly to the efforts of a particular correspondent, he
could be stringent on his ruling. Conversely, if he liked a correspondent,
he might allow a liberal interpretation of a release. Both circumstances
presented problems: if he were too strict, it only added to the poor impression of Fleet public relations, but if he were too liberal, he faced a possible
reprimand from Nimitz or others on the staff for not properly concealing Navy secrets. The latter situation Drake tried hard to avoid. Most disputes occurred when Drake censored for the morale of U.S. forces or the
American public, or for security restrictions. Consequently, Drake earned

the animosity of the correspondents who disagreed with him about what material needed to be removed.

For example, International News Service's Richard Tregaskis arrived in Honolulu in early 1942, and like many correspondents, his first stories dealt with his transport convoy to Oahu. Tregaskis submitted one of his stories to Drake, who blocked its publication because, contrary to Navy censorship guidelines, it contained the names of enlisted men. Tregaskis asked Drake why the names of enlisted men couldn't be mentioned.

"Because there was a rule that said one could not," Drake replied, which mystified Tregaskis, since the names of officers could be included in stories.

The correspondent harped about the seemingly inconsistent restriction for weeks, but he didn't push Drake too far, noticing that the Fleet's PRO often appeared "vexed" and "extremely worried."[47] Tregaskis realized it was better to avoid antagonizing the Fleet's PRO and *chief censor*.

The timing of releases also created headaches for Drake. A crisis erupted when OPR officials in Washington, D.C., jumped the gun on releasing stories of Fleet raids of Japanese bases in the Marshall Islands and Gilbert Islands. The raids had occurred in early February and been carried out by two separate carrier task forces. The action was highly symbolic, an effort to demonstrate to the American public that the Navy was hitting back. Drake had timed the release dates to ensure fairness for all press outlets seeking to entice readers with fresh headlines from the Pacific, but OPR fumbled the handoff in Washington, D.C., riling journalists and editors who saw it as evidence that Secretary Knox was pulling strings to benefit his own newspaper and its affiliates.[48] Adding to the tension, Casey—Knox's man in Pearl Harbor—had been out with one of the task forces heroically "dodging enemy bombs," appearing, ironically, to have benefited from Drake's favoritism.[49]

Drake recognized he needed OPR's guidance on how to handle the growing tension before fingers were pointed at him. On February 20, 1942, Drake handed a confidential letter to Capt. Willard Kitts III, USN, to take to Washington, D.C. Only a few years older than Drake, Kitts had served on Kimmel's staff and was well-connected. Kitts had been tasked with a visit to the Bureau of Ordnance, but Drake thought he might be able to help him at OPR as well. In the letter's first paragraph, Drake implored Kitts, "[W]ill you please ask Admiral Hepburn and his Assistant Director, Commander Bob Berry, (if he has not already gone to sea), to give you an outline of what they expect from the Commander-in-Chief in the public relations field? Please emphasize that we have had no directives from the Office of Public Relations since the outbreak of hostilities except several despatches about specific situations."[50] Drake was unsure exactly what the Fleet's public relations role should be under wartime conditions. He instructed Kitts, "The point should be emphasized whether public relations in the Fleet is to be solely (a) a collection agency for Washington or (b) whether it should be both a collection agency and a distribution headquarters. If the latter, then what limitations are prescribed." In absence of guidance from OPR, Drake had charted a course somewhere between (a) and (b), distributing material locally after OPR's official release, but the uncertainty left him uneasy.

In his letter, Drake proposed the "continuance" of an extensive list of practices he'd improvised, asking Kitts to check with Hepburn and Berry whether "the following procedure by the Commander-in-Chief is in accord with the Director's [Hepburn's] policies." Drake's proposals included continuing to release stories and photographs locally for distribution immediately following OPR's own release in Washington, D.C.,. Correspondents were then free to transmit those stories to their stateside bureaus. In this way, the Fleet was not merely a collection point for news and publicity shipped to OPR for final release. Drake had instead arranged for the Fleet to play a central role within the Navy's overall public relations effort.

In hindsight, OPR officials' failure to provide Drake directives concerning the Fleet's wartime public relations is stunning. The Pearl Harbor crisis understandably created chaos in the Navy Department in Washington, D.C., but the failure to issue Drake any guidance for nearly three months must be interpreted as a lapse that contributed to the problems of war reporting in the Pacific, problems that also permanently marred Drake's reputation. In his letter to Kitts, Drake was blunt: "Please emphasize that Admiral Nimitz is anxious to cooperate fully with the press, but that lack of information on definite policies and desires of the Director of Public Relations, as evinced by recent despatches from SecNav, has left our Fleet press relations pretty much up in the air." One is left to speculate whether Kimmel's earlier rebuke of Hepburn somehow contributed to OPR's decision to keep Drake in the dark.

Drake's letter to Kitts drew attention to the needs of the correspondents assigned to the Fleet. These correspondents were, for the most part, brave and self-sacrificing professionals who, like almost everyone else, worried about the security of their jobs and prospects for advancement.[51] Understandably, these interests shaped their conflicts with Drake and contributed to their dissatisfaction with Fleet public relations. For example, soon after the Pearl Harbor attack, OPR proposed creating a press pool to share the limited news emanating from the Fleet. The idea was met with scorn in Honolulu. Drake explained why in his letter to Kitts: "All of the present friction out here with newspaper representatives is caused by their feeling that they are not living up to their jobs, and they fear they will lose them if all the releases are centered in Washington thereby eliminating any need of correspondents out here. The reaction of the pooling idea now is 'why bother to risk my life in a Task Force at sea if John Jones is going to do it for me.'"

Drake understood the financial stakes involved. "In spite of the dangers they faced while in combat," one scholar observed, there were plenty of perks for war correspondents, including a decent salary, expense account, and a fine room at one of Honolulu's splendid hotels: "No BOQ [bachelor officers' quarters] for him unless all the hotel rooms were booked."[52] One reporter confessed that the "war correspondent was pursued by book publishers and travel agents, and he could usually find time for these people pressing money upon him."[53] Drake's position afforded him considerable influence in determining which correspondents found themselves in the middle of a story that could bring notoriety and financial reward.

Robert Sherrod, correspondent for *Life* and *Time*, who would later gain fame for his reporting of the Battle of Tarawa, described how correspondents occupied a privileged position. As honorary Navy officers, they were not subject to the same responsibilities and burdens as enlisted personnel, and they were often called on by senior officers to share frank discussions about the war and world affairs that could not be had with others in the chain of command.[54] Correspondents' civilian salary also came in handy when buying a few rounds of drinks for friends and acquaintances at watering holes in Honolulu. Most importantly, correspondents were free to come and go from the theater of war, which allowed them to maintain their connections to their stateside bureaus as well as devote time to professional projects. In Sherrod's case (as in several others), that time included writing an acclaimed book. Reporting on action in the Pacific could be lucrative. Correspondents' criticisms of Drake thus reflected multiple motivations.

While he understood the professional stakes for correspondents, Drake's loyalties were strictly with the Navy. He explained to Kitts, "Correspondents accredited to the Fleet are continually importuning us for permission to release a greater percentage of 'fresh' news copy under Honolulu date line."[55] Drake thought it prudent to acquiesce, however, because it advanced the Navy's interests. He noted, "If this can be permitted without discomfiting the procedure of Admiral Hepburn's office I earnestly recommend that it be done, as a measure of both diplomacy and propaganda," a comment that underscores how he understood his job. He aimed to use public relations tactics to promote the Navy's interests, rather than simply distribute wartime information. Drake began to see the correspondents' requests as akin to harassment. Navy officers had traditionally kept the press at arm's length, and as the journalists pressed CINCPAC for more information, Drake's dealings with them began to resemble a struggle between adversaries.

In all conflicts, Drake held loyal to Nimitz. Time and again, in letters to OPR officials and others, Drake depicted Nimitz as sincere in his desire to find harmony between the press and the Fleet, even at times serving as an advocate for their interests. From Drake's perspective, however, harmony remained elusive through no fault of his own. For example, in the letter to Kitts, Drake explained, "I also feel that, in fairness to the Commander-in-Chief, Admiral Hepburn should be apprised that the recent difficulty on press censorship in Honolulu was entirely a district matter, in which the Fleet had no part—except to correct the situation." While mostly true, some correspondents apportioned blame to Drake and the Fleet. If Drake had taken a more strategic view of public relations, pivoting from reactive response to proactive collaboration, some of that blame may have been avoided. But Drake never gave any ground in accepting the criticisms leveled against him.

The problems, as Drake saw them, were with the District, absent or unclear guidance from OPR, or the flat-out falsehoods of disgruntled correspondents. In warning Berry about an incoming letter from Casey in late March, Drake stated, "Like the usual 'Casey letter', it will start more trouble just when 'trouble' would be poor policy."[56] There is scant evidence Drake accepted (let alone considered) that strategic planning could be used to improve Fleet public relations. In the first year of the war, he advocated on behalf of correspondents with Nimitz and OPR officials, but he was outright dismissive of his most vociferous critics. Drake did not seek systematic input from correspondents nor strategize *with* them about how to best improve conditions and coverage. He failed to recognize how his role as censor chilled critical feedback that might otherwise have been offered in the spirit of collaboration.

At the end of the letter, Drake asked Kitts to convey his regards to McCollum at ONI, offering an inside joke: "Meanwhile, sir, keep your powder dry until you resume command at Bad Manor. With regards from the 'depth charge committee.'" Bad Manor was the name Drake had given his "menage," his housemate being thirty-eight-year-old Lt. Cdr. Francis Black, USN, aerological officer of Patrol Wing 2 (later Fleet personnel officer). Black's profile in the Naval Academy's 1926 *Lucky Bag* stated, "He is a mean man to get in an argument with, for he never admits defeat but will hold his ground against all logic."[57] After Mary and the children had departed Oahu, Drake had returned to Pearl Harbor, moving into bachelor officers' quarters with the tenacious Black. The Drake-Black menage was located among a stretch of houses on the road running from the new CINCPAC headquarters building on Makalapa Hill, then still under construction, toward Honolulu. A shared bathroom divided the double rooms in the spartan house, giving privacy. A servant made the beds, took care of the laundry, and kept the place clean.[58] While Drake and Black took most of their meals in the officers' mess, the house had an icebox wherein could be found a few bottles of Bass Ale, chicken fricassee smelling of cold storage, nut ice cream, and discarded cake.[59]

Bad Manor was the site of memorable "wingdings," where Drake and colleagues gathered to consume "small libations" (the euphemisms provided by Lovette, according to Bassett).[60] Bassett tried to reassure Willie that Bad

Manor's bawdy reputation was overblown, writing, "As for Navy nurses, my cherub—you are all wrong. They are for the unmarried ensigns and j.g.'s; we old married men just sit on the sidelines like chaperons at a junior high school hop, nuzzle our beer, and sigh for the Old Days when we, too, were young and full of Vitamin-B."[61] In reality, the wingdings at Bad Manor were subdued affairs. For Black's birthday, Bassett reported, "Waldo and I bought Francis a new silver cap insignia as a present. Genevieve (Black's wife), who is as crazy as a bug, sent him three large Mexican pig-banks, of which two arrived looking like a blitzed Japanese city; a book of children's poems; and four offcolor birthday cards about dogs that couldn't control themselves."[62]

At birthdays and other times, the small libations might include depth charges. When in command at Bad Manor, Kitts would drop shots of whiskey or local Okolehao spirits into pint glasses of beer, and the others partaking in the ritual—usually Drake (the eldest of the group after Kitts), Black, Crosley, Lovette, and their guests—would belt them down. Bassett explained to Willie why he usually abstained, noting, "Hard liquor is scarce, and considering the climate and the horrible effects of a hangover in these latitudes (I remember them from old!), it's just as well. They've drummed up a potion alleged to be a Canadian whiskey called Dumbars, which obviously springs straight from the House of the Boggias [sic] or from the three witches' cauldron on Macbeth's heath. I have smelled of its cork; and I found that even a whiff brought blisters to the skin, so to date I am a true puritan."[63] Primed with a Dumbars depth charge or two, Drake's tendency toward "injudicious language" might rise to the surface. He could, for example, disparage an importune (read: son of a bitch) correspondent who was giving him a hard time.

One reason Drake did not deny an adversarial relationship with the press is because he suspected foul play. In a February 23, 1942, memorandum routed to senior CINCPAC staff members, Drake asserted, "Local representatives of the three wire services, UP, AP and INS, call me so consistently on movements and operations of Fleet task forces that I believe they secure their information from some leak in secret radio traffic."[64] One passage of the memorandum implicated Tremaine: "Frank Tremaine, UP bureau chief here, called late last night and asked for Fleet release on story of a task force action, which he said he had been told had taken place early

yesterday, near Australia. In his efforts to pry some indication from me
he told me that Col. Walter Dunham, aide in the Governor's office, had
told him 'to see if the Fleet will not give you a release on a hot news story.'
Tremaine's tips have been accurate and timely over a period of months."
Drake sounded the alarm: "Consistent repetition of similar instances con-
vinces me that Tremaine and Haller [Richard Haller from INS] have some
regular, accurate sources of information on official traffic."[65] The tips may
have come from errant military radio signals picked up by the United Press
radio receiving station on the northeast edge of Oahu, which the Navy
had inexplicably failed to shut down following the Pearl Harbor blackout.[66]
Either way, correspondents were forbidden at Bad Manor, and in addition
to scrutiny from Drake and Navy censors, some newsmen were soon under
FBI surveillance.[67]

It is tempting to second-guess Drake's adversarial approach to his PRO
duties, but it must be remembered the conditions he confronted in the
aftermath of Pearl Harbor were unusual: the need for strict security to
protect military secrets, a nascent public relations profession with emerging norms and practices, the Navy's uncertainty about how to establish
effective media relations in the expansive Pacific theater, and technolog-
ical constraints on the transmission and reception of internal and exter-
nal messages. But the interpersonal dynamics Drake faced were (and are)
enduring: hostile reporters, superiors who neither understood nor cared
for public relations, and the need to cultivate organizational allies to protect and advance one's interests. In facing these dynamics, organizational
politics made it difficult for Drake to know who to trust. To say the Navy
was "political" is not an accusation; the term is a metaphor for the struggle
that occurs in all large-scale organizations among groups of people who
compete for scarce resources.[68] Drake's PRO position was quintessentially
political in that *influence*—of the press, U.S. lawmakers, military officials,
and citizens (U.S., allies, and adversaries)—was its raison d'etre.

≈≈≈≈≈≈≈≈≈≈≈

Drake's February 20, 1942, letter to OPR via Kitts had not yet reached its des-
tination when Knox decided Casey's troubling reports required an on-site

investigation. Given Hepburn's dressing down by Kimmel in August, he was reluctant to interfere with Drake and risk a repeat of the "two masters" lecture from Nimitz. Knox himself ordered Berry to Oahu to investigate the situation and propose improvements.[69] Lovette had returned to Washington, D.C., as deputy director of OPR—his sea command having literally been sunk as a result of the Pearl Harbor attack—freeing up Berry for the visit. Berry departed Washington, D.C., on February 22, 1942. His plan was to spend one week with Drake and Riddick to understand their activities for the Fleet and the District, then another week with correspondents, local reporters and editors, and business leaders, learning their side of the story before returning to OPR. He was tasked with sending back reports every few days via airmail to Hepburn and Knox. He immediately noted, "Drake is in a position as a result of [his authority to censor and release all public relations matters] to be better informed on action of the PacFleet than Admiral Hepburn in Washington."[70]

Berry met with more than thirty stakeholders: Army, Navy, and federal officials, Fleet and District officials, members of the press, and local business leaders. He organized a luncheon for a large group of them at the Royal Hawaiian Hotel. Bassett's handiwork was evident in the preparations, with participants' names and rhyming ditties typed upon radiogram cards for the seating arrangements. Among them were "Frank Tremaine, UP's pride, Takes all censors for a ride," "Bob Casey unlocks by calling Frank Knox," and "Here's to Waldo, that old tar, He stuck his neck out just too Farr."[71] The Farr ditty was a reference to a controversial story about a Navy convoy written by the *London Daily Mail*'s Washington, D.C., correspondent, Walter Farr. The story, which Drake had passed, resulted in Farr's temporary deaccreditation from the Fleet while OPR officials investigated.[72]

With multiple group meetings and individual interviews, Berry's work was thorough. He identified the major problems: having separate PROs for both the Fleet and the District; Fleet and District PROs' censorship activities; the poor attitude of certain Navy officials toward public relations; and the lack of Army-Navy coordination. At root, many of the issues stemmed, Berry wrote, "from the conflict between 'Security' and 'Publicity' as interpreted by Navy officials."[73] He dubbed the censorship situation the "Dr. Jekyll and Mr. Hyde" problem. For example, Riddick welcomed publicity for the District, but not only had he deleted portions of correspondents' stories without notifying them, he'd also attempted to re-edit them himself. Riddick and Drake were also standoffish with each other. According to Riddick, Drake treated him with indifference, a sign of Drake's air of superiority. Rear Admiral Bloch, the District commandant, acknowledged that "Riddick was a good man but not a newspaperman, being an advertising man instead."[74] Riddick had also been given no written instructions from officials on how to perform his censorship duties. Correspondents and business leaders found Bloch uncooperative and Riddick "particularly obnoxious," Berry reported.[75] By contrast, Berry received positive reports about Drake, while Nimitz was considered "very understanding about public relations."[76]

But Berry's March 8, 1942, summary warned, "Drake and I had quite a talk with Admiral Nimitz who said that he hoped he could put an end to all public relations problems. I voiced my opinion that these would never end—at least, they hadn't in Washington where we had a Secretary of the Navy, Admiral Hepburn and as efficient and experienced advisors in the press world that could be had. He wasn't too happy and I am reluctant to report that I believe he hasn't too much confidence in Drake's abilities."[77] In a later summary, Berry commented, "He [Nimitz] also said that he would be glad to have some regular Naval Officer who is conversant with public relations to head his staff, and asked me if I would like to take the assignment."[78] Berry claimed to have replied, "I had better get back with the active service," whereupon Nimitz reiterated he "would be very glad to have a regular officer who had had such experience." Berry appeared to be setting the stage for Drake's removal.

Coincidently, a story appeared in the March 16, 1942, edition of *Newsweek* explaining that officials had decided the *London Daily Mail's* Farr had so egregiously misrepresented facts in his March 7 convoy story that he would not be reaccredited to the Fleet. An unnamed Navy source added grimly, "Farr could consider Honolulu his abode for the duration unless The Mail discovers commercial transportation to fetch him home."[79] The dateline for Farr's March 7 article had been "written at sea," implying he'd been traveling with a convoy witnessing battle; in truth, he'd been ensconced in his hotel in Honolulu. Stateside editors were livid that Farr, a British correspondent, had seemingly been allowed to publish an eye-witness account while their own American newsmen were pounding sand in Honolulu. They wanted Drake held responsible. Complicating matters, Farr claimed that Drake had told him to change the dateline from Honolulu to "at sea." The *Newsweek* article declared, "The censor himself, Lt. Comdr. Waldo Drake, former Los Angeles waterfront reporter, was relieved of duty at Honolulu and started back to the mainland to assume new, unspecified tasks."[80] The March 19, 1942, edition of the *Calgary Albertan* carried the same story but placed Drake's removal in the headline: "U.S. Navy Censor 'Fired.' "[81] Presenting a Washington, D.C., dateline, the unnamed writer for the *Albertan* cited the same unnamed Navy source included in the *Newsweek* article. "While disagreeing with the censor's judgement in passing the story, the Navy department added they could 'understand why the censor might not have regarded the story as news.' " Given Berry's reports to OPR—and the challenge Drake's influence presented to Hepburn's authority—the *Newsweek* and *Albertan* articles were suspicious. They were also presumptuous: Drake had not, in fact, been relieved of duty.

The next day, March 20, 1942, Berry provided his final report to Hepburn and Knox. It offered several recommendations. At the top of the list was a reorganization of Fleet public relations centered on the proposed position of "Fleet press censor." This new position differed from "Fleet censor," a position held by the Fleet's intelligence officer, Layton, but in practice was delegated to Drake for press duties. Berry recommended Drake be assigned to the Fleet press censor position—a job he'd already been performing—thereby opening the PRO position for a "regular line officer." Berry wanted Riddick reassigned too, urging that he be transferred to the Office of Censorship, which handled domestic and civilian censorship. Moreover, Navy and Army public relations, while maintaining separate tasks, should be placed in the same office under Nimitz's command, given his overall responsibility for forces in the Hawaiian area. Some of the problems Berry had identified, especially those concerning the District, were addressed with the reorganization of the Office of Censorship in Washington, D.C., which occurred on March 15, 1942.

The Fleet's PRO position remained unassigned in his report, but Berry himself was a "regular line officer." His weeks-long facilitation of press matters in Pearl Harbor may have been less an investigation and more an audition. Who planted the erroneous stories of Drake's removal in *Newsweek* and the *Albertan* was a mystery, but Berry's claim that Drake was better informed about the Fleet than the director of OPR may have provoked the admiral. Berry himself could have inadvertently implied to Farr or a sympathetic correspondent in Pearl Harbor that Drake's relief was imminent. A smart editor would have known to use a Washington, D.C., dateline to mask the source of such explosive information.

Knox's intentions became clear in his June 2, 1942, confidential letter to Nimitz wherein he revealed having asked the admiral to add Berry to his staff earlier in the spring. Having been rebuffed, Knox implored Nimitz to reconsider:

> I have carefully considered the point of view you expressed in your letter concerning Berry and his coming to Honolulu. I feel a great deal of confidence in Berry and I do know that he has, to an unusual degree, an understanding knowledge of the newspaperman' point of view. Why not put him on your staff, say for a six months trial and see how it works out? I say put him on your staff because I think unless he is put in the posture of a staff officer where he can get the information he must have, he cannot function successfully. I have no hesitation in saying you will find Berry a thoroughly trustworthy subordinate and also a highly intelligent one. I do wish you would try him out and I feel that, after a time, you will come to agree with me about the matter.[82]

Whether the secretary helped orchestrate the erroneous report of Drake's removal as PRO is a possibility that cannot be ruled out. Despite Knox's pleas, Nimitz would never add Berry to his staff. Knox was unwilling to force Nimitz's hand. Drake would remain in Pearl Harbor.

Berry's references to Drake in his daily summaries could be plausibly interpreted in three ways. First, Nimitz may have sincerely invited Berry to serve as his PRO, as claimed in Berry's March 13 meeting summary. If true, it means Nimitz had a change of heart sometime between that date and when Secretary Knox asked Nimitz to add Berry to his staff. What could have caused Nimitz to reconsider is unclear, but if Drake suspected

Berry's involvement in the *Newsweek* and *Albertan* articles and told Nimitz about it, the admiral may have soured on Berry joining his staff. But because Berry's March 13 meeting summary claims he demurred when Nimitz offered him the PRO position, it is possible Berry wasn't gunning for Drake's position. A second possibility is that Berry's March 13 meeting summary mistook Nimitz's graciousness as evidence of a desire to replace Drake. Nimitz may have simply been engaging in diplomacy with Knox's emissary from OPR. A final possibility is that Berry interpreted Nimitz's graciousness self-servingly, that is, he deliberately overstated Nimitz's support for replacing Drake to encourage Knox to lobby Nimitz for the PRO position for himself. Whether or not one of these interpretations is accurate, the *Newsweek* and *Albertan* articles, along with Knox's rebuffed requests, suggest there was a struggle over Drake's position.

Earl Thacker, the wealthy real estate investor and OWI liaison Drake had befriended while organizing the Moon Festival gala in 1941, came to Drake's defense. Thacker's letter to the editor of *Newsweek* was published in the May 18, 1942, edition and read,

> Your issue of March 16 carried a story about young Farr of The London Daily Mail in which he was supposed to have a big scoop, and in the article you stated that Lt. Comdr. Waldo Drake, who is head of the Navy Public Relations here on the staff of Admiral Nimitz, was being relieved and sent back to the mainland. Waldo Drake is still very much here, and doing a splendid job for the Navy as well being a great credit to his own paper, The Los Angeles Times, and highly respected and regarded here by the civilian community. I feel you have done Waldo Drake a very great injustice.[83]

Newsweek printed a nonapology, stating only, "Newsweek regrets its story caused discomfort to Lt. Comdr. Waldo Drake, who is still very much on the job in Hawaii." Bassett wrote to Willie that thereafter he'd catch Drake in the office "perusing the morning *Advertiser*, grimly, looking for libel and betrayal of confidences."[84]

Drake kept his head down and plodded forward. On June 3, he wrote to Berry, "I appreciate your explanation of the Secretary's policy on damaged ships. We will comply."[85] The policy prohibited Drake from approving publicity photographs of damaged ships that had managed to return to port. Drake continued, "I presume that you have by this time seen the copy forwarded on the Coral Sea action [May 4–8, 1942]. I hope to get the pictures off tomorrow." Drake also updated Berry on some of Berry's recommendations. "Buck Riddick has received orders to Com-12 and expects to leave today." Most of Berry's recommendations, however, took time to be implemented, and some were abandoned. Drake sought a Fleet press censor, but the position took four months to fill because he couldn't find a candidate he deemed qualified. Drake therefore continued to censor press copy; he played the thoughtful PRO in the morning ("Dr. Jekyll") while reviewing and censoring correspondents' copy at night ("Mr. Hyde"). He believed he was doing correspondents a favor by performing censorship duties himself as it expedited transmission of their copy to the mainland. Berry was convinced that reassigning Drake to the position of Fleet press censor would resolve the major complaints, and it might have done so, but Drake continued to censor copy throughout his entire tenure as PRO. A visiting OPR official noted, "[The Fleet press censor's] word is final but in actual practice he consults with the Public Relations Officer and it's generally a compromise between the two that results in release of all picture and story material."[86] Some correspondents and their editors detected a whiff of arrogance, ensuring that their criticisms of Drake's management of Fleet public relations persisted.

If Berry coveted Drake's Fleet PRO position (and there is room for doubt), it can hardly be condemned. As long as people interact with each other in organizations, groups and individuals will pursue their interests, bringing them into conflict with other groups and individuals; organizational politics is the game that must be played if one is to accrue and maintain power.[87] In this instance, Drake either made the right moves or was lucky. By mid-1942, Drake had learned the value of loyally serving Nimitz and staying in his wake; it allowed him to avoid some of the hazards that Knox and OPR officials placed in his way.

6

Father Neptune

Frankly, we are still having as much difficulty—in getting
news copy and sufficient pictures released—as a couple of
handcuffed fellows trying to climb a greased pole.

—Waldo Drake

T HE FIRST BATTLE REPORTS from Midway reached CINCPAC headquarters on June 4, 1942. Under the overall command of Vice Adm.
Frank "Jack" Fletcher, USN, Task Force 16 and Task Force 17, with Rear
Adm. Raymond Spruance, USN, in command of the former, sank four
of the Japanese carriers that had conducted the Pearl Harbor raid: *Akagi*,
Kaga, *Sōryū*, and *Hiryū*. The CINCPAC staff erupted into cheers upon con-
firmation of the victory. Drake was euphoric. The action would provide him
material for communiques, interviews, press releases, and features for
weeks. The day after the battle, Nimitz was to radio President Roosevelt
at the White House to discuss the success. To celebrate, Drake picked up
Alec MacDonald, a recent Navy volunteer, former *Advertiser* staff member,
and Hawaiian handball champion who monitored radio and cable traffic
flowing in and out of Pearl Harbor for the District. Nimitz was about to call
the president, and Drake asked MacDonald to monitor it from radio station KGU. MacDonald proudly announced to his District colleagues that
he was honored to be monitoring the admiral on this historic occasion. To
Drake's amusement and MacDonald's bewilderment, all MacDonald heard
through his earphones as Nimitz gave his report to the president was a

meaningless, garbled message. Drake laughed, telling MacDonald the conversation was going through a "scrambling device," protecting its content
from enemy (and friendly) ears. Drake played practical jokes on his colleagues to lighten the atmosphere. As revealed later, Nimitz's message to
the president could be summed up, "We are Midway to victory."[1]

There was more good news. Drake had arranged for famed Hollywood
director John Ford (a reserve officer) to fly to Midway Atoll right before the
battle. On June 2, Ford cabled Drake about the arrangements, "Boy that's
service thanks."[2] On June 4, Ford obtained epic footage of the Japanese
attack on the outpost. Drake had previously interacted with Ford in March
when the director had first arrived in Pearl Harbor to make films for the
Navy. Drake had initially been unaware of the VIP's presence, complaining
in a letter to Berry at OPR about the oversight. When Berry later arrived in
Pearl Harbor, Drake helped arrange a private screening of Ford's Academy
Award–winning film *How Green Was My Valley* for Nimitz, Berry, Ford,
and himself in Nimitz's quarters,[3] with Ford making "a neat little talk just
before the showing."[4] In late May, Drake hinted to Ford something film-
worthy was likely to happen on Midway. After the battle, Ford reported
that while he'd nearly been killed himself, the footage he'd obtained was
excellent.[5] In addition to the thanks from Ford, Drake received praise for
his handling of the Midway coverage even from his critics. Berry wrote to
Drake, "The UP Navy Department representative, Sandor Klein, has stated
that they have had word from Honolulu [Tremaine] telling of the excellent
work that has been done by your crowd out there in handling the Midway
Battle reports. To this I would like to add my own congratulations on the
good speedy handling of it."[6]

It wasn't long after the initial praise however, that the problems began.
On June 9, Drake wrote a memorandum to Wiltse (Nimitz's assistant chief
of staff for administration) explaining that national radio networks were
clamoring for a statement from the admiral about the victory. Drake suggested that since the date that Task Force 16 and Task Force 17 would return
to Hawaii was uncertain, they should confer with Army officials and agree
on a joint eyewitness press conference once all parties were back at Pearl.[7]
Drake sensed danger in the Army being first to publicize its version of
events, and he tried to ensure equal play for the Navy. But after the Task

Forces returned, Nimitz wanted no word of their presence mentioned in the press. On June 16, he penned a note to Drake: "I wish to convey the impression carriers are at sea."[8] It would be three months before news of the loss of the carrier USS *Yorktown* (CV 5) at Midway was released to the public.

Despite Nimitz's misdirection, Drake was able to arrange a press conference with Ens. George Gay, USN, the sole survivor of Torpedo 8, a torpedo plane squadron from the USS *Hornet* (CV 8), one of the participating carriers at Midway. Ensign Gay described feeling the dorsal fins of sharks swimming under the life raft that he'd spent the night in after his plane had been shot down. Gay said the blood in the water from the many casualties attracted the sharks. United Press' Tremaine included Gay's description of the sharks in a story for publication. As usual, Tremaine submitted the story to Drake for censorship. Drake immediately ran his red pencil over Gay's description of the sharks. Tremaine soon began shouting at Drake in the public relations office at CINCPAC headquarters, attracting attention from the nearby staff members and correspondents. "You can't take that out!" Tremaine yelled. "There's no security involved in that."[9]

"I'm not going to let the mothers of America read that!" Drake fired back. Back and forth they went, each getting more and more frustrated. Finally, a red-faced, scratchy-voiced Drake yelled, "If you don't like it, take it up with the admiral!"

"All right, I will!" Tremaine hollered back.

Tremaine grabbed his copy and headed for Nimitz's office, which was on the same floor. He charged through the swinging saloon-style doors that separated the outer office from the hall. Nimitz's flag secretary, Crosley, sitting at his desk inside, scrambled to halt him. "Hey, where are you going?" Crosley said.

Before Tremaine could reply, Nimitz came out from his office accompanied by two other admirals and a Marine colonel. "Why, Frank, what's the matter?" Nimitz asked.

"Commander Drake said to see you about this," he said.

"All right. Let's go into my office," Nimitz said, putting his arm over Tremaine's shoulder.

Once inside, Tremaine handed the admiral the censored copy. "I don't see anything wrong with this," Nimitz admitted.

"Drake said he wasn't going to let the mothers of America read about blood and sharks in the water," Tremaine said.

Drake hadn't expected Tremaine to call his bluff. Nimitz summoned Drake, and when he appeared, Nimitz scolded him. "Your job is to censor for security. The mothers of America are not your concern. There is nothing wrong with this story."

From one point of view, Nimitz was correct. Appendix B of the April 12, 1942, "Regulations for Correspondents Accredited to the Pacific Fleet" reiterated earlier guidance. "In general, correspondents' copy will be passed if it is: accurate in statement and implication; does not supply military information, aid or comfort to the enemy; does not injure the morale of our forces, the people at home, or our Allies; does not embarrass the United States, its Allies or neutral countries."[10] Appendix B then explained, "More specifically, the following subjects should not be treated in press copy," listing security-related topics such as "strength, efficiency, location or organization of Fleet forces." One could read the regulations as emphasizing only the explicitly prohibited security subjects.

From Drake's point of view, however, stories about sharks devouring downed Navy pilots could dent the morale of "our forces" and "the people at home." It was well-known that the only thing downed airmen in the Pacific feared more than sharks was capture by the Japanese.[11] In other words, the censorship regulations were interpretively flexible. Their ambiguity served as a perpetual source of conflict between Drake and the correspondents. Tremaine's story eventually ran, but without reference to the sharks: "Ensign George H. Gay, Jr., his own plane shot down, saw his comrades attack the two Kaga class carriers and a smaller one, and he saw them burst into flame from direct hits."[12] In the same story, Tremaine mocked the Navy's secrecy amid its victory. "The navy's latest communique said: 'There is nothing to report from the central Pacific area.'"

☙☙☙☙☙☙☙☙☙

Only a few days after the blowup with Tremaine, Drake and Bassett were in the public relations office at CINCPAC scanning newspapers when Bassett watched the blood drain from Drake's face. As he'd feared, a story implied that Army pilots, not Navy flyers, were to credit for the Midway victory. Army aviators returning to Pearl Harbor and the mainland had been the first to talk to the press and had conveyed the impression that the Army had played the essential role. In truth, Army bombers had inflicted minimal damage, and it was the Navy that had destroyed the carriers of the Japanese fleet. Despite Drake's attempts to control the news, Army censors on the mainland had released the self-serving and inaccurate information.

Hepburn, Nimitz, and other top Navy officials had watched for years as Army advocates of a separate Air Force had steadily gained public support and political influence. Before Pearl Harbor, while at the Bureau of Navigation, Nimitz had issued a memorandum explaining why a separate Air Force was undesirable from the Navy's point of view.[13] For Nimitz, establishing the Air Force as a separate service undermined the principle of unity of command, and it risked developing aviators who lacked understanding of naval doctrine and tactics. Drake had long agreed with Nimitz's sentiments, writing in a November 21, 1926, feature in the *Times*, "All of this work that the Navy has done in the air is to one purpose, increase of the fleet's striking power."[14] Now, following the Battle of Midway, the Army had robbed the Fleet of what should have been its greatest public relations success of the war.

Nimitz, however, forbade Drake to disclose details of the battle, ordering him not to publicly contradict the Army's pretensions to maintain security. Hamstrung, Drake watched helplessly as erroneous reports passed through his hands. United Press' Robert Miller wrote in his diary on June 12, "Had my first run in with Drake and won. Did a think piece on what would have happened had Midway fallen and he was against passing it. However, it went to someone higher up and came out without emasculation."[15] The next day, Miller submitted another story. This time, Drake sat on it. Nimitz's new flag secretary, Lt. Cdr. Preston Mercer, USN, stepped in and "did wonders in getting it loose, much to Waldo's disgust," according to Miller.[16]

Drake complained to Berry, writing, "Admiral Nimitz insisted that all of the Army's releases on Midway should be censored by us [the Fleet] for security, but for security only."[17] The ramifications of holding back the truth were enormous. Fights broke out between the services over credit for the victory. Correspondents were outraged when Drake refused to provide details of the battle, and the situation caused the near defeat of a congressional appropriations bill for the construction of several aircraft carriers.[18] Until Midway, Drake had been anxiously awaiting releasable news to satisfy hungry correspondents. Ironically, when the Navy won the most decisive battle of the war, the real extent of the victory went underreported due to Nimitz's reticence in publicizing it.[19]

Desperate to set the record straight, on July 9, 1942, Drake wrote to his former colleague Warren Francis, chief of Washington Bureau at the *Los Angeles Times*. "I will be most grateful if you can tell me who is the motivating influence behind the persistent false propaganda that Army planes were chiefly responsible for the victory at Midway. I assure you nothing could be farther from the truth."[20] Nimitz wouldn't permit disclosure of information supporting Drake's claim, so Drake apologized to Francis: "I can't show you the official report of the action to substantiate my statement." Drake pointed to recent coverage that reported the Army's false claims. Although his letter appeared on CINCPAC stationery, Drake stated, "Please let me emphasize that I am not making this request officially, but as a sincere personal effort to see justice done to the people who deserve the credit, namely: the Navy and Marine flyers who—many times risking almost certain death from enemy anti-aircraft and fighter opposition—took their torpedo planes and dive bombers close in to the Jap carriers and cruisers and destroyed them." On July 12, Drake sent a similar letter to Hanson Baldwin of the *New York Times*, this time pointing out Baldwin's reporting that repeated the Army's false claims. "The Fleet has been prohibited from telling a complete story, because publication of certain facts would disclose the weight of our surface forces participating," Drake repeated.[21]

However, the Midway news only got worse. On June 7, 1942, the *Chicago Tribune* published a front-page story, "Navy Had Word of Jap Plan to Strike at Sea," that divulged the composition of the Japanese fleet assembled for the battle. It would have been clear to the careful reader that the U.S. Navy had cracked IJN's secret code. An aide showed the *Tribune* article to King, who later remarked that whoever in the Navy had leaked the secret information should be shot, and he was not joking.[22] King had assumed duty as Commander-in-Chief U.S. Fleet—later renamed COMINCH—in

December 1941, relieving Stark as CNO in March 1942. King presumed that when enemy intelligence agents discovered the *Tribune* story, Japan would change its code and eliminate the Navy's hard-won advantage.[23] Within days, King learned that forty-two-year-old *Tribune* reporter Stanley Johnston had drafted portions of the story while on board the USS *Barnett* (APA 5) when it was en route to the West Coast after Johnston's transfer from the carrier USS *Lexington* (CV 2). The carrier had been fatally damaged and scuttled during the Battle of the Coral Sea in May. How Johnston had gained access to the secret information, and who had permitted its disclosure in the *Tribune*, became the focus of FBI and Navy Department investigations. Drake, Bassett, and OPR officials were soon involved.[24]

The once officer-in-charge of the Los Angeles District Intelligence Office was now the focus of the FBI. On June 18, 1942, Drake provided a memorandum to Berry that mirrored the statement he'd made to an FBI investigator.[25] He explained that Johnston had been accredited to the Fleet since March, and he asserted that proper procedures had been followed in verbally communicating censorship rules to Johnston upon his arrival at CINCPAC headquarters. In Bassett's presence, he'd also furnished Johnston a copy of a memorandum specifying prohibited content. Drake explained that Nimitz had approved Johnston's assignment to the *Lexington*, and on the morning of April 14, Bassett had met Johnston at the dock. There was no time for an additional security lecture before boarding, but Bassett claimed in a June 17 memorandum to Drake that he'd given Johnston another copy of the regulations "in company of other correspondents then intending to leave with task forces."[26] The commander of the *Lexington* had been furnished with a copy of the rules governing correspondents as well. Critically, however, Johnston had not signed the written pledge to uphold Navy censorship regulations that was required of every correspondent in Pearl Harbor. This oversight would be significant if Johnston was later charged with a crime. Drake shifted blame for the oversight to OPR, stating, "It was assumed all Naval regulations had been complied with before Johnston was dispatched to the Pacific fleet by authority of the Secretary of the Navy."[27] He nevertheless later wrote to Berry that "we are insuring that all correspondents execute the Pacific Fleet agreement, as well as those you send with their credentials."[28]

In an earlier telephone call with Berry, Drake stated he had given "no specific verbal instructions" to Johnston, demonstrating a laxity at odds with Drake's usual rule-bound behavior.[29] In documents the FBI assembled concerning the case, Drake appeared chummy with the genial and outgoing correspondent. A letter Johnston had written to Drake while filing his stories from the Battle of the Coral Sea in early May contained this line: "What a pal you turned out to be—wait till I get back to Honolulu—hope to see you inside next ten-twelve days if luck holds."[30] Drake reported to officials that Johnston had complied with censorship regulations when in Pearl Harbor and on board the *Lexington*. The security breach appeared to have occurred during Johnston's transit to the West Coast. Attention shifted to officers on board the *Barnett*, *Tribune* employees, and officials in Washington, D.C. President Roosevelt, Secretary Knox, and others urged prosecution of Johnston and the *Tribune* under the Espionage Act of 1917, empaneling a grand jury. King, however, was unwilling to risk further disclosure of the Navy's secret intelligence-gathering techniques via cryptanalyst testimony provided during a public trial; the grand jury was soon dissolved.[31]

The fiasco nevertheless took a physical toll on Drake, who'd come unnervingly close to shouldering the blame for Johnston's calamitous security breach. A June 21, 1942, letter from Bassett to Willie omitted reference to the situation but noted, "in his passion for everlasting youth and the slim figger, [Drake] has become too thin, I'm afeared."[32] Drake's heart-stopping run-in with the FBI, OPR, and COMINCH crystalized his commitment to the principle that security should trump publicity. A thank you letter from Johnston on September 30, 1942, tested Drake's diplomacy. "I am glad to see that you came up smiling," Drake replied, adding, "Everyone here thought you turned in an excellent series of articles on the last adventures of the LEX [USS *Lexington*, the carrier lost in the Battle of the Coral Sea in May 1942], except censorship was rather lax in several instances."[33]

By mid-July, however, the Midway coverage flap finally seemed to be receding. Correspondents began turning their attention to other topics. One correspondent, Charles Arnot, who worked for United Press, arrived at Pearl Harbor after the victory and needed a fresh story. Arnot was intrigued that Honolulu was the only place in the United States and its territories where prostitution was legal and even encouraged by military authorities. Arnot decided to write an article about it as a lead for a report on life in wartime Hawaii. The piece began like this, "Hawaii is the only place in the entire United States or its possessions where there is legalized prostitution today. Most of the 'houses' catering to our love-starved servicemen are located on a certain downtown Honolulu street known as 'River Street.' They operate between the hours of 11 A.M. and 3 P.M. Mondays through Saturdays. Apparently the military authorities who have authorized and oversee the operations of these joy houses still figure that Sunday is sacred."[34]

Following standard procedure, Arnot made four copies of the proposed dispatch and took it to the CINCPAC public relations office to wait for a censor, usually Drake, to review it. Arnot had heard the rumors about Drake and his autocratic ways from Tremaine and others, and he doubted this first article was the best way to establish rapport. Indeed, Drake was not too happy about the article. He read it and reread it. Brow furrowed, he picked up his telephone and called a senior officer whose duties included overseeing public relations. There was a long conversation between Drake and the officer. Arnot decided his story was about to get a big, fat "K" for killed. Finally, Drake concluded the conversation by stating, "That's exactly how I feel about it, admiral."[35] He hung up the phone. Ceremoniously, Drake produced a small razor blade and cut out of Arnot's dispatch only two words—"River Street"—handing it back to him for final review. The sentence thus read, "Most of the 'houses' catering to our love-starved servicemen are located on a certain downtown Honolulu street." Arnot concluded that the houses of prostitution on River Street were a military secret, and that the next time the Japanese attacked Hawaii, they would ignore Pearl Harbor and concentrate their assault on River Street, "thus killing most of the American enlisted personnel."[36]

Correspondents were rarely so politic. International News Service's Richard Tregaskis barreled into Drake's office one afternoon, pleading for permission to "go with the landing party," a rumor he'd learned about from a friend.[37] Puzzled, Drake replied he knew of no landing party, but that he would check with Nimitz. Surprising both men, Nimitz issued Tregaskis secret orders to accompany a landing party, then called by the code name "Watchtower." Ever conscious of security, Drake warned Tregaskis to say nothing about Watchtower to anyone. They stared at each other as though playing poker, each man having no idea what Watchtower was nor where the landing party was heading. Tregaskis later wrote, "Probably Admiral Nimitz was the only man in Pearl Harbor who knew that the invasion was going to be made in the Solomon Islands."[38]

Drake's spirits were rising. In a July 14, 1942, letter to Willie, Bassett remarked, "Fr. N. has a birthday coming up, and Francis B. [Black] has dreamed up a 'hunt breakfast' for him at Earl T.'s [Thacker's] cliffside mansion. (Earl's wife, too, has gone back to Blighty; so the fat boy is in his prognathous glory.) That one, my infant, you may look up for yourself! I anticipate it will be a slightly dull affair, not being anything to do with either 'hunt' or 'breakfast'. When it's over, I shall give you a full report, omitting nothing, not even the most gruesome details."[39] Fr. N. was an abbreviation of "Father Neptune," the moniker Bassett used when referring to Drake in letters to Willie. A few days later, Bassett reported, "Fr. N's birthday party went off nicely, with every one jovial and gay in a funny sort of way; and nobody tight despite the fact that Frank B. brought four bottles he'd been hoarding for the occasion; and Waldo overcome with such gifts as a wristwatch bought by FB [Francis Black] by proxy for Mary; and a fine birthday cake . . . and all hands scurrying like white mice to make port before the blackout snuck down on us, as if we'd be suddenly changed into pumpkins when the lights went out."[40] Drake received a birthday present from Nimitz as well. On July 18, 1942, in a memorandum to the director of OPR and the chief of naval personnel, Nimitz recommended Drake for promotion to commander, commenting he'd "organized and administered the public relations activities of this command with efficiency and accurate judgment" and had "performed all duties assigned him in an outstanding manner."[41]

Nimitz's recommendation cemented Drake's loyalty to his admiral. Despite Drake's missteps and fumbles, Nimitz supported and protected his PRO. After Midway, the stakes shifted. Damage control had characterized the first six months of the war, but now Drake began to imagine a glorious scene: triumphantly sailing into Tokyo Bay on board Nimitz's flagship with the Fleet. If Drake could make it to the end of the war, his legacy would be etched in the history books forever.

Amid the good news, Drake and Bassett engaged in some uncommon strategic planning. On July 22, 1942, Drake wrote to his old boss at the *Times*, L. D. Hotchkiss, with news he and Bassett hoped to soon launch a Fleet newspaper. "We propose to call it BLUEJACKET," he wrote.[42] Drake was seeking help from his alma mater: "Would you, therefore, ask Bruce Russell and Charlie Owens if, at their leisure, they will sketch us their idea for a masthead. We would like something on the order of THE TIMES masthead, with a little seagoing atmosphere." Drake's pivot from reactive damage control to proactive planning was short-lived; Captain Lovette at OPR shelved the Fleet newspaper idea due to distribution and duplication issues (ships often produced their own newsletters).[43]

As Drake turned the corner on the Midway mess, Berry wrote to him on July 19, 1942. "Admiral Hepburn informed me that the Secretary had directed that I be ordered out to Cincpac's staff as PRO to proceed as soon as relieved by Lieut. Comdr. W. G. Beecher, Jr., who has just checked in from the Naval Hospital here."[44] Beecher had served as assistant to the director of ONI's Public Relations Branch from 1938 to 1940. After Secretary Knox's failed attempts in the spring, it appeared he'd finally succeeded in replacing Drake as PRO. Berry's letter continued, "This is about all I know on the situation except that Adm. Hepburn called me in to state that Admiral Jacobs had been in conversation with Adm. Nimitz when the latter was on the coast and the subject of a 'Fleet Press Censor' had again been raised. I suggested that if agreeable, why not 'Drake' for that billet which would not require any change at all." Berry explained everything was on hold until he got to Pearl Harbor after official orders had been written.

But Drake hadn't received Berry's letter. On July 23, Berry wrote to Drake again. "The Secretary sent for me yesterday and there in his office I saw your old friend, Bob Casey."[45] Drake did receive this one, and when he read that line, he deflated. In his mind's eye, he watched his glorious entrance into Tokyo Bay with Nimitz and the Fleet recede over the horizon and vanish. "As you may expect, Casey was unhappy about some of the things at Pearl Harbor and did not hesitate to bring them to the Secretary's attention," Berry wrote. As one commentator would later put it: "Waldo Drake was his [Casey's] favorite bull's-eye," referring to him as "that swabby in charge of suppressing news in the Pacific."[46] Casey's complaints involved the "triple censorship" of news material when assigned to ships of the Fleet: (1) commanding officer, (2) Fleet censor (Drake), and (3) downtown Honolulu radio and cable censor. Another complaint related to correspondents' access to the Navy Yard and their movements once on site: "He wouldn't be surprised if he were required to swim from the dock to the ship if he ever went out there again," Berry reported.[47] Casey also objected to the delay in moving cleared press copy from CINCPAC headquarters to the commercial cable company offices downtown. Berry saved the worst for last. "Casey, in general, reported to the Secretary that he felt that all correspondents were looked upon out there as general nuisance and wound up by telling the Secretary that in all of his years of coverage of various military establishments, he had never seen anything quite as bad as the Navy at Pearl Harbor." Berry concluded, "The Secretary was considerably disturbed about these allegations," adding, "The conference broke up with the Secretary telling me to take steps to remedy the situation as soon as I get out there."

Drake replied to Berry on July 29, 1942: "Your letter was the first news I have had that you are coming as my relief."[48] Drake had not yet received Berry's letter of July 19, but he did not give up his PRO position without a fight. "Concerning Bob Casey's complaints, none will hold water." Triple censorship? Drake did not consider "security examination" by a ship's captain a burdensome form of censorship. Moreover, he claimed, "The cable censor, by agreement with Cincpac, does not further censor or delay press copy bearing Cincpac's release stamp, Casey's charges notwithstanding." Access to the Navy Yard? While armed escort had indeed been required earlier, new processes allowed correspondents to carry special passes and officers' tags for their automobiles. Taxis bearing Pearl Harbor tags could also come and go freely. Delays? Drake denied problems in passing cleared copy to the cable operators and vetoed the motorcycle idea, but he added that an "automobile available at all times to Public Relations would be desirable." He declared, "There is not the faintest truth in Mr. Casey's charge that correspondents are regarded as 'general nuisances'. They are accorded every possible courtesy by Capt. Wiltse, Bassett and me, as well as by Capt. Scanland, (Captain of the Yard) and by Comdr. Stephens, (Exec. of the Sub Base). Finally, Admiral Nimitz has taken a direct personal interest in the correspondents assigned to him and has been kept closely informed of their movements and our treatment of them and their copy." Drake fought to save his job, but he maintained decorum: "Please let me know if there is anything that I may do here for you in advance of your arrival."

Miraculously, Berry would not come to Pearl Harbor to relieve Drake after all. Three overlapping events may explain why. First, Drake's reply letter to Berry may have been persuasive. Knox and Hepburn had earlier dispatched Berry to Pearl Harbor to investigate Casey's complaints, but despite Knox's maneuvering, Drake was still there as Fleet PRO. Knox and Hepburn may have decided an encore from Berry was unnecessary to confirm the accuracy of Drake's rebuttal. Critically, Nimitz's support for Drake's removal was doubtful; he'd just recommended his PRO for promotion to commander. If Knox pressed the issue a third time, there is no record of it. Second, Lt. Cdr. Bonney Powell, USN, recently in Pearl Harbor, had conducted a review of naval photography for the Bureau of Aeronautics and provided a glowing report of Fleet public relations to OPR upon his return to Washington, D.C.. Powell praised Drake and Bassett's efforts. Third, and most importantly, fate intervened. Berry had been serving as assistant to Hepburn since Lovette had returned from Pearl Harbor and taken over Berry's deputy director position at OPR. As a result of Hepburn's announced transition to lead the General Board the following month (August), Lovette would move up to director, and Berry would need to again serve as deputy director. Lovette was a strong supporter of Drake's, having worked with him in Washington, D.C. in the late 1930s when Lovette headed ONI's Public Relations Branch. In Pearl Harbor in the months before the Japanese attack, Lovette was a regular presence at Bad Manor. He saw no need to replace the Fleet's PRO. In contrast to Nimitz's intervention in May, the Navy's bureaucratic machinery had vaulted a Drake ally to power at OPR, ensuring that Father Neptune stayed put at CINCPAC headquarters.

🙟🙞🙟🙞🙟🙞🙟🙞🙟🙞

Francis, the *Times'* Washington, D.C. bureau chief, replied to Drake on July 28, 1942. The content of his letter confirmed Drake's suspicions and came as a relief.[49] Drake showed the letter to Nimitz as evidence the Army had engaged in credit-grabbing behavior outside of Drake's control. But Francis also pointed out the Navy had not been without fault. He wrote,

> I am thoroughly aware of the situation in which you're interested, as I've seen a lot of incidental evidence of what *looks like* a deliberate plot. Actually, this credit-grabbing is merely one facet of an involved situation. Back-stage, there is a lot of pulling and hauling, much political intrigue, and considerable jealousy. No single individual or faction can be blamed for the unfortunate state of affairs. Frankly, there is an element in the Navy seeking to discredit the Army and there is an element in the Army seeking to discredit the Navy. There are a lot of volunteer knife-throwers on both sides. Hap Arnold feels very sincerely, I believe, that the Navy is trying to claim an excessive amount of credit, and everybody around him has that point of view. The Air Forces gang feel they were treated like step-children for many years, while Roosevelt pampered and petted the Navy, and they are out to win their place in the sun. I'm not mentioning these names in any attempt to fix blame but merely to illustrate the process. But the people like the Doolittles, Al Williamses, Seversky's and others of the Billy Mitchell school of thought have been very industrious in chanting "We told you so." That is one of the principal reasons for the columns and articles which have come to your attention.

No longer skilled at handling crises, the Navy was losing its public relations battle to the Army. Francis explained, "A considerable part of the blame—if that's what you want to call it—for the bad press the Navy has received can be laid right at the Navy's doorstep. There are too many competent naval officers and too few experienced public relations men in Navy public relations, so there is a pretty wide distrust here among the press corps of Navy statements." Hepburn's preference for regular naval officers to hold PRO positions, and Berry's push for a "regular line officer" to hold the Fleet's PRO position, merely perpetuated the "too many naval officers" dilemma. Francis continued, "Col. Knox hasn't helped improve matters with his ill-advised remarks, wise-cracking generalities, and miscellaneous boners."

He concluded, "The Navy used to be aces with most Washington correspondents, but in recent months the Army has proved far smarter, professionally and politically, the same goes for relations between the services
and Congress; the Army now stands in much better on The Hill than the
Navy." It was no coincidence Hepburn was on his way out of OPR to head
the General Board.

Despite Francis' bleak assessment, positive news reached Drake a few
weeks later. Director John Ford wrote to him on August 18, 1942, concerning the Midway footage. "Admiral Draemel [Nimitz's chief of staff]
happened to be in L.A. the day the composite print came off and was terri-
bly moved and enthusiastic."[50] Ford had evaded Navy censorship, secretly
editing his footage in Los Angeles and showing it directly to President
Roosevelt, whose son had been strategically edited into the film to win
the president's favor. Ford boasted to Drake, "Now everybody, from the
President, Admiral King and General Marshall on down are screaming to
have it released to the public." The director was appreciative, "May I take
this opportunity to thank you for the many courtesies you have shown to
me and the lads in my unit."

Drake could do little to protest Ford's evasion of Navy censorship and
replied, "Was delighted to hear that the Midway stuff turned out so well
and hope that proper disposition will be made. It is a fine new feather for
the old Ford bonnet."[51] Ford's *The Battle of Midway* would go on to earn the
Academy Award for Best Documentary of 1942.

Drake had weathered the two biggest storms of the year in Pearl
Harbor: the Midway coverage flap and the Stanley Johnston fiasco. He'd
survived Knox's attempts to have Berry replace him as Fleet PRO. He'd
repelled attacks on Fleet public relations from correspondents including
Casey and Tremaine. Through a combination of professional skill, organizational savvy, and pure luck, Drake survived the crises. He even snagged
a new office. In August, Nimitz and the CINCPAC staff transferred their
headquarters to the new (and supposedly bomb-proof) rectangular, three-
story "Cement Pot" on Makalapa Hill. The public relations office was on
the second floor, directly above Nimitz's office, overlooking a small stream
flowing down the hill from Aiea.[52] It consisted of three rooms still smelling of fresh paint, one of which was the photographic laboratory that

handled all negatives and prints received for clearance. The second room was reserved for correspondents (and later, Army and Marine Corps representatives) and clerical staff. The third room held Drake, Bassett, and the new Fleet press censor, Lt. Cdr. Murray Ward, USNR, whom Drake had picked to join the CINCPAC staff in July. Ward was known to Drake; they'd crewed together as teammates (and opponents) in yacht races in the 1930s in Southern California.[53]

Soon, maps of the Pacific adorned the walls of Drake's new office, along with a poster of Douglas SBD Dauntless dive bombers flying in tight formation.[54] A poster of a majestic thunderhead rising above the Pacific, a waterspout in the foreground and a rain-veiled cruiser in the distance, hung near a window. Drake also placed an oversized, framed photograph of Nimitz where all visitors could see it. The correspondents reporting to Drake's office every day to submit their stories and photos, as well as to send and receive their personal mail, had to confront the oversized admiral hanging on the wall. Wearing a khaki shirt and garrison cap, grinning and squinting in the bright sun, the admiral was there to remind visitors that Drake spoke for the commander-in-chief.

After relocating to the Cement Pot, Drake wrote to Powell at the Bureau of Aeronautics. "Jim and I are both grateful for your kind words, both in your report and to Captain Lovette and Bob Berry."[55] He noted, "I have not heard from Bob for many weeks, but I understand he is not coming out for perhaps six months." "'Bad Manor' still continues on its bawdy way," he added, while declining Powell's invitation to relocate. "Your effort to sell us on Washington as 'a grand old place' is appreciated, but I would much rather move out to the firing line." Despite the recent good news, Drake admitted, "Frankly, we are still having as much difficulty—in getting news copy and sufficient pictures released—as a couple of handcuffed fellows trying to climb a greased pole."

****

Nimitz had good reason to promote Drake to commander despite his foul-ups. Drake was a loyal and hard-working staff member. After an article supporting the Fleet had been published, Drake drafted a short letter bearing

Nimitz's signature thanking a journalist, editor, or publisher for the coverage. In this way, Drake ensured that Nimitz appeared especially thoughtful, building goodwill with members of the press. Drake recognized that public relations was more than positive press coverage; it was about building long-term relationships with stakeholders. Drake also fielded requests for publicity photos, forwarding requests up the chain of command that aligned with Nimitz's self-image. The Associated Press asked Nimitz for "a picture of you on the pistol range at headquarters." Drake routed the request to Nimitz, who wrote on the letter, "Drake—OK CWN."[56] Drake carefully constructed Nimitz's public image and ensured the admiral conveyed his personal touch.

Bassett's letters to Willie throughout 1942 describe how he and Drake often worked from 0800 to well past midnight. It was probably at the end of one of those long nights that Bassett complained their job was "to handmaiden a lot of correspondents who want to see the world at the Navy's expense."[57] Nevertheless, with their loved ones on the mainland, the two men settled into a routine of lengthy work hours punctuated by tennis at noontime, cribbage in the late afternoon, and a glass of beer in the evening. Drake reported to his former boss at the *Times*, L. D. Hotchkiss, "We both have knocked 20 pounds from our weight by playing tennis instead of eating lunch this summer, but scarcity of tennis balls and increasing work load has disrupted our schedule of late."[58] They might occasionally watch a movie, but the air in the CINCPAC theater resembled "warm consommé"; Bassett suggested bottling and selling it to the Campbell Soup Company.

Nimitz often joined the two men for their noonday tennis ritual. If Bassett bowed out, others might step in for doubles. A regular duo facing Nimitz and Drake was Gen. Lawton Collins, USA, and Gen. Ralph Smith, USA.[59] After their tennis match, Nimitz might invite Drake and the other officers to join him in the evening for cocktails, dinner, or a game of cards. There, Drake might overhear one of the Admiral's droll stories. His favorite one, Drake later reported, was about a lady bridge enthusiast in a Texas town and her inept husband. The lady aspired to the day when she'd be invited to play bridge with the number one woman expert in the town. Finally, she and her husband were invited for dinner and bridge with the expert and her husband. Naturally, when they sat down to play, the expert, the hostess, asked the inept husband to play with her and he did a horrible job: he trumped his partner's aces and forgot the suit and did everything imaginable. His wife was embarrassed all through the evening, and finally he excused himself and went to the bathroom and he left the door open, and you could hear all the noise that was going on, and his wife blushed and turned to her hostess and said, "My dear, I feel terrible about this. Just you wait till I get him home." The hostess said, "Now . . . I beg of you don't say a word to the poor fellow. This is the first time this evening I've had the faintest idea of what he'd had in his hand!"[60]

Bassett was equally proud as Drake to be supporting Nimitz and the Fleet. Bassett's feelings about Drake (and Mary), on the other hand, were mixed. In a May 15, 1942, letter to Willie, Bassett remarked that Gennie Black, the wife of Drake's housemate Francis Black, had traveled to Big Pine to visit Mary and the children. "In her last letter, Mary D. said she wondered 'if Willie were going to drop up and see me—or did I do something to make her mad.'"[61] Bassett added, "I didn't tell Waldo. But it's my suspicion that you're not fussing about seeing that portion of our life in these charmed scenes." Willie had not developed close bonds with Mary. While Bassett was a supremely loyal colleague, he often teased Drake, writing for example, "Waldo's nearby, but out-of-sight, viewing of all things, Shirley Temple's latest movie. This sounds a bit incredible; but it's gospel-truth."[62] He occasionally seemed to pity his mentor, once mentioning to Willie, "Like square root, this sorry business of being away from those we love seems to cause some staggering multiplication in the amount of that love. Even Mary D. seems to have caught that bug: a cablegram from her to Fr. N., which I read to see if it was important enough to telephone the message to him ashore, contained the brief words, 'We love you'—impelled, I should imagine, by something like an anniversary or Easter or something."[63] Bassett had noticed the lack of intimate feeling between them; the "we love you" stood out. Later, in another letter, Bassett remarked, "Waldo hasn't heard from Mary for two months; and only indirectly, through Chick Hanson [of the *Times*], who visited the Drake menage in the Sierras and reported completely on the landed *gentry*, does he know they're still inhabiting what *Time* calls 'the globe's face.'"[64]

Mary proved a poor correspondent. When receiving mail at CINCPAC headquarters, nearby officers and correspondents could hear Drake exclaim, "Four sacks of mail and not one letter from my wife!"[65] Like her notorious husband, Mary could rub some people the wrong way. In one letter, Bassett remarked, "Mary wrote Waldo recently and asked about you (wanted your address; which made me laugh a little to myself because I knew damned well that was a Mary-gag of some sort). She's on, so help me, a 150-acre farm in the Sierras and doing God-knows-what. Remember how she used to berate even the isolation offered by Haleiwa?"[66] Drake, of course, was devoted to Mary, but with his wife and children absent and infrequently heard from, he dedicated himself to serving Nimitz and the Navy. When Nimitz returned to the office after dinner to read dispatches, he found Drake and Bassett hard at work on the second floor.

Nimitz was also generally inclined to give his staff members a second chance. Nimitz himself had been given a second chance after facing a court-martial for running the USS *Decatur* aground in the Philippines in 1908. His naval career could have been sunk by the mishap, but the minor reprimand he received shaped Nimitz's response to his subordinates' errors; he ensured problems were understood and not repeated, but he believed that if an officer could learn from a mistake, the Navy was better for it. Of course, some errors were unforgivable, and staff members did not take Nimitz's patience for granted. While Drake had fumbled in failing to ensure Johnston had signed the correspondents' pledge, Nimitz also heard from people he respected that his PRO was doing a good job. In thanking Nimitz and the Fleet's public relations staff for his successful visit to the Pacific, the *New York Times'* Hanson Baldwin wrote, "Commander Drake was particularly helpful." Berry had praised Drake's Midway coverage before the U.S. Army Air Forces and Johnston flaps had occurred. On September 17, 1942, OPR's new director, Capt. Lovette, wrote to Nimitz, "From our point of view, Waldo Drake is doing a very fine job for us. I hear that he is up for Commander and hope that he will make it."[67] Nimitz wrote in the margin of the letter next to this passage, "Hear! Hear!" adding his initials.

Drake was also learning how to navigate the Navy's organizational politics. When Nimitz presented awards for heroism stemming from the

Battle of Midway on June 17, 1942, Drake drafted the admiral's remarks, ensuring a key portion of them quoted Secretary Knox at length. Drake transformed these remarks into Fleet Press Release No. 58 (Drake often transformed Nimitz's public remarks into Fleet press releases). Likewise, when Undersecretary Forrestal provided remarks (his own) at the annual "E" awards ceremony at the Navy Yard in Pearl Harbor on September 6, 1942, Drake transformed them into Fleet Press Release No. 72. The undersecretary earned widespread publicity for his visit to the South Pacific and Pearl Harbor thanks to Drake's promotional work.

Drake also cultivated allies to help him manage politics outside the Navy. In one mysterious case, Drake believed someone in the press was trying to sabotage him. A July 27, 1942, letter Drake wrote to one of his supporters, Roy Howard, the powerful chairman of Scripps-Howard news service, alluded to the plot: "Please let me thank you for the numerous kind and thoughtful things you have done in my behalf since your return to the mainland. I assure you that I have never laid eyes on the particular hatchet man who has been so busy recently making my life miserable."[68] The letter suggests that Howard suspected the identity of the culprit and had moved against him. Drake continued, "I hope and believe that your able efforts have effectually stymied his plans for the present. I am deeply grateful for your promptness in passing the word about the last incident and likewise appreciate your kind words." Both the identity of the "hatchet man" and the nature of the "incident" remain a mystery, but a connection to the earlier *Newsweek* and *Albertan* hatchet jobs seems likely.

Drake was also well-positioned to survive his mess-ups because he could write in Nimitz's voice well enough to satisfy the admiral. Nimitz's edits of Drake's draft remarks and letters were minimal.[69] In Fleet Press Release No. 43, in honor of Mother's Day, Drake (with an assist from Bassett) had Nimitz declare, "I can tell you that your sons are defending their Country with courage and valor" and "no amount of toil, hardship, adversity or danger can deter us from our final triumph." Drake was even skillful enough to draft messages that reflected Nimitz's proud Texas identity. In a memorandum in response to the governor of Texas designating July 22, 1942, "Admiral Nimitz Day," Drake suggested the following text be sent back as a dispatch: "The officers and men of the Pacific Fleet are now engaged in the tremendous task before them, fully aware of the power and resourcefulness of the enemy. The spirit displayed by all Texans, in actual conflict with the enemy and their response to the Navy's call for volunteers, is an inspiration to the Fleet and the nation and a source of great pride to me. Deeply sensible of the honor accorded me by the State of Texas, I consider it a tribute to all Texans in the Fleet." Nimitz removed five minor words from the draft before initialing his approval. Having a PRO skilled enough to intuit how a son of Texas would compose a speech to medal winners from the Battle of Midway, a tribute to the mothers of America, and a response to the governor of Texas must have pleased Nimitz.

Nimitz played an active role in Fleet public relations. He intervened in security-related matters, carefully controlling what information was released (for example, concealing the presence of task forces in Pearl Harbor after the Battle of Midway). Nimitz was also involved in the timing of news releases (for example, the issuance of communiques concerning the Wake-Marcus raids). Given his vast responsibilities, Nimitz's level of involvement in public relations is astonishing. Nimitz's signature was used to convey information or orders to correspondents and members of the Fleet, but as anyone who has worked in a large bureaucratic organization knows, subordinates often draft documents for the boss to sign, and as trust grows, the boss' signature is obtained without much questioning. Records show that Drake prepared innumerable documents for Nimitz's signature in this way. Day-to-day involvement in public relations is inconsistent with what we know about Nimitz's managerial style, and it is improbable that Nimitz reserved for himself a micromanagerial role in public relations: paperwork was Drake's responsibility.

Nimitz was remarkably aware, however, of the details of how Fleet news and publicity were generated and disseminated as well as of the identities, interests, and locations of correspondents in his command area. Still, engagement was not the same thing as enthusiasm, and Nimitz was soon complaining to King about the ever-increasing number and never-ending requests of reporters. In his April 22, 1942, secret "Estimate of the Situation" provided to King, Nimitz identified public relations as a security risk, writing that "a national weakness is that through gossip, carelessness, etc., we do not deny information to the enemy that is of value to him. Included are ship movements, building program, press releases, some future plans, and land military installations of all kinds."[70] By January 15, 1943, Nimitz's comments dripped with sarcasm. He wrote to King that "our press keeps Japan well posted on the progress of our war effort."[71]

Nimitz and King met for quarterly conferences throughout most of the war, usually in San Francisco, but occasionally in Washington, DC, or Pearl Harbor. The topic of public relations rarely made the agenda; instead, topics usually focused on officer and enlisted personnel matters, operations, strategy, planning, ships and equipment, logistics, and general warfighting concerns. When public relations did appear on the agenda, it was usually in response to negative publicity. The first mention of the topic appears in a set of King-Nimitz conference conversation notes dated July 5, 1942, in the aftermath of the Midway debacle. The notes state only, "The Public Relations situation at PacFlt is satisfactory to Cincpac."[72] Drake had developed enough goodwill to remain Nimitz's PRO and earn promotion. King, however, wanted to ensure no repeat occurred of the still unfolding Stanley Johnston fiasco. The notes state, "Cominch outlined the President's policy that one representative of a news service and no others should be allowed to go out in Task Forces." Johnston had been the only correspondent assigned to the *Lexington* and its task force, but King wanted to ensure tighter control of reporting from the Pacific, and limiting the number of correspondents requiring Drake's supervision was one way to do it.

As Fleet PRO, Drake ostensibly served two stakeholder groups: the Navy and the public, but the close ties he developed with Nimitz ensured that Drake would never attempt to advance Fleet public relations beyond what he thought the admiral would support. Constraining the buildup of news and publicity in the Pacific may have eased Nimitz and King's anxieties, but it also may have undermined the Navy's broader ambitions. Drake confessed in a September 5, 1942, letter to Hotchkiss, his former boss at the *Times*, "I don't know about Bassett, but aside from the fact that I don't see the family—I thank my lucky star for being yanked loose from the Spring Street Navy [the *Times*]. . . . (Goes for me, too, Boss! Jim.) You are right. We are censors besides doing several other odd jobs, but the story will have to wait awhile before we can tell it."[73] Drake sensed that censorship and security had skewed public perception of the war: "May I also add, Hotch, that this is going to be a tough grind? I hope that the citizens back home are becoming aware of this fact. We note with recurring pride the intelligent efforts of the old paper to bring home to the population the realization that the country is embarked upon a job that is going to require the combined efforts of everybody able to lift a productive finger."[74]

There is no way to know for sure what postwar outcomes might have resulted had the Navy's public relations activities in the Pacific been more widespread and effective during the first years of the war. Nevertheless, Nimitz was loath to broadcast Navy victories and tell the service's larger story if it risked security. Even so, Nimitz's reticence was nothing compared to King's. Even if Nimitz had wanted to develop a more aggressive Navy public relations campaign (and he didn't), King would have taken a very dim view of that. Toward the end of 1942, Nimitz and King were united on the need to reduce the number of correspondents in the Pacific. "Cincpac states that he is bedeviled by reporters," noted the King-Nimitz conference minutes for September 19, 1942, adding, "Wishes Elmer Davis [the director of OWI] to know that he assumes that release of war news to the press means release to the enemy."[75] King was unsympathetic: "Cominch replied that he fights that battle every day."

That night, September 19, back in Pearl Harbor, Drake, Layton and two other CINCPAC officers celebrated their promotions to commander with a "wetting-down" party at Bad Manor. Bassett reported the scene to Willie:

> Francis B. did the impresario-ing, and did it up brown. Even to helium-filled balloons that blustered around the overhead, in black, yellow, white and red; and which will go aloft tomorrow . . . as radio-meteorgraphic balloons for stratosphere soundings. There was a great deal of talk, but little enough said. Also much drinking and a bit of nibbling on the inevitable cold storage turkey and canned ham. A few Navy nurses looking antiseptic and one or two wives of District officers, who didn't look antiseptic. Then it was over, and a lad I know and I went somewhat glumly off to a sweaty movie where we thrilled to Rita Hayworth in tights and Technicolor.[76]

The newly promoted Commander Drake understood that if he wanted to maintain Nimitz's goodwill, he needed to decrease his boss' encounters with bedeviling reporters. The conscientious and extremely loyal Drake, driven by an emotional need to win Nimitz's approval, ensured that the admiral got what he wanted. With his eagerness for a game of tennis, reliability for a humorous story, and his occasional use of injudicious language to put an overzealous correspondent in his place, Father Neptune was the kind of newsman the admiral liked having around.

7

Dog Team

I agree that the press job is a terrific headache, but a few poor souls, such as we, must do it. It has been a constant battle since I came here a year-and-a-half ago.

—Waldo Drake

NIMITZ WAS BACK in Pearl Harbor four days after his September 19, 1942, conference with King. CINCPAC's ambivalence toward the press didn't prevent him from visiting United Press correspondent Joe Custer at Queen's Hospital in Honolulu. Thirty-three years old and a sportswriter before the war, Custer was recuperating from injuries sustained in the South Pacific. On August 8–9, he had been on board the USS *Astoria* (CA 34) when it had come under ferocious attack from Japanese naval forces during the nighttime Battle of Savo Island. Surgeons had successfully removed a 15-mm shell fragment from behind Custer's left eye, but he would never regain its sight. On September 23, 1942, Drake accompanied Nimitz to Custer's bedside, ensuring that the press reported the admiral's act of kindness. Nimitz was glad Custer's injury "was not worse," and he hoped the correspondent would soon be "back in action."[1] Stories of Nimitz's call on Custer appeared in scores of major American newspapers, earning the admiral praise for extending to war correspondents his policy of visiting all officers and enlisted men wounded in action.

Not mentioned in any of the coverage of Nimitz's visit, of course, was the name of Custer's ship, news that it had been sunk, or the location or outcome of the battle. Only morale-lifting reports of Custer's recovery made it past Drake and the Fleet censors. Nevertheless, *Editor and Publisher* ran the Custer story next to a longer feature headlined, "INS Man Dies in Pacific; Missing AP Writer Found."[2] The article described how International News Service's Jack Singer (formerly Drake's colleague at the *Times*) had been reported missing in action in the South Pacific under circumstances the Navy Department left unexplained. Only a week earlier, Singer, twenty-seven-years-old, had made national news with an electrifying eyewitness account of riding in a U.S. torpedo bomber as it attacked a Japanese aircraft carrier. Prophetically, in that story, Singer reported that after gaining permission to accompany the squadron commander on the mission, he'd rushed back to his room, "stuffed several stories I had ready for mailing into envelopes and left a note to my roommate . . . to mail the envelope to Lt. Com. Waldo Drake, the fleet public relations officer, if I didn't come back."[3] A week after Singer's story appeared in print, he was gone. But the missing AP writer, thirty-four-year-old Vern Haugland, had been found alive after bailing out of an Army bomber over New Guinea. He'd endured forty-five days alone in the jungle, nearly starving to death. September's news reminded readers of the deadly risks correspondents faced covering the Pacific War. It reminded Drake that the assignments chosen (by lot) for correspondents—Custer to the *Astoria*, Singer to the USS *Wasp* (CV 7)—could be their last.

September also marked a pre-U.S. midterm election surge of publishers expressing disdain toward the Navy's censorship practices.[4] One editorial in response to the Navy's September 16 disclosure that the carrier *Yorktown* had been sunk during the Battle of Midway three months earlier declared, "There is the uncomfortable suspicion that the American people, instead of being told the truth as soon as the truth can be told, are being fed bits of good news and bits of bad news according to a scientific dietary program worked out by morale experts who look upon us as a mixture of boobs and fraidy-cats. There is a growing feeling that military information is being tampered with not to confuse our opponents but to pump up public approval of our war leadership."[5] Although Drake was implicated as one of the Navy's "morale experts," disclosures of Fleet losses were generally under the control of OPR officials in Washington, D.C., in coordination with Nimitz and King. Nevertheless, no compromise on publicizing Fleet losses could be had.

The same month Drake and Nimitz visited Custer's bedside, Bassett walked into the public relations office at CINCPAC headquarters to find an older gentleman with a "battered face in an open-necked blue shirt" plugging away at a typewriter.[6] Uniforms and neckties had been required at headquarters. Nimitz had relaxed the necktie mandate in July, but Bassett assumed that the gentleman in shirt sleeves was a local typewriter repairman. It was actually Navy Undersecretary Forrestal, who'd toured the South Pacific to get a closeup view of the problems facing the Solomon Islands campaign. He'd returned to Pearl Harbor to discuss the need for reinforcements with Nimitz. Although Drake ensured that Undersecretary Forrestal earned publicity for his remarks at the annal "E" awards that week, the "typewriter repairman" was dismayed about the problems in the combat area.

Vice Adm. Robert Ghormley, USN, in command of the area, had been headquartered first in Auckland, New Zealand, then Nouméa, New Caledonia, an island under Free French control nine hundred miles off the Eastern coast of Australia. The fighting in the Solomon Islands was nearly a thousand miles to the north, creating logistical challenges in gathering correspondents' stories for relay to Pearl Harbor, where Drake or Ward, the Fleet's new Press Censor, reviewed them before releasing them locally or transmitting them to the Navy Department in Washington, D.C. Photographs were handled under a new, separate review and disposition process in place in Pearl Harbor that Powell had helped create.[7] Luckily for Drake, fewer logistical challenges confronted the handful of correspondents who joined U.S. forces in the Aleutian Islands in Alaska as the campaign in the northern sector unfolded. Despite two far-flung combat areas, Drake was unequivocal. "Admiral Nimitz has directed that he control the censorship of all press material, (whether copy or photographs), concerning any combat operations in the Pacific Ocean Areas, whether originated by the Navy, Marine Corps or the Army."[8]

The cover of the August 17, 1942, edition of *Time* magazine featured Ghormley, steering public attention to the South Pacific. Anticipating that most correspondents in Pearl Harbor would be clamoring for task force assignments as Operation Watchtower on Guadalcanal gained momentum, Drake tried to prepare Ghormley's PRO, Lt. Cdr. Gene Markey, USNR, for the inevitable surge. By late August, twenty-two of the fifty correspondents in the Pacific were at sea, the "largest number yet," Drake reported to Berry.[9] Drake acknowledged to Markey, however, "Admiral Nimitz has just reiterated, to the Secretary of the Navy, his desire to reduce this number."[10]

Drake wrote to Berry, "Concerning ComSoPac [Ghormley], I have explained the whole set-up by letter to Gene Markey, (who did not stop here enroute), and have admonished him about permitting any person not fully-accredited to take passage in ships under that command."[11] Drake was referring to a handful of unaccredited correspondents who'd arrived in the South Pacific attempting to gain transport via Navy ships and file their stories through CINCPAC censors. Markey relied on Drake's guidance, as he possessed little public relations experience himself. He was, however, a celebrity, a noted Hollywood producer and screenwriter who'd gained press attention for his romances with famous Hollywood actresses. Drake wrote to Markey throughout the summer of 1942, advising him on broad public relations functions and mundane tasks, including preparing accreditation requests for correspondents and printing identification cards to hand to those who arrived at Ghormley's headquarters. He warned Markey, "Sec-Nav has insisted, since the Stanley Johnston affair, in going slow about accrediting new correspondents until their backgrounds have been carefully investigated."[12] Drake also reiterated the need for Markey to ensure all correspondents signed three copies of the Pacific Fleet Agreement for War Correspondents, the same document Drake himself had failed to have Johnston sign. Drake also kept the Army's PROs on a short leash. The Midway flap had taught him a harsh lesson, and he required press material concerning U.S. Army Air Forces planes operating in the South Pacific to be routed through Pearl Harbor so it could be forwarded to King for disposition.[13] He explained why in a letter to Berry, which read, "Maj. Gen. Hale's Seventh Air Force has been attempting to claim credit for the Solomons campaign."[14]

Markey got along well with Drake but reminded him, "I am only pinch-hitting on this job."[15] Ghormley neglected public relations, leaving Markey in Auckland after transferring his headquarters to Nouméa. Due to his remote location and short tenure, Markey did not have much incentive to tackle the growing list of public relations problems in the South Pacific. At the top of that list was one neither Markey nor Drake could do much about: the careless handling of mail. Drake lamented to Hotchkiss, his former editor at the *Times*, that weeks-old mail arriving in Pearl Harbor over the Pacific that summer was "probably brought by dog team."[16] In September, Drake urged Markey, "Make every effort to insure that your correspondence goes out to us via official Navy air mail."[17] He added, "I appreciate that everyone in the combat area is busy with purely military jobs, but anything done to keep copy coming will help much."

But it was already too late. Foster Hailey of the *New York Times* complained about the delays to his editor, who protested to OPR officials.[18] Additionally, the *New York Times*' Hanson Baldwin arrived in Pearl Harbor, meeting with Nimitz to "emphatically" voice his displeasure "with the Navy's, (and the Fleet's), press policy," which, he declared, "originates at the top [read: King]."[19] Sitting outside Nimitz's office, overhearing Baldwin's rant, Drake glanced at Mercer, the admiral's flag secretary, and just shook his head. Drake tried to explain the mail situation to Berry on September 17, 1942, writing, "It is regrettable that Hailey's copy was delayed, but I assure you that everything possible has been done to expedite the forwarding of copy of correspondents covering the Solomons campaign. Admiral Nimitz sent Admiral Ghormley a dispatch directing him to so instruct unit and ship commanders. Short of my going down south and speeding the copy along I know of nothing more that could be done. I am sure you will agree if you comprehend the operating situation in the combat area."[20]

By October, the situation in the South Pacific was dire. Drake pleaded with Markey, "I have written to Lt. Arthur Train [a member of Ghormley's staff], asking his cooperation, and likewise bespeak your help. Main trouble has been that the mail clerks in your area toss the stuff in a bag, which goes merrily by this place [Pearl Harbor] and is sent back to us by Fleet Post Office, San Francisco."[21] On October 10, Drake wrote to Lt. Cdr. W. G. "Slim" Beecher, USN, Berry's relief as head of the press section at OPR (by then, Berry had moved up to deputy director), "Majority of our 55 accredited correspondents are now in the South Pacific. Admiral Ghormley, with a small staff, is already so snowed under with operating exigencies that

I feel I should be down there to take the press load from his staff and to expedite the flow of copy."[22]

Drake's good intentions did not ease correspondents' complaints. On October 16, 1942, United Press' Frank Tremaine wrote to Nimitz, copying Drake, to protest the way eyewitness accounts of naval action in the Solomon Islands had been held up even after the same news had been released by the Navy Department in Washington, D.C. He explained, "I am in hearty sympathy with the restrictions on the release of news while it may be of the slightest assistance to the enemy. However, I am puzzled to know why the story of our correspondent, Joe Custer who witnessed the action from the Astoria, and those of the other correspondents who obtained interviews with eye-witnesses were not released after the Navy Department saw fit to announce loss of the three ships."[23] Drake tried to explain the mix-up in a letter to Beecher, blaming mail delays and calling Tremaine's criticism "unfounded."[24] Yet for Tremaine, Baldwin, and other correspondents, a solution to the mail problem was obvious: censor press material in the South Pacific and ship it directly to the mainland (via the Twelfth Naval District headquarters in San Francisco) instead of routing it through Pearl Harbor. Once the Navy Department had issued its official communique on an action, the censored material could then reach mainland newsrooms immediately. It took a letter from Knox to Nimitz eight days later suggesting this same approach to compel consideration of the change.[25] But it would take Nimitz another three months to approve "Comsopac's" direct censorship of press material in his command area.[26]

Drake's offer to "be down there to take the press load from [Ghormley's] staff and to expedite the flow of copy" demonstrated concern, but it also illustrated how his management of Fleet public relations tilted toward personal control rather than effective delegation. He did not relocate to Nouméa. Two days after Tremaine's letter reached Nimitz, the commander-in-chief replaced Ghormley as overall commander of the South Pacific area with Vice Adm. William "Bull" Halsey, USN. The timing was coincidental: public relations problems were not the cause of Ghormley's relief. With Drake's support, Nimitz reassigned Bassett to serve as Halsey's PRO, replacing Markey, who received new orders for intelligence duty and was glad to be done with COMSOPAC public relations. Drake sympathized, writing to Markey, "I agree that the press job is a terrific headache, but a few poor souls, such as we, must do it. It has been a constant battle since I came here a year-and-a-half ago. Jim Bassett and I have each lost 30 pounds in the process—believe it or not—but we are still alive and swinging."[27]

For Drake, having Bassett in place as Halsey's PRO was the next best thing to serving in that position himself, but coordinating public relations remained difficult, especially because Halsey and his staff declined to support correspondents. Halsey's stubbornness was puzzling since reporters relished the admiral's outrageously quotable public statements (a favorite was Halsey's promise to one day ride the emperor's white horse through the streets of Tokyo). In addition to Halsey's roadblocks, an overhaul of divisions and personnel at OPR in Washington, D.C. added to Drake's challenges. The Marine Corps also maintained its own public relations unit and had recently created a combat correspondent unit. Coordinating with the Army as well as with allied forces, added further complexity. Keeping tabs on the ballooning public relations activities of the various branches of the military in the Pacific soon became impossible. Drake complained to Powell on September 5, 1942, "Unknown to CINCPAC, the Marines have recently sent a number of public relations outfits, (reporters and photographers), to the South Pacific and one group to Pearl Harbor. Their first copy of the Tulagi-Guadalcanal battle hit the newspapers here before we even knew they were in the Pacific."[28]

Director John Ford's evasion of Navy censorship also came back to bite Drake. A letter drafted for Nimitz's signature, written to the commandant of the Marine Corps, illustrated why publishers perceived political motivations behind some of the military's press releases:

> On August 12, the *Honolulu Star-Bulletin* published the following United Press article: 'PRESIDENT'S SON WAS UNDER FIRE AT MIDWAY' WASHINGTON, Aug. 12. (U.P.) Maj. James Roosevelt, son of the president, was under fire during the Japanese attack on Midway Island in June, U.S. marine headquarters announced today. Earlier it was reported that Mj. Roosevelt had been under fire in Iraq in May of last year.' Inasmuch as the statement made therein that Roosevelt was under fire at Midway is untrue, I was surprised to note that it was

attributed to official Marine Corps sources. I note that the August 24 issue of *Time* carries a similar report. I am sure that you, too, will want to ascertain the source of this statement.[29]

The Marine Corps source could be forgiven for the error; in his documentary, *The Battle of Midway*, Ford had spliced in frames of Major Roosevelt to win the president's favor. Like most Americans, members of the Marine Corps could have believed the president's son had participated in the battle. The incident illustrated how Drake's actual span of control (subordinates a supervisor is directly responsible for managing) was limited, yet he was still responsible for controlling Navy public relations in the Pacific.

The South Pacific forces under Ghormley (later Halsey) had started off with too few (and too inexperienced) public relations personnel, inadequate transmission facilities, and ineffective censorship processes. But even though Drake knew that structures and staffing in the South Pacific risked repeating the same mistakes the Navy had made prior to the Pearl Harbor attack, there was little he could do about it. Nimitz and King were united in halting the buildup of public relations in the Pacific Ocean areas; they held the number of correspondents to sixty. Drake had been telling colleagues since July, "Admiral Nimitz will not take additional public relations personnel on his staff."[30] He commiserated with OPR's Lovette: "I feel that Bassett and I appreciate what you expect from us and likewise understand what the working press wants and requires. Please let me add, likewise, that Captain Wiltse [Nimitz's assistant chief of staff], as our immediate superior, is sympathetic. There are other factors, however, which prevent the output that I know you hope for. We are most grateful for your forbearance in this respect and assure you that we are struggling constantly for an increase in the flow of news and pictures to the mainland."[31] The unnamed other factors were, of course, the press-avoidant Nimitz, King, and Halsey.

As COMSOPAC, Halsey banned correspondents in the South Pacific from traveling by airplane unless authorized to do so. Halsey deemed a hundred pounds of "gas, bombs, and mail" more important than a hundred pounds of correspondent, even though reporters watched airplanes depart the area with plenty of room on board.[32] In one incident, Halsey asked Secretary Knox to revoke the accreditation of the Associated Press'

Jack Rice, who unknowingly disobeyed the ban and boarded a flight from Espiritu Santo to Nouméa.[33] The ban had gone into effect after Rice had departed Oahu for the South Pacific by Army B-17. Drake had assured Rice before his departure that formal orders were unnecessary to secure further air transport in the combat area. Rice had spent seven months at sea with the Fleet and had a clean slate. When Bassett read Rice's letter to Drake blaming the Fleet's PRO for the mix-up, COMSOPAC counter-manded the revocation of Rice's accreditation. But the correspondent had already had enough; he requested transfer out of the Pacific.[34]

Almost no one in the Navy's public relations hierarchy was willing to second-guess Nimitz, King, or Halsey, not even Secretary Knox. When an intermediary asked King why he chronically failed to keep Knox informed on various developments, King remarked, "Why should I? The first thing he does is tell reporters everything he knows."[35] As the topmost command-ers in charge of executing the war against Japan, Nimitz, King, and Halsey compelled from their subordinates (and often from their superiors) almost total deference to their public relations wishes.

Adding to the challenges was another variable Drake could do little to control: MacArthur and his Southwest Pacific Command. Correspon-dents accredited to the Army in the Southwest Pacific area cleared copy through MacArthur's headquarters in Brisbane, Australia, while corre-spondents in the neighboring South Pacific area cleared copy through Nimitz's headquarters in Pearl Harbor. Nimitz was the anti-MacArthur in terms of his relationship to the press. Personal publicity and mythmak-ing were anathema to the humble Texan, but they were second nature to MacArthur. MacArthur's near daily communiques, which he often wrote himself, depicted the general as singlehandedly prosecuting the war.[36] In response, Nimitz kept a magazine photograph of MacArthur on his desk. The image reminded Nimitz about the dangers of personal publicity and the foolishness of making "Jovian pronouncements complete with thun-derbolts."[37]

Nimitz kept a low profile with the press. In one of the first articles about himself he permitted Drake to release in May 1942, the Newspaper Enter-prise Association's Tom Wolf described the admiral as "A Cheerful Man of Confident Tomorrows."[38] That description had lingered since Nimitz's days as a midshipman at the Naval Academy. Wolf's article ran in scores of American newspapers, introducing readers to the Pacific commander who held a "poised, calm manner" and who "has enjoyed life." Tremaine amplified Nimitz's humble, hometown hero image in an August 19, 1942, profile: "White-haired, square-jawed Nimitz, a Texan, is exceedingly popular with the navy men here and with correspondents covering the fleet."[39] Tremaine noted, however, that the admiral remained tight-lipped: "Since he took command after Pearl Harbor, Nimitz has issued only six communiques—five on the Midway battle and one on the Solomons—and he has held only three press conferences. He told reporters several months ago that he was not talking for publication 'until I get out from behind the eight-ball.'"

By contrast, *Life* and *Time*'s Robert Sherrod, who covered MacArthur's command as part of his assignment in Australia, claimed that MacArthur was high on rhetorical drama but low on action. Even though he'd been forced to abandon his garrison and evacuate the Philippines, MacArthur, Sherrod observed, could "talk the best war."[40] For American news consumers hungry to satisfy their desire for stories of heroes, MacArthur played the role perfectly. By early 1943, forces under MacArthur's command were on the move in New Guinea, drawing the press' attention away from the Fleet.

To some extent, the press' focus on MacArthur (as well as the accelerating North Africa campaign against Axis forces) in early 1943 eased pressure on Drake. After eighteen months of nonstop work, he needed a break. On January 21, 1943, Drake's housemate, Francis Black, was killed along with nine other Navy officers (including Admiral English, Pacific Fleet Submarine Force commander) when the Pan American Clipper they were on board crashed near Ukiah, California, while en route from Pearl Harbor to San Francisco. Five days later, Bassett wrote to Willie, "We've got word (as have you) that our good friend Frank Black was in that missing Navy clipper."[41] Bassett mourned the loss but noted, "Poor Waldo will miss Frank, too, and more than I will. Because the Black was a steadying influence on him." With his wife and children far away, Drake's colleagues had truly become his family. Bassett concluded, "Well, this sort of life doesn't make you callous. But it does make these things easier to take, I guess, because it happens so often. And it's all in the line of duty . . . trying to refashion for everyone the sort of world we want most to have. And for this reason it's not in vain, or fruitless, to go."

Drake's grief likely darkened his reaction to the *Honolulu Star-Bulletin*'s January 27, 1943, profile of B. J. "Barney" McQuaid, correspondent for the *Chicago Daily News*.[42] McQuaid had replaced his vituperative colleague, Robert Casey, in June 1942 after Casey had returned to the mainland. Thirty-four years old and a native of New Hampshire, the stocky, dark-eyed McQuaid declared in the *Star-Bulletin* article, "I believe we have an ideal setup in the Aleutians for an offensive whenever we care to launch it." He added, "In my opinion, we could take Kiska [in the Aleutian Islands] at any time we wished to pay the price in manpower." Drake found McQuaid's Monday morning quarterbacking as irritating as Casey's public relations policymaking had been. In the article, McQuaid described himself as "an authority on aviation, having learned to pilot a plane in 1930 and later conducting an aviation column." Why McQuaid thought that made him qualified to opine on CINCPAC's broader warfighting strategy mystified Drake. Ward had passed McQuaid's *Star-Bulletin* feature without issue, but Drake bristled at the reporter's presumptuousness. He balled up the broadsheet and threw it in the wastebin.

Drake did not have time to dwell on why *Daily News* correspondents aggravated him. Complaints about Fleet public relations continued to reach the *Daily News*' publisher, Secretary Knox. In response, Knox directed OPR's Lovette to organize a PRO conference to try, yet again, to improve the situation. The dates of the conference were set for April 26–28, 1943. Drake was invited as a featured participant, handing him an opportunity to smooth over the growing frustration that increasingly positioned him at the center of conflict.

★★★★★★★★★★

Before the PRO conference, Nimitz dispatched Drake to the South Pacific for two weeks to investigate the problems firsthand. He traveled more than fourteen thousand miles, meeting top commanders in the region. He earned his "Neptunus Rex" card, crossing the equator for the first time on March 17, 1943, in an airplane 6,500 feet above it. His card stated,

Specification: In that one Waldo Drake did masquerade as a Commander in the Navy and did both while in such character and previously thereto feloniously, crassly and with no regard to his own lowly insignificant stature attempt to chronicle and report upon the august occurrences within my royal kingdom such action jeopardizing the sense of security of my loyal subjects and resulting in unwarranted disclosure of the mysteries of the deep to other vulgar pollywogs and freshwater sailors and constituting a crime of lèse-majesté punishable by the most severe means at my disposal, the U.S. then being at a state of war. Findings: *Guilty as Hell.*[43]

Drake's "sentence" was to compose a "sycophantic" poem eulogizing his namesake: Neptune (the poem has not been found).

Drake and Bassett rendezvoused on Guadalcanal, dining on fresh oysters harvested from the mangroves, raising their tin cups to the seven thousand U.S. servicemen who'd died fighting on the island. A second toast remembered their fallen Bad Manor comrade: Francis Black. Bassett reported to Willie, "Waldo and I sat around by the light of a dim little lantern and daubed ketchup on the raw oysters, placed them daintily on exceedingly damp crackers (everything is damp up there), and washed them down with a bit of beer that had been miraculously provided from the medical shack cooler. After that even an air raid seemed like little more than the icing on the cake."[44] When Drake returned to Pearl Harbor, he conferred with his new assistant PRO, Lt. Cdr. Kenneth McArdle, USNR, recommending an extensive set of changes to how the Navy handled public relations in the combat area.

Drake's memorandum to Nimitz bluntly declared, "I found that Commander, South Pacific Force [Halsey], and leading members of his staff, (with one notable exception, Captain H. R. Thurber), are strongly unsympathetic to the legitimate needs of the press in the South Pacific area."[45] Thurber had previously served in ONI's Information Section in the mid-1920s.[46] Not mentioned by name in Drake's memorandum was Halsey's chief of staff, Capt. Miles Browning, USN. According to correspondent Joseph Driscoll of the *New York Herald Tribune*, Browning was "a Cap'n Bligh in khaki, a tough profane seadog with saber-scarred face, steely blue eyes, uncompromising manner and entire absence of cordiality. Rawboned, erect, forceful, he was handsome in an unlovable way. For no apparent reason he radiated hostility toward the press."[47] In addition to staff problems, Drake observed, "Embarrassing delays in release of copy by ComSoPac have resulted because of his ignorance of issuance of communiques [by COMINCH and SECNAV] concerning operations in the SoPac area."[48] Drake recommended Halsey and his staff receive a daily summary of command dispatches.

Another critical issue was the lack of air transport for correspondents, as well as the lack of transmission facilities for their copy, with the radio transmitter at Nouméa limited to only 12,000 words per day. Drake recommended that correspondents be allowed to travel by plane, and that Press Wireless be authorized to establish a transmission facility on the island. Nimitz approved Drake's recommendations, although Halsey's staff nixed the Press Wireless transmitter due to security concerns. Nimitz told Halsey confidentially, "During my incumbency in my present job, I have been slowly but surely pushed into the position of lending all facilities to newsmen which will not prejudice operations, and of releasing factual material which is of no assistance to the enemy."[49] He added, "In doing the above, I have kept just one jump ahead of Col. Knox, who has almost taken the matter out of my hands once or twice." With several improvements in the South Pacific secured from Nimitz and Halsey, Drake headed to Washington, D.C..

The April 24, 1943, issue of *Editor and Publisher* described the PRO conference as a "'Cards-on-Table' Parley."[50] Mirroring Drake's framing of Navy-press relations as a struggle between adversaries, *Editor and Publisher* explained that the conference was intended to "clear up censorship difficulties." OPR officials extended "an invitation to all war correspondents and editors to send to the Navy Department before or during the conference any complaints or problems, so that there will be thorough discussion of all phases of the situation at one sitting." Despite its invitation, the Navy limited the collaborative approach: only the last thirty minutes of the conference were reserved for interactions between the attendees and members of the press. OPR allowed a sole press "observer," a reporter from *Editor and Publisher*, to attend the conference in its entirety.

Shoulders slumped from his long flights from Hawaii to Washington, D.C., Drake's disorientation showed. He'd missed the two previous PRO conferences held in July 1941 and September 1942, and much had changed in the capital in the sixteen months the nation had been at war: auto cannons ("ack ack" guns) dotted the rooftops of the government buildings packed along the Mall. The balmy spring weather did little to ease Drake's fatigue, but he squared himself away before entering the Bureau of Ordnance Conference Room at the Navy Department on Monday morning, April 26. There, he greeted friends: Lovette, Berry, and PROs from the West Coast naval districts he'd known before the war. Despite the ever-present possibility Berry would replace him as Fleet PRO, he'd proven a reliable ally since his August 1942 promotion to deputy director of OPR. Drake spied Earl Thacker in the room. Thacker had accompanied him on the flights from Hawaii and was attending the conference as an OWI representative.

The high-ceilinged, antiseptic conference room had a thick blackout curtain covering the windows on one side, with framed photos of severe-looking admirals hanging from the room's other three walls.[51] Three conference tables had been placed end-to-end in the center of the room, around which sat, in highbacked leather chairs, seventeen OPR officials and PROs including Drake. Dozens of flimsy folding chairs were arrayed around the room, with most placed in rows in the back as a kind of gallery for participants. Drake tugged at his shirt cuff under his jacket, noticing that the three stripes on the sleeve of his commander's uniform were a common site around the conference table. But his status as Nimitz's newsman elevated him in the pecking order. Combined with his exhaustion, the bright lights and clouds of cigarette smoke gave Drake a stunning headache; Main Navy was a long way from the fresh breezes of Oahu.

Nearly a hundred participants from the Navy, Marine Corps, and Coast Guard flooded the room before Lovette began his opening remarks. He acknowledged the unique circumstances surrounding the largest conclave of PROs the Navy had ever assembled. He explained, "You have been called here because we have some problems only partly solved. Because of the peculiar and rather unique nature of the work that is ours, these problems can be better approached by the direct face-to-face conference than by the formal letter, the directive or the order. We all learned some empirical formula and equations to solve engineering and mathematical formula but I believe that you all agree there is no touchstone or rule of thumb that will definitely and precisely help us in dealing with our problems of human relations and public relations."[52]

With *Editor and Publisher*'s Walter Schneider seated in the back of the room for the entirety of the three-day conference, the Navy needed to demonstrate its seriousness in improving public relations or risk more bad feeling from correspondents and their editors. Monday's remarks were reserved for the bigwigs: Secretary Knox and top admirals in the Navy Department, OWI's director Elmer Davis, the Office of Censorship's director Byron Price, and senior OPR officials. On Tuesday morning, it was Drake's turn. He sat at the head of the conference table and faced the audience. He informed the participants that Nimitz was committed to addressing the problems of war reporting in the Pacific. He noted there were sixty-eight correspondents and photographers in the theater presently. He explained how Nimitz had dispatched him to the South Pacific before the conference to investigate what could be done to improve the situation in the combat area. After briefing Nimitz upon his return to Pearl Harbor, CINCPAC immediately secured Halsey's agreement that correspondents should be allowed to use airplanes for transport instead of having to waste weeks traveling by ship. Vice Adm. Aubrey Fitch, USN, commander of Aircraft, South Pacific Force, had agreed to place a press officer on his staff to facilitate correspondents' transport. Drake also announced that a senior officer would regularly review the war—every week if possible—with available correspondents to ensure they were informed of developments. Yet Drake repeated the caveat that had become his mantra and the source of so many conflicts with the press: all the changes would need to be "compatible with security."[53]

Drake confessed he and the CINCPAC public relations staff had learned to place security above publicity "the hard way," a reference to the Stanley Johnston fiasco and other security breaches that had ensnared the Fleet's PRO. The former *Times* newsman also acknowledged his transformation from journalist to PRO/censor. "Correspondents," he declared, "have to change their concepts of news when they get into war zones."[54] He continued, "Winning the war is the major job we have to do and after that Admiral Nimitz believes in doing all for the press that is compatible with security." Most of the participants knew about Drake's struggles with correspondents. "90% of the trouble," he asserted, "has been caused by a few newspapermen."

After Tuesday's meeting, the PROs and officials gathered for a reception in the Willard Hotel. The private room included a piano. Once the attendees were assembled, Beecher sat down to play a tune. A Navy Department photographer captured the PROs' tight-lipped expressions as "Slim" began his impromptu serenade, but soon, Lovette—a gin and tonic in one hand and a cigarette in the other—began tapping his toe.[55] Beecher's tempo increased, and before long his bawdy lyrics had the crowd in stiches. Drake, his skin pale and voice scratchier than ever, helped himself to a cup of tea. The energetic Earl Thacker tried to cajole him into staying longer, but Drake retired early to his room at the Willard, long before Lovette stood upon a chair next to the piano to regale the crowd with one of his incredible stories.[56]

Scanning newspapers before bed, Drake noticed the New York Times reported that the Senate Judiciary Committee had decided to extend its study of official war news to the War and Navy Departments. The committee was investigating "the question of possible propaganda in the news," as well as suspicious delays in the disclosure of Army and Navy losses. The Times noted, "The heads of the War and Navy Departments will be asked to bring their public relations staffs with them so that news releases can be traced from source to final production."[57] Drake chuckled at the irony of it all. He folded the newspaper, setting it on the bedside table before turning out the light. He'd be back in Pearl Harbor by the time Knox, Lovette, and Berry faced the committee. Several floors below him, his OPR colleagues, oblivious to the day's news, were loosened up after several "small libations" and heavy hors d'oeuvres.

On the final day of the conference, Berry came to the front of the conference table. Berry fired the closest warning shot he could muster. Staring directly at Drake, he reminded the PROs, "Never confuse your mission with that of censorship."[58] He continued, "One of the most effective government offices is that run by Byron Price. Where we come in on the deal is assisting newspapers and other public media in the release of stories where normally the censorship code precludes such release. Then we act as an appropriate authority to permit publication. We are the antithesis of censors. Instead of acting as censors to stop news we help to push it over the fence." Berry once again advocated for the assistive approach to public relations he'd been urging Drake to adopt since March 1942. But *Editor and Publisher*'s subsequent summary of the conference emphasized Drake's "hair down" session, placing Berry's comments at the end of its three-page article.

Berry had lobbied for a frame that management scholar Judi Marshall might describe as "feminist" (although Berry did not use that term). Public relations can be considered through a gendered lens, with Berry's approach reflecting "interdependence, cooperation, receptivity, merging, acceptance, awareness of patterns, wholes and contexts, emotional tone, personalistic perception, being, intuition, and synthesizing. Underlying themes are openness to the environment, interconnection, and mutual development."[59] Drake, on the other hand, had always approached Fleet public relations from a stereotypically masculine frame. He emphasized persuasion, influence, and control,[60] digging in his heels against the approach Berry advocated. Nimitz's newsman faced a dilemma. The more he performed the masculine frame, the more he avoided conflict with Nimitz and King. The more he performed the "hair down" approach, the more goodwill and praise he earned from members of the press. There was no easy way to resolve the conflict.

Drake confers with *Chicago Tribune* correspondent Harold Smith following his wounding by a Japanese mortar shell during the Battle of Eniwetok, February 18, 1944.
Courtesy Scott Drake

Admiral Nimitz pins a Purple Heart on Drake in an impromptu ceremony in the CINCPAC public relations office, Makalapa, Hawaii, March 1944. *Courtesy Scott Drake*

CINCPAC public relations staff, August 1944. Seated second from left is Captain Mercer, CINCPAC flag secretary; followed by Lieutenant Commander McArdle, assistant PRO; and Drake, PRO. *Courtesy Scott Drake*

Drake and Mary with their children Bill, John, and Errol, Haleiwa, Oahu, fall 1941
Courtesy Jennifer Drake Schroeder

Drake conducts a press conference in the CINCPAC public relations office, date unknown. *Courtesy Jennifer Drake Schroeder*

For my good friend and shipmate
WALDO DRAKE
Comdr. USNR
whose invaluable help
has meant much to me

McCLELLAND BARCLAY
USNR

Sketch portrait of Drake by McClelland Barclay *Courtesy Jennifer Drake Schroeder*

Portrait of Drake after his promotion to commander, September 1942
Courtesy John Drake

Drake and Bassett somewhere in the South Pacific, 1943 *Courtesy John Drake*

Drake at mess, March 1944 *Courtesy Jennifer Drake Schroeder*

Admiral Nimitz and Drake shake hands at net, CINCPAC headquarters, Makalapa, August 1944. *Courtesy of John Drake*

8

Game, Set, Match

You can't blue-pencil a mortar shell!

—Harold Smith, *Chicago Tribune*

ONE EVENING IN July 1943, Nimitz invited Drake to his quarters, coaxing him into joining his daily target practice. The admiral and his housemates, Spruance and Capt. Elphege Gendreau, USN, the Fleet surgeon, had rigged up an air rifle target inside their house between the entrance hall and across the dining room leading to the pantry. Spruance mixed old-fashioned cocktails for Drake and Nimitz but helped himself only to a thimble full of spirits (Gendreau was at the time in the South Pacific inspecting medical facilities). They took turns plinking the paper target. Nimitz divorced himself from talking about the war during such times, and Drake waited until they were back at the Cement Pot to raise, yet again, the problems in the South Pacific that had persisted despite his promises at the April PRO conference.[1]

Drake and Nimitz formulated a plan to ask the Associated Press' Tom Yarbrough, a trusted correspondent assigned to Halsey's command area, for a candid assessment of the situation. Yarbrough's subsequent report alarmed them both. "The difference between Admiral Halsey's headquarters and General MacArthur's headquarters regarding the work of correspondents is the difference between a crossroads country store and a big city department store."[2] Yarbrough berated Halsey's press unit as "lumbering, timid, and operated largely by thumbs." Drake rushed to defend

Bassett, arguing that he wasn't to blame and was equally as frustrated as Yarbrough. The principal problems continued to be the delayed receipt of dispatches from MacArthur's headquarters and the slow outbound transmission of press copy that rendered eyewitness accounts old news once they finally reached the mainland. One sympathetic assistant PRO on Halsey's staff admitted, "Despatches containing the text of the communiques have been sent to us with deferred precedence, arriving here usually four days after the action. Any elaboration here of a four-day-old communique is like trying to warm up a dead fish."[3]

Correspondents who found their hard-won stories on page sixteen instead of above the fold on page one due to transmission delays often blamed Drake. The *Chicago Daily News*' Barney McQuaid discovered one of his stories had arrived so late on the mainland that it was unprintable. John O'Keefe, who'd stepped in at the *Daily News* to manage publisher duties while Knox served in government, wrote to Nimitz and accused Drake of sabotaging McQuaid as payback for the PRO's earlier run-ins with the newspaper's Robert Casey. O'Keefe remarked that McQuaid's delayed copy "indicates that something happened which is difficult for me to completely justify in my own mind." He asked Nimitz to "see whether we can eliminate the possibility of a recurrence."[4]

One correspondent in the South Pacific, the North American Newspaper Alliance's Ira Wolfert, found Halsey and his staff more intimidating than "timid." Halsey confronted the unfortunate newsman over his story claiming U.S. forces on New Georgia were burying casualties without confirming they were dead. CINCPAC censors had passed the story, but Halsey's director of intelligence, Capt. Julien Brown, USMC, glowed white hot and accused the correspondent of "yellow sensationalism and nothing else."[5]

"I resent that!" Wolfert shouted back at Brown.

"I hoped you would," said Brown, who unclenched his fists and began removing his khaki shirt, signaling his intention. No fight ensued, but Halsey ordered the correspondent back to Pearl Harbor under armed guard to have his accreditation re-examined. Finding a prohibited camera and photographs in his gear while en route, the Navy Department revoked Wolfert's accreditation. The incident was notable for its rarity: few correspondents wrote anything that so outraged the Navy (Wolfert would win a Pulitzer Prize for his earlier reporting on Guadalcanal).

The South Pacific headaches continued, but Drake dealt mostly with security concerns rather than with claims of sensationalism. In one case, during a conversation with Drake, United Press' Charles Arnot let slip the name of an island in the South Pacific to be occupied by U.S. forces that he wasn't supposed to know about. Despite the military's efforts to squelch loose talk (and much to King's consternation), correspondents befriended officers who routinely disclosed secret information. Drake reported Arnot to the Army, sparking an investigation that identified a loose-lipped sergeant who'd inadvertently tipped off the correspondent.[6] With cases like Arnot's multiplying—and despite Berry's urging of an assistive approach to public relations at the April PRO conference—Drake doubled down on security.

The next major campaign was about to commence in the Gilbert Islands. In October, in anticipation of a new combat zone, Drake drafted a six-page confidential memorandum for the PROs who were to aid correspondents during the amphibious assaults in the Central Pacific. The memorandum was meant to serve as an "informal summation" of the policies of the commander-in-chief of the Pacific Fleet and Pacific Ocean Areas "concerning accredited press representatives, the handling of their material, (written and pictorial), and measures to promote the dissemination of information concerning the Pacific campaign by both civilian, naval and military personnel."[7]

In the Fleet's hierarchy of values, Drake asserted, security superseded publicity. He wrote, "In field press relations, two considerations are paramount: (a) SECURITY of military operations and classified information pertaining thereto. (b) PROVISION OF FACILITIES for the adequate coverage of operations, by both civilian correspondents and naval and military personnel, and the expeditious transmission of all material, either to mainland destinations or higher authority." In contrast to Berry's admonition at the April conference that PROs were the antithesis of censors and should help to push news over the fence, Drake held firm. "While press relations officers have immediate responsibility to all news-gathering personnel within their jurisdiction, they have a primary responsibility to promote the security of all classified information."

Drake nevertheless tried to strike a better balance, one that had eluded him since the start of the war. "Remember, you have equal responsibility for the indoctrination of all naval and military personnel under your cognizance in (a) earnest cooperation with all accredited civilian and combat correspondents; (b) preservation of security while imparting or otherwise making available necessary information to correspondents." Drake's guidance risked repeating the arbitrary censorship practices that had earned him correspondents' antipathy. As before, instead of pointing to specific, written restrictions, Drake instructed the Fleet's PROs, who were empowered to censor or withhold copy in the field, "In determining disposition of material, keep ever in mind the question: WILL IT HELP THE ENEMY? It must be presumed that every bit of written and pictorial material regarding the war will eventually find a way into enemy hands." Drake anticipated PROs' objections to such vague instructions, writing, "It is not possible to prepare a complete list of subjects which if published would help the enemy; each case must be judged on its merits and in light of existing general censorship directives." In other words, Drake's guidance left room for speculative decision making and differences of opinion.

While Drake empowered PROs, his guidance also guaranteed conflict because information that could "help the enemy" was typically unclear, subjective, or rapidly changing. Therefore, PROs were instructed to rely on the expertise of the military officers in their combat areas. Drake wrote, "The Fleet Public Relations Officer in the field should acquaint all necessary officers, as early as possible, with the function of the public relations officer. On the flagship, the admiral, chief of staff, intelligence officer and flag secretary are the chief functionaries, and the PRO's battle station should be the signal bridge and flag plot." Ultimately, the success of a PRO depended on the goodwill and cooperation of senior officers. Effectively gathering, reviewing, and transmitting press copy from the field was beyond any individual PRO's control.

On October 25, 1943, Drake drafted a formal memorandum for Nimitz to accompany his "informal summation."[8] As he'd requested of Kimmel before the war, Drake asked Nimitz to provide "a brief directive to the Fleet and Pacific Ocean Areas . . . emphasizing the importance of public relations and enjoining all force, group and unit commanders concerned to lend all practicable support to the press in the field: expressly directing them to facilitate the availability of information and transportation and transmission of material." The consequences of not doing so were clear. "Without such a directive the present opposition and inertia will not be overcome." Nimitz initialed his agreement with the recommendation.

Drake also asked Nimitz to direct the CINCPAC communications office under the command of Capt. John Redman, USN, to supply him with "copies of despatches reporting results of our operations" to facilitate preparation of communiques and press releases and "intelligently reply to queries from the press concerning enemy announcements of our operations against him." Drake also requested sufficient information on *projected* operations to allow him to "intelligently assign war correspondents" to task forces. Nimitz initialed his approval of both requests. But Nimitz did not approve Drake's request to provide transmission facilities from distant headquarters' bases, writing in the margin of the memorandum that further study and recommendations based on each locality were called for. Drake cited as support for his appeal the problems that still plagued radio transmission at Nouméa. Drake wrote, "This decrepit French station is fantastic in its snail-like inefficiency and will never be otherwise." Despite requesting consideration of a Press Wireless transmitter in March, King required the continued use of the French commercial station on the island.[9] Mercifully, the Army eventually permitted Navy PROs at Nouméa to instead use its radio facilities for transmission.[10]

Critically, Drake lobbied for release of combat news only at Guadalcanal or Pearl Harbor, "where accurate stories giving proper credit to all hands and ships concerned can be assured, rather than risking highly-discriminatory accounts of releases at Washington, San Francisco, or Philadelphia." Nimitz initialed his approval. To ensure tighter control of other military services, Drake requested an Army officer and Marine officer be assigned to his staff at CINCPAC, noting, "Adequate supervision cannot be maintained over Army forces unless steps are taken." Nimitz agreed "in principle" but asked Drake to speak to another official about the request.

Drake additionally asked Nimitz for (a) a new staff member to help handle mail censorship, (b) permission to publish the names of personnel attached to various units, and (c) a weekly "off-the-record" briefing for correspondents at Pearl Harbor given by the CINCPAC plans officer. Nimitz approved all three requests.

Finally, Drake recommended a subordinate Fleet press office—with a full complement of staff and censors—be established in downtown Honolulu next to the cable and wireless office to expedite transmission to the mainland. It had been nearly twenty-two months since the *Chicago Daily News*' Robert Casey had first suggested a similar arrangement. Nimitz approved the expansion "in principle," but once again instructed Drake to seek additional guidance. The Fleet's subordinate public relations office in Honolulu was soon established inside the Office of Censorship. Drake's preparations for the first drive of the Central Pacific campaign culminated in Nimitz's issuance of the requested directive. "Fleet, force and unit commanders are directed to provide all practicable cooperation, including information and physical facilities, consistent with security operations, to accredited representatives of the press and of the naval and military forces assigned to coverage of the Pacific campaign."[11] Nimitz also wrote a letter to Lovette, OPR's director, explaining the changes: "To further facilitate the efforts of the press to adequately cover the Pacific campaign, I sent Drake to Halsey's area. He has just returned and I have taken action which I believe will insure that news from the South Pacific will be delivered as promptly and as completely as news from our Central and North Pacific operations."[12] But Nimitz and Drake still faced an unmovable obstacle: MacArthur. Drake tried to console Bassett, writing to him, "I was deeply sorry to hear about disinclination of General MacArthur to permit Admiral Halsey to issue his own communiques."[13]

While laudable, Drake's steps toward a more assistive approach did not reflect any fundamental transformation of his thinking: security still superseded publicity, and arm's length cooperation still precluded closer, collaborative planning and decision making with correspondents. Nevertheless, from the Fleet's sole PRO in 1941, brushed aside by Kimmel, Drake had by November 1943 become the head of a multifaceted public relations organization supporting ninety correspondents across the Pacific Ocean areas. When he'd gone on active duty in August 1940, the Navy had treated intelligence, public relations, and censorship as "one ball of wax." Three years later, the Fleet's PRO had learned the value of better separating the functions. All the recommendations Drake had first made to Kimmel in June 1941 were now in place: expanded public relations staff; directives from CINCPAC requiring PROs to be appointed to subordinate commands; a fleet photographic officer; and textual and photographic coverage of Fleet operations at sea. Drake's influence could not be denied. When an opening for the PRO position of the Twelfth Naval District, headquartered in San Francisco, became available in November 1943, Drake was considered, but Nimitz torpedoed the idea. "I do not want to make any change," he informed his loyal and trusted PRO.[14] Bassett would eventually be tapped to serve as the PRO for the Twelfth Naval District·

ørørørørørørø

On November 20, 1943, Drake's preparations were put to the test: the Battle of Tarawa had begun. Drake arranged for more than two dozen writers, photographers, film crew members, and illustrators to accompany the invasion force. The press contingent "was the same size as the one for the invasion of North Africa, which had sprawled over nearly 1,000 miles of Mediterranean coastline."[15] By contrast, Betio, where much of the fighting on Tarawa was concentrated, was a "crowded strip of sand the size of New York's central park."[16] As fighting commenced, assistant PRO McArdle was on board the battleship *Pennsylvania*, flagship of the commander of the Amphibious Force, Rear Adm. Richmond Kelly Turner, USN. In an unprecedented move, Turner granted McArdle use of the *Pennsylvania*'s radio facilities to transmit initial press copy back to CINCPAC headquarters in Pearl Harbor.

Meanwhile, Drake remained at his desk, vowing not to move until he'd cleared the first dispatches. That afternoon, Drake tapped his red pencil on his desk awaiting news from Redman's communications office and the initial stories from McArdle. The three censors, lieutenants under the supervision of Fleet press censor Ward, nervously rocked in their chairs. Ward and the lieutenants sat across from Drake, but nobody made eye contact.

The first reports of the battle that came through Redman's communications office were shocking: the situation on Tarawa was "in doubt."[17] Once the probable outcome became clearer, Nimitz allowed the staff to prepare the first communique and wire stories.

It was past 0330 before Drake retired to a cot he'd set up in a corner of the office, not daring to return to his quarters. Once the sun had risen, Drake finished drafting CINCPAC Communique No. 17, routing it to staff officers for security review. After Nimitz approved it, the communique was released at 1630 in Washington, D.C.: "Marine Corps and Army forces covered by powerful units of all types of the Pacific Fleet have established beachheads on Makin and Tarawa Atolls, Gilbert Islands, meeting moderate resistance at Makin and strong resistance at Tarawa. Fighting continues during these operations. Army LIBERATORS made diversionary attacks in the Marshalls."[18] With the communique issued, the CINCPAC staff flooded the wires with material: "News stories of the battle were on editors' desks in twenty-four hours and still photographs within forty-eight."[19] At first, McArdle, Drake, and Ward tried to tone down correspondents' descriptions of the Marines' "savage" and "bloody" assault, but they soon gave up; the battle was among the most brutal in the Pacific.[20]

Drake soon discovered that McArdle had not disembarked the *Pennsylvania* until D-day plus two. The assistant PRO asked to have a seaplane schedule altered to pick up additional press copy at Tarawa, but when he arrived on the beach, McArdle learned that the Marine PRO who was supposed to round up correspondents' dispatches had been killed. The assistant Marine PROs didn't know where any of the correspondents were. The correspondents had already returned to their ships, told by the on-site intelligence officer that the seaplane supposed to pick up their copy would not land in the lagoon until three days later. The next day, however, a handful of correspondents found McArdle, who told them the seaplane was, in fact, landing that afternoon and leaving almost immediately after receiving the press copy. Word passed that correspondents had better get their stories to the seaplane immediately. McArdle also decided to return with the seaplane to Pearl Harbor to provide Drake and the CINCPAC censors with an eyewitness account of the situation to help guide their work, although he'd only received a fraction of the correspondents' stories.[21]

When McArdle arrived in the public relations office, Drake assured him he'd made the right decision, but the correspondents who'd failed to get their copy out because of the confusion did not share Drake's opinion. Those who'd returned to their ships to wait for the seaplane had showered and retired to bed, but when they awoke in the morning, they discovered their ships had sailed on to a nearby atoll. They had no chance of filing a story until they returned to Tarawa. What most upset them was Drake's decision that the first wire story that made it back from Tarawa would be "pooled," making it available to all three major wire services: Associated Press, United Press, and International News Service. Back in February 1942, Drake had sided with the correspondents in rejecting the pooling idea, but now he embraced it. No news organization was given sole credit for its correspondent's work. Like the Battle of Midway, initial accounts of Drake's public relations success at Tarawa had morphed into a more complicated and contentious picture.

Capping off the struggles, correspondents returning from Tarawa soon learned that a Japanese vessel had launched a scout plane that followed an American plane back to Hawaii. The "snooper" was detected at the shoreline, where a barrage of antiaircraft fire blacked out the sky and forced the pilot to flee. Within hours, the story was common knowledge in Honolulu. When two dozen correspondents piled into the CINCPAC public relations office to ask why the Japanese plane had not been picked up by radar out at sea, Drake explained that the American plane had "screened" the Japanese plane behind it. The correspondents asked if they could write that in their stories, arguing if they did not, the American public would have a poor opinion of the Honolulu defenses. Drake responded with a firm "No." Radar capabilities were one of the military's most closely guarded secrets.[22]

Most of the correspondents relented, but Barney McQuaid of the *Chicago Daily News* loomed over Drake's desk. It had been seventeen months since McQuaid had first arrived in Pearl Harbor in June 1942. His inaugural article gushed over the Navy; Drake couldn't have written better promotional material himself. McQuaid's account of transiting from California to Oahu depicted life at sea as a party. "We were all genuinely sorry when the day of arrival came and wished for a few days more of swing concerts, boxing matches and volleyball. We had even begun to enjoy the blackout."[23] McQuaid's second article, however, earned him Father Neptune's ire. In the wake of the Midway mess, McQuaid tried to smooth things over: "Army and Navy Argue but Both Won Battle of Midway," declared his headline.[24] "In my opinion many of the Japs ships were hit again and again within relatively short time intervals by both Army and Navy pilots and by both land-based and carrier-based air power." Hamstrung by Nimitz's order to censor only for security and not accuracy, Drake twisted himself into knots allowing McQuaid's erroneous assessment to pass censorship.

Following his Midway article, Drake had sought to rid himself of the troublesome McQuaid. He was glad to oblige the correspondent's request to accompany a task force to the Aleutian Islands. There, McQuaid spent the next six months, often as the only correspondent in the gloomy, frigid region. His remote location did not prevent him from criticizing CINCPAC's warfighting strategy. He'd gone back to the mainland for the holidays but had returned to Pearl Harbor in January 1943, where he proceeded to undermine the Fleet by calling for the abandonment of the planned Central Pacific campaign in favor of an Army advance through China. Drake couldn't help himself: he loathed McQuaid.

On the other side of the desk was McQuaid, who suspected Drake of delaying his dispatches and sabotaging correspondents he didn't like. The tough Chicago newsman was unafraid of the grim-faced PRO, so he pushed back against Drake's prohibition on the mention of radar and the screening of the Japanese snooper. With a certainty that must have read to Drake as disrespect, McQuaid protested, "It's been said before."[25]

Drake contemplated McQuaid's "It's been said before" logic. Stanley Johnston had said in June 1942, "Navy Had Word of Jap Plan to Strike at Sea," in a *Chicago Tribune* headline, but that did not make it okay to publish further articles disclosing the Navy's cryptographic secrets. Saying something before was no justification for saying it again if it undermined security. At the April PRO conference, Drake had admonished participants, "Correspondents have to change their concepts of news when they get into war zones." Now here was McQuaid, determined to undermine security and, in Drake's mind, help the enemy.

"True, but just the same it can't be said now!" Drake roared back.

The room fell silent as the two men stared one another down. McArdle, Ward, and the three lieutenant censors didn't breathe.

Correspondents like McQuaid, Casey, and Tremaine couldn't take no for an answer. Drake couldn't take it anymore. He rose to his feet, eyes locked on McQuaid.

In an instant, Drake and McQuaid were toe-to-toe, tapping each other on the chest, daring each other to take the first punch. Desks and chairs skidded across the floor as staff members and correspondents rushed to pull the two men apart. Alerted to the melee, Mercer, Nimitz's flag secretary, stepped in, forcing the two men to sit down. Mercer said McQuaid could use the phrase "detection devices similar to those used before Pearl Harbor" but could not mention radar. McQuaid ranted, threatening to take his case to Secretary Knox.

"Go ahead," Drake goaded him, thrusting his index figure toward the oversized photo of the grinning admiral hanging on the wall, "I'm still talking for C. W. Nimitz!"[26]

Fortunately for Drake, McQuaid returned to the mainland a few days later. "The sun already seems brighter," Drake wrote to his old boss at OPR, Jimmy Stahlman.[27] Indeed, brighter days had arrived. Despite the fumbles, the Battle of Tarawa "marked a triumph of Drake's campaign for reportorial access in the Pacific—a campaign motivated by the desire to bring the public into closer contact with the realities of combat."[28] As one scholar has written, "When a group of correspondents formed an organization to bargain with the military over professional issues in the South West Pacific the following year, they lauded Drake as an exemplar of transparency."[29] Drake's management of public relations was positive enough to earn him *Time* magazine's praise. The December 6, 1943, article, "The Press: The Not-So-Silent Service," declared,

> For nearly two war years U.S. newsmen covering the Pacific Fleet had chafed at red tape, slow censorship, slow transmission of dispatches. Now things changed. Twenty writers, five photographers, two artists and a newsreelman flew over, cruised near or landed with combat troops on the Gilbert Islands. In the weeks before the Gilberts invasion

CINCPAC Chester W. Nimitz issued a directive ordering fleet, force and unit commanders to extend fullest cooperation to correspondents everywhere. His brusque public-relations officer, Commander Waldo Drake (onetime Los Angeles Timesman), picked the correspondents to be taken along, decided which should go in planes, on carriers, in landing parties. Faster transmission of news had already been arranged. Correspondents got the use of the Army's radio transmitter on Guadalcanal, no longer had to suffer from the French-owned station at Noumea. Last week the new policy began to pay off. Reporters' eyewitness dispatches of the Gilberts offensive reached U.S. readers with only three-day delays. And for the first time names of units and commanders were promptly given. Naval activity was not yet being covered as fast or as well as Army operations (examples: the invasions of Sicily and Italy). But Navy coverage was better and faster than it had ever been before.[30]

When he read the *Time* article, the brusque PRO of Bad Manor smiled; he couldn't fault the writer for the accurate description. Sitting across from Drake at CINCPAC headquarters, McArdle, Ward, and the lieutenants watched him lean back in his chair, clasp his hands behind his head, and take a deep, satisfying breath. The press' "brickbats" had become "bouquets," and Father Neptune had finally caught the fair breeze he'd long hoped for.[31]

§§§§§§§§§§§

Ten days after publication of the *Time* magazine piece, Bassett wrote to Drake offering "congratulations on long-overdue recognition in Mr. Luce's publication. Remembering a somewhat different piece in *Newsweek*, I read this one with a vast deal of pleasure."[32] But the letter handed to Drake the following week knocked the breeze out of his sails and the air out of his lungs. Signed by thirty-four civilian correspondents, editors, and photographers in the Pacific, the letter announced the establishment of the Pacific War Correspondents Association.[33] The association's "entirely constructive" purpose was to "afford an avenue of cooperation between the Public Relations Office and the correspondents as a group in the solution of such problems as they arise." "In many instances," the writers claimed, "the problems of the correspondents are also the problems of your Public Relations Office." The correspondents hoped "to save time by collective rather than individual presentation" of these problems. Most of the signatories had covered the Battle of Tarawa, but notably absent from the list was Robert Sherrod, whose publication, *Time* magazine, had praised Drake only days before. All but one member of the local Honolulu press corps also declined to sign the letter.

The association attached a list of nineteen problems and recommendations it hoped to address. At the top of the list was the association's desire to cease the practice of Drake being allowed to read correspondents' personal mail while simultaneously working on their behalf. Even U.S. service members whose mail was checked for security didn't endure such awkward invasions of privacy from their own unit commanders, the association noted. The remaining eighteen points offered a litany of complaints ranging from a desire to confine censorship to security considerations, with each censor "given a list of items barred," to halting bothersome "interruptions of interviews" by the Fleet PRO.

Although the association claimed it earnestly desired its recommendations "not be considered as criticisms of present practices in the Fleet's press relations," Drake had no doubt its members were telling him how to do his job. The *Times*' antiunion maritime editor now had to deal with a union of nearly three dozen Pacific War correspondents. The correspondents anticipated Drake's defensiveness and tried to disarm him. "The Pacific War Correspondents Association and the Pacific Fleet Public Relations Office are on the same side in the same war . . . we assure you of our cordial intent." Drake scoffed, recalling his near fisticuffs with McQuaid only weeks before and how one "cordial" hatchet man had fabricated the 1942 *Newsweek* and *Albertan* articles announcing his relief, hoping their publication might somehow make it true.

A less committed PRO might have read the nineteen indictments and decided to call it quits, but Drake believed his duty was to protect security, not only for the Navy but for the nation. A less security-conscious PRO might let slip a secret as consequential as the one Stanley Johnston had disclosed, endangering not only U.S. military personnel but America's overall war-fighting advantage. He couldn't let that happen. Instead of acquiescing to the association, Drake urged Nimitz and Mercer to ignore the association's letter. In a memorandum drafted on Christmas morning, he wrote, "Official acknowledgement of the specific demands of the association would commit both CINCPAC and the Navy Department to recognition of the association per se; whereas, if the complaints and recommendations were signed by each individual correspondent over the name of his service or newspaper, as requested by the Admiral, no such commitment could be attributed to CINCPAC."[34] Counseling a strategy of *divide et impera*, Drake struck down each of the association's nineteen points. He argued some correspondents used their personal mail to evade Navy censorship and therefore his scrutiny of their mail should continue. His strict controls were in place to protect security, morale, and fairness, he wrote. Awkward interruptions of interviews were necessary to halt disclosures of secret information. He also stated that several of the association's recommendations had already been accepted.

In reporting to the association's members the outcome of a meeting with Mercer, the association's president, *New York Times*' Robert Trumbull, offered a conciliatory gesture, agreeing that many of the recommendations had indeed already been accepted, and when not, the reasons given were "logical."[35] The Fleet PRO had escaped relatively unscathed but confessed to a friend from his yacht racing days, "Haven't been in a sailboat since before the blitz and would give my right eye for an afternoon in CAPRICE again with you and Tommy [Lee]."[36] Drake didn't make it back to Southern California; he was ordered instead to Washington, D.C., to brief COMINCH and SECNAV. Afterward, he visited Mary and the children in Tennessee. Critically, the major amphibious operations that followed—Kwajalein (January), Eniwetok (February), and Saipan (June)—saw the newly promoted Captain Drake further improve in the volume, speed, and leniency of censorship and release. Nimitz received no further letters from the association about his PRO, although individual complaints about Drake continued.

Sea duty was usually a requirement for promotion from commander to captain. Therefore, to soothe nervous Navy officials and escape disgruntled correspondents at CINCPAC headquarters, Drake and McArdle switched places: Drake served as the PRO at sea on board the *Rocky Mount*, which entered service as Turner's flagship on January 10, 1944. When not out with the Fleet, Drake resumed his duties for Nimitz in Pearl Harbor. But in January 1944, before the Battle of Kwajalein, Drake just missed the "Old Texas Roundup," an epic, beer-fueled picnic in Honolulu that reflected and reinforced Nimitz's proud "son of Texas" persona. Drake had been en route to Pearl Harbor after his six-day visit to Washington, DC, and one-day visit with Mary and the children. The remarks drafted for Nimitz on the occasion were notable; they were among the first to honor women serving in the auxiliary service. Under the probable influence of his wife, Catherine (who objected to fraternization), Nimitz had forbidden WAVES (Women Accepted for Volunteer Emergency Service) from serving in Hawaii since the unit's creation in July 1942, claiming it was too dangerous for women in the combat area.[37] But Nimitz used the roundup to pay tribute to the women's auxiliary service, not only to the "sons" of Texas but also to its "daughters."[38]

Nimitz's roundup remarks differed from the letter the admiral wrote to Lovette endorsing the *American Legion Magazine*'s women-in-war-work campaign six months earlier. Drake warned Wiltse, "I consider that the Admiral should not make the statement requested," but Nimitz overruled him, penning, "I have no objection to issuing a statement as amended."[39] The statement began, "The increasing shortage in the Nation's civilian manpower, as new millions of young men are called to military service, must be filled largely by the women of America." Ignoring women's contributions to the military, Nimitz asserted, "Unless our women do their share there will not be enough [men], in time, at the right place, to bring victory." Drake sensed the statement's chauvinist tone. Nimitz's evolution concerning the role of women in the military was slow, and it would take until December 1944 for him to finally permit the first contingent of WAVES in Pearl Harbor.

The Fleet's policies toward Black correspondents mirrored the services' broader segregation. Bassett wrote to Drake,

> Fletcher Martin of the Negro Publishers' Association arrived several days ago, after we accepted him from SoWesPac on a temporary basis. He is quartered with Negro Army units and will continue with them

up-the-line. He has seen Admiral Halsey and written a decently constructive piece about his people on the basis of it; ditto Negro Marines
and SeaBees, using some MarCorps combat correspondents' copy. Martin's stuff is censored by us and USAFISPA, and then sent to the War
Department for release to all Negro newspapers. Accepting him caused
us no little concern; but there was no choice in the matter. And as it is
working out, it may actually prove to be of advantage. Certainly if we
had denied him, as representative of the pooled Negro press, the opportunity of seeing this area, considerable trouble might have ensued.[40]

Battling the Pacific War Correspondents Association at the time, Drake
offered Bassett few replies.

The admiral's public relations gaffes were rare, and Drake never criticized Nimitz's approach. Just before the Old Texas Roundup in January,
while visiting Mary and the children in Columbia, Tennessee, Drake
granted an interview to Margaret Sanders of the *Nashville Tennessean*. In
the interview, Drake lavished praise on the admiral. "Picture a tall, lean
58-year-old Texan who can whip any young ensign at tennis, who swims
two or three miles every morning, who rarely misses a daily turn at the pistol range; a man who holds the respect and confidence of all his associates;
a man who flies to the front lines, directs sea, land and air offensives in his
war zone, a diplomat and warrior."[41] If Nimitz had read Drake's statement,
it would have embarrassed and annoyed him; it reflected the kind of personal publicity he abhorred. Drake's statement is noteworthy due to its rarity; he seldom promoted the admiral using such gallant imagery. Instead,
he reinforced Nimitz's preferred homespun persona. He later remarked,

> Well, he professed to be a Texas farm boy, but he had a hidden suavity
> that put everybody at their ease much better than lots of people who
> wore their good manners on their sleeve. I mean there was no pretense
> about the fellow at any time, whether he was meeting with the Presi-
> dent of the United States or playing horseshoes with his Marine chauf-
> feur. He just had the common touch to make everybody at all levels of
> society feel at ease, and that's how he was able to extract from his own
> officers and the people under his command so much.[42]

Drake, of course, ensured that the admiral's innumerable letters, speeches, and statements evidenced this common touch.

Nimitz successfully evaded the press' spotlight, but Drake found it. Walter Cochrane, a Marine combat correspondent, mentioned Drake in his February 10, 1944, story of "Death and Carnage" on Kwajalein. "Near our flagship transports were loading assault troops into landing craft. Shortly afterward three waves were ashore. Four hours later I hit the beach with Capt. Waldo Drake, Pacific fleet public relations officer with whom I worked in the Los Angeles Times."[43] Cochrane explained what happened once they were ashore. "I crawled into a crater and met Army sergeant Ray Woodworth of Walkerville, Mich. As we peered over the parapet Jap bullets sang around our heads." Cochrane pulled no punches. "I happened to glance at my feet and saw I was standing on part of a Jap's head. The shells had gotten him. I slithered into another hole where five soldiers crouched. On the far side of the hole lay a headless Jap." The gruesome dispatch, by now commonplace, rendered quaint Drake's earlier handwringing over bloody, shark-infested waters at Midway. Another story that February mentioning Drake underscored how much the security situation in the Pacific had changed. "We've got so much stuff and power now we don't have to give much of a damn what we tell the Japs . . . what he does find out will scare him."[44]

King did not share the spokesperson's point of view. On February 17, 1944, Eniwetok D-day, King wrote to Nimitz, cautioning him against talking to the press. "You may be surprised to know how widely you are quoted as the basis for comment and speculation as to what we are doing next in the Pacific Ocean Areas."[45] King added, "In fact you said nothing much but what would be obvious to military men of high status—but—the use of it has, I fear, verged on giving aid and comfort to the enemy. You must watch your step in dealing with the press, etc.—basically, they care for nothing except their own 'kudos' and the news—or interpretation of the news—that will enable them to peddle more papers! . . . Press and radio here can have left no doubt in the minds of the enemy that our next objectives were Eniwetok and Ponape."

While King composed his letter to Nimitz, Drake was reaching the rendezvous point on Eniwetok Island, relieved that there were few signs of

Japanese resistance. He'd stood near Hal O'Flaherty from the *Chicago Daily News* in the LVT that had brought them to the beach from the *Rocky Mount.* They'd just arrived at the rendezvous point when a group of correspondents and photographers joined them: Sgt. John Bushemi and Sgt. Merle Miller from *Yank,* Harold Smith from the *Chicago Tribune,* 1st Lt. Gerhard Roth and Sgt. Charles Rosecrans, both G-2 photographers, and CPO D. A. Dean, the master at arms of their transport. Drake saw that Bushemi's left arm was still in a sling from fracturing his hand at Kwajalein only a few weeks before.[46] Bushemi, twenty-six years old, had earned the nickname "One Shot" for his combat photography. He and Miller (twenty-four years old and the correspondent of the duo) opened *Yank*'s Pacific bureau in Honolulu in 1942. Until Kwajalein, Bushemi had disapproved of Drake, complaining to his editors at *Yank* about the lack of news in Pearl Harbor. But the vibrant and daring Bushemi had an unfailing sense of humor, and he and Drake traded jokes when crisscrossing the Central Pacific.

The high-pitched ring of Japanese Type 99 rifle fire suddenly erupted in front of the group, and Type 89 mortar shells slammed into the sand behind them. The men dove for cover. In the chaos that followed, Drake and O'Flaherty became separated from the other correspondents. The two men ended up following a group of Marines, soon discovering the Japanese had carved out holes in the sand which they'd then covered with corrugated tin, palm fronds, and mangrove leaves. The American troops had passed over these positions earlier without detecting them. Now, in a full-on ambush, the Japanese were hitting back. As each hole was discovered, American rifle shots, grenades, or flamethrowers dispatched their occupants. The pace was slow, and it would take another day to secure the entire island. Yet by 1445, most of the holes near the beach had been cleared. Air support was called in to hit machine-gun nests, snipers, and mortar positions further inland. While this was carried out, the troops lit their Lucky Strikes and waited.[47]

Drake and O'Flaherty found Bushemi, Miller, Smith, Roth, Rosecrans, and Dean crouched behind a tank, waiting alongside the troops. The group was about seventy-five yards from the front line. With air support called in, the men ambled away from the tank to examine a strange sight: a bullet-riddled chest full of Marshallese books. Boobytrapped, they presumed.

Drake, O'Flaherty, Bushemi, and Smith had walked about twenty paces away from the chest of books when a 60-mm mortar shell exploded right in front of them. A shell fragment hit the lip of Drake's helmet with such force that it blew him over backwards.[48] Roth, Rosecrans, and Dean sprinted back toward the beach, while Miller jumped into a hole next to the chest of books. Drake, O'Flaherty, Bushemi, and Smith flattened themselves on the open ground as mortar bursts continued without pause for two minutes. When they finally ceased, Drake watched Bushemi attempt to rise to his feet but fall back to the ground. Bushemi lay only a few yards away from Drake, bleeding profusely from wounds in his cheek and neck, his left leg badly damaged. Smith was nicked in the arm. O'Flaherty looked at Drake, who had blood pouring down his face from a gash above his right eye. Bushemi cried out, "Where's my camera?"[49]

They needed to get Bushemi back to the beach fast. Although conscious, he couldn't move on his own. O'Flaherty stayed with Bushemi while Miller, Smith, and Drake ran to the beach to get medics to help transport Bushemi. Drake's head wound was serious, but he pleaded with the medics to get the litter to his more severely wounded colleague before attending to him.[50] Once the medics were on their way with Miller, Drake wrapped bandages around his head, but the blood soaked through and streamed down his cheeks and dripped off his chin. A photographer snapped a picture of Drake conferring with Smith about what had happened. Moments later, as Smith turned to leave, he couldn't help himself, "You know, Captain," he remarked over his shoulder, "you can't blue-pencil a mortar shell!"[51]

Medics carried Bushemi to an aid station near a demolished coconut log emplacement as he joked about his condition. Instead of focusing on his own injuries, he asked how badly Drake was hurt and instructed Miller, "Be sure to get those pictures back to the office right away."[52] Medics rushed Bushemi to the transport ship, but surgeons were unable to tie off the artery in his neck before he died. He became the eighth correspondent killed in combat in the Pacific and the second to die in the Marshall Islands that February. Nobody blamed Drake for Bushemi's death: correspondents accepted the risks of combat. Drake had barely escaped death himself, but he would make sure that in the next major operation on Saipan that each correspondent was handed an M1 carbine for self-protection, Navy rules notwithstanding. The correspondents bragged they were members of the "Waldo Drake Rod and Gun Club."[53]

In the weeks ahead, scores of American newspapers and magazines featured stories of the Battle of Eniwetok filed from the *Rocky Mount* anchored off the atoll. Drake, who'd been there to assist the correspondents in gathering and filing their stories, found himself the subject of a few of them. The photograph of the bandaged and bleeding Drake appeared on newspaper front pages from New York to Los Angeles. Correspondents, editors, and Navy officials who'd earlier accused Drake of being an impediment to public relations now had to eat crow. The Navy had a great story, and even the press-avoidant Nimitz couldn't help but be amused that his own newsman was at the center of it. They'd lost Bushemi, but overall casualties from the battle had been low. For Drake, the day had been a victory for Navy public relations and for himself personally. He knew it would take time for the letter he wrote to Mary and their children to reach them in Columbia, Tennessee. Drake presumed they'd see the photograph before his letter arrived, and he was right. Out shopping one afternoon with her sister, Mary felt a pull on her sleeve. Pointing toward a newspaper rack, Lois exclaimed, "Look, Mary. My God, that's Waldo!"[54]

◆◆◆◆◆◆◆◆◆◆◆

After the Battle of Eniwetok, a wounded Drake returned to Pearl Harbor on board the *Rocky Mount*. While en route, *Life* photographer George Strock captured the PRO's gleeful expression despite two swollen black eyes.[55] For Drake, they were proof of his bravery. Nearly two weeks after returning to CINCPAC headquarters, an upbeat Nimitz pinned a Purple Heart on Drake in an impromptu ceremony in the public relations office. Afterward, officers and correspondents inclined to mock the *Times* newsman for sailing a desk to become a "Captain in old Chet's Navy" might have hesitated just a second more. Drake reported on the Eniwetok action to his sons in a letter dated March 10, 1944:

> I hope that neither of you lads were scared by the picture which you
> may have seen in the papers. It was only a small hole in my forehead

and already is as good as new again. I am most thankful for my steel helmet, however, because it undoubtedly stopped the slug from going clear through my skull. The fragment cut a quarter-inch gash through the bottom edge of the front of the helmet and then hit me just above the right eyebrow. The worst part of the business was two gorgeous black eyes, the right one hanging on for two weeks.[56]

Drake noted,

> The third salvo landed a few feet from where Sergeant John Bushemi, *Yank* Magazine photographer, and I were lying in a shallow depression in the beach. Bushemi, who was five feet to the right of me, got the full blast of the shell. He was badly-hit in the leg and neck, and also received an arterial wound in the side of the head, from which he lost so much blood that he died shortly after he was taken on board a transport. So you can see that I was quite lucky. First, I might well have been in the spot where Bushemi was lying. Second, had the fragment been an eighth of an inch lower it would have snuffed out my right eye. Admiral Nimitz himself gave me a Purple Heart, which I will send to you for safekeeping. Henceforth, I expect to keep myself out of harm's way.

Bushemi's death troubled Drake. In a letter composed to no addressee, Drake praised the photographer, writing, "He showed himself to be a courageous soldier, many times going beyond the line of duty to get the best possible pictures for his publication, and intent on the best possible fulfillment of his mission, without regard for his personal comfort or safety."[57] Whether Drake later sent a similar letter to Bushemi's parents is unknown.

Drake's PRO duties had transformed from his days on Kimmel's staff. Once marginalized, he now officially served "as advisor to the Commander in Chief, Pacific Fleet in all public relations matters."[58] In directing "administration of public relations matters in the Pacific Ocean Area, ashore and afloat," much of his work involved personnel management.[59] In letters to Bassett about prospective staff members, Drake was harsh. He called one potential PRO "a former classified ad solicitor for the San Pedro News-Pilot and the Honolulu Advertiser [who] is an unreliable windbag of the first water."[60] Drake's observations about correspondents could be equally severe. "[Associated Press' bureau chief] is of such selfish, combative, small-principled nature that he consistently incurs the displeasure of both commanding officers and flag officers in the ships to which he is assigned," Drake wrote to a CINCPAC staff member.[61] In addition to never-ending personnel decisions, Drake established a public relations and censorship unit in the forward area, assisted correspondents covering the Battle of Saipan, and, on July 29, 1944, organized an outdoor press conference at the Holmes Estate in Waikiki for President Roosevelt, who'd arrived in Pearl Harbor for a meeting with Nimitz and MacArthur.[62] Drake ensured that each correspondent was introduced to the president and allowed to shake his hand.[63]

Following the president's successful visit to Hawaii, and as they'd done countless times before, Nimitz and Drake began their warmup at the Maka-lapa tennis court, hitting tennis balls back and forth to check both the tuning of their rackets and the flexibility of their joints. While other officers on the CINCPAC staff scurried away when Nimitz sought an opponent for his noonday tennis ritual, Drake could be counted on to appear on the court. Both men were skilled tennis players. Nimitz was a "placement expert" who could run Drake ragged with shots "chopped along the lines."[64] Drake was as fit as he'd ever been, but Nimitz threatened him, "Drake, if you ever give away a point to me, I'm going to kick you out of here."[65] The Maka-lapa court, surrounded by a high fence, was nestled among administrative buildings that partially blocked the breeze. The overcast sky blotted out the noonday sun, but the two men were soon bare-chested to keep cool. The day's match was unusual: Drake had arranged for a Fleet photographer to capture images of the admiral's serve and volley for publicity purposes. It was a glorious afternoon on the court. For both men, it was beginning to feel like game, set, match against the Japanese. The day they'd sail tri-umphantly into Tokyo Bay was approaching. Smiling at each other while warmly shaking hands at net, the photographer captured Drake and Nim-itz's good humor and the spirit of their friendship.

9

Forrestal's Crosshairs

It would be very helpful if Captain Drake could make periodic visits to Washington every year.

—James Forrestal

K ING, NIMITZ, AND a handful of their staff members gathered in the nondescript conference room near the Twelfth Naval District in San Francisco on September 29, 1944, for the first day of their three-day quarterly meeting. Joining them was an unexpected participant, James Forrestal. Five months earlier, almost to the day, word had reached CINCPAC headquarters that Secretary Knox had died of a heart attack. Drake wrote (and Nimitz approved) CINCPAC's statement to the press: "In the passing of Mr. Knox the Navy has lost one of its truest champions. The Nation has lost one of its most able and loyal servants."[1] In Knox's stead, President Roosevelt appointed Forrestal. The new secretary had observed the Fleet's public relations problems during his inspection trips to the Pacific over the past three years, but public relations had been Knox's purview. Now, as secretary, Forrestal was under pressure in Washington, D.C., to finally resolve the issues. American publishers told Forrestal they'd been fighting with the Navy for the entire war about censorship and communications. Forrestal, in return, complained to the publishers, "You don't tell about this battle. Why don't you write our story?"[2]

The publishers replied, "We can't write it. You've got a guy out there who won't let us write it."[3]

Forrestal worried that without better public awareness and support, the Navy would, after the war, be forced to yield to the creation of a separate Air Force, and the Navy itself would be subsumed into a single Department of War. In a September 2, 1944, letter to his friend Palmer Hoyt, the publisher of the *Oregonian*, Forrestal asked about the "public drift" on the matter. "I have been telling King, Nimitz and company it is my judgment that as of today the Navy's lost its case and that either in Congress or in a public poll the Army's point of view would prevail."[4] Something had to be done.

Fleet public relations had rarely been on the King-Nimitz conference agenda. Since the beginning of the war, the conferences had addressed public relations matters only a handful of times, and usually in a perfunctory way. In July 1942, after the Battle of Midway, Nimitz expressed his satisfaction with the Fleet's public relations "situation" (read: Drake), and no further discussion occurred. In September 1942, Nimitz complained he was "bedeviled" by reporters, and he and King agreed to reduce the number of correspondents in the Pacific. In September 1943, Nimitz again expressed his wish to keep Drake as Fleet PRO, despite the suggestion that a regular naval officer take over that position. "Cincpac wishes to keep commander Drake," the conference notes recorded.[5] King concurred with Nimitz, arguing that "it was up to Cincpac to decide who and what type of officer he wants for this job." Each time public relations surfaced as a concern, Nimitz backed his newsman, and King, in turn, backed Nimitz. Forrestal had arrived at the September-October 1944 conference in San Francisco to persuade Nimitz and King to change course.

"[It's] extremely important for the Navy to keep the public fully informed with respect to the war against Japan," Forrestal declared.[6] From Nimitz's perspective, that's exactly what Drake had been doing for thirty-three months. By traveling with the Fleet during recent operations in the Marshall, Mariana, and Palau Islands, Drake had improved the amount and timeliness of news reaching the United States. Two months earlier, at Drake's urging, Nimitz had established a public relations and censorship unit in the forward areas under the command of Vice Adm. John Hoover, USN, who was soon complaining about the "over-emphasis placed on operations and activities of certain air units and personal advertising by various officers."[7] Nevertheless, with the triumvirate of (a) Drake in the forward area or afloat with the Fleet, (b) McArdle, the assistant PRO, back at Pearl Harbor, and (c) Ward, the press censor, and his team of lieutenants clearing copy, Fleet public relations ran like a smooth diesel engine, it seemed to Nimitz. King would also soon approve the inclusion of a "Public Relations Annex" for each major operation plan or order.[8]

Despite Nimitz's cool reception, Forrestal kept trying. "With the collapse of Germany," he continued, "unless 'fresh' news and pictures were given to the American public . . . it might act very disastrously against the Navy. It would also aid in the Navy's argument against a single Department of War."[9] What "fresh" news meant in this context was confusing because Drake and the Fleet's public relations staff had been releasing news as quickly as possible. In fact, Drake had used the same term—"fresh" news— in early 1942 when advocating that OPR permit him to release correspondents' copy locally under Honolulu dateline.

Having witnessed Forrestal's bureaucratic machinations before, Nimitz perceived something amiss. Nimitz himself had earned Forrestal's animosity in 1941, when the new undersecretary's friend, Joseph Shaw, claimed to have been working in an unofficial capacity for the Navy in Washington, D.C. Forrestal told Shaw he would advocate for his commission once Shaw's conviction for selling civil service positions in his brother's mayoral administration in Los Angeles was overturned. As chief of the Bureau of Navigation, Nimitz had opposed Shaw. With Drake's assistance at the *Times*, they'd refuted Shaw's claims. According to Mercer, "Mr. Forrestal didn't like that very well, and he tried very hard to get this man commissioned. But at that time it was the policy in the Navy that you didn't commission people as officers who had spent time in jail. So he wasn't commissioned."[10] Old animosities undergirded Forrestal's effort to break up the Nimitz-Drake duo.

At the King-Nimitz conference, Forrestal introduced information about how the director of OWI, Elmer Davis, sought a deputy director at the agency. King saw where Forrestal was headed and flatly stated, "A Naval officer on active duty would not be satisfactory in such a job."[11] Forrestal framed the OWI position for Drake as a possibility to be explored, but it wasn't optional: he'd already taken steps to reassign Drake to it while feigning that the situation remained fluid. Nevertheless, Forrestal demurred, stating he'd merely like to issue Drake "temporary orders" to report to Washington, D.C., "at this time to discuss Public Relations matters in general."[12] He reassured Nimitz that the assignment was temporary, stating "it would be very helpful if Captain Drake could make periodic visits to Washington every year."

Forrestal's invitation to Drake to make periodic visits to Washington, D.C., was wholly insincere; the secretary was determined to remove him as Fleet PRO. Anticipating resistance from Nimitz and King, a month earlier Forrestal had launched a two-pronged attack on Drake. The first prong involved enlisting the help of a visiting delegation of OPR and OWI officials in Pearl Harbor. The second prong involved adding a new member to the Fleet's public relations staff, Capt. Harold "Min" Miller, USN. Miller had accompanied Forrestal on a trip to London shortly after the D-day landings in Normandy, and his handling of the British journalists had impressed the secretary.[13] Forrestal did not mention either of these efforts during the King-Nimitz conference. Instead, he turned the conversation to Fleet photographic issues. Again, however, he used the discussion to urge Drake's reassignment to OWI. This time, he asked Nimitz directly if he'd be willing to release Drake to Davis at OWI. King and Nimitz exchanged a knowing glance, both men bristling at Forrestal's repeated and unwelcome attempts to remove Drake. "It would create trouble" if Drake worked for Davis, they finally claimed, hoping that would end the matter.[14] Forrestal capitulated, allowing Nimitz to steer the conversation in a different direction.

Nimitz returned to Pearl Harbor unaware of the larger plan Forrestal had already set in motion. Even if he had thought of pulling Drake aside to warn him about the secretary's intentions, it was too late. Drake was out with the Fleet managing public relations in the leadup to the Battle of Peleliu.

※※※※※※※※※※

By mid-1944, several officials in Washington, D.C., and Pearl Harbor were pushing for Drake's removal as Fleet PRO. In May, Cdr. E. J. Long, USNR, chief of the pictorial section at OPR, traveled to Pearl Harbor to investigate how to better coordinate Fleet photo clearance policies with those in Washington, D.C. Long noted that "there is always someone who says that they were 'in the shower' when the word was passed, and the press is quick to take advantage of pictures that can be released in Washington, not be released in the fleet, and of pictures which are released in the fleet and which are refused in Washington."[15] The situation was maddening. Long proceeded from San Francisco on board the new submarine tender, USS *Proteus* (AS 19), under the command of Captain Berry, OPR's former deputy director, who'd returned to sea duty. What Berry might have said to Long about Drake during the five-day voyage to Pearl Harbor is unknown. Long's investigation led him to conclude the Fleet press censor and Fourteenth Naval District PRO, while nominally independent decision makers, deferred to Drake. Drake, of course, had influenced both men's appointments to maintain his control. The subtext of Long's conclusion was that Drake impeded photographic clearance and publicity.

Forrestal, aware of Drake's unsavory reputation with the press, wrote a letter on June 15 to OPR's new director, Rear Adm. Aaron "Tip" Merrill, USN, whom Secretary Knox had picked to replace Lovette (who'd returned to sea duty in June 1944 on his way to promotion to rear admiral). Forrestal's letter noted that part of overhauling Navy public relations should involve Drake's reassignment: "Relieve Captain Waldo Drake, USNR, now Public Relations Officer at Admiral Nimitz's headquarters, replacing him with a younger, more vigorous officer who would be designated a Deputy Director of Public Relations."[16]

Also in June, Drake began reporting to Nimitz's newly assigned assistant chief of staff for administration, Capt. Bernard Austin, USN. Austin, five years younger than Drake, was a slim South Carolinian and distinguished commander of submarines and destroyers who'd served as a deputy to Ghormley in London at the outset of the war. Austin was no public relations neophyte; he'd worked closely with Lovette, Beecher, and Berry as a press relations officer in Washington, D.C., from 1937 to 1940 in ONI's Public Relations Branch, briefly leading the unit when Lovette had returned to sea duty. Unlike Nimitz's prior assistant chiefs of staff, who'd deferred to Drake on public relations matters, Austin was an experienced and confident interlocuter with the press. He had no qualms about requiring Drake to resolve the complaints that constantly dogged the Fleet.

Later that month, Austin called Drake into his office. "You draw up for me, with the help of your staff, the organization that, in the light of your experience here, would be able to cope adequately with the need to know, and the desire to know on the part of the various media, and bring it down to me," he instructed.[17]

Drake signaled he understood; he'd been proposing such plans to Nimitz since 1942. He walked back upstairs to his office. Sitting at his desk, Drake reflected on the situation. Austin had just handed him a blank check. Here was his chance to finally get the staffing and resources he needed to keep correspondents, their editors, and their publishers off his back. With Austin running interference, Drake wouldn't have to approach Nimitz with an unappreciated request to build up the public relations staff to handle even more "bedeviling" reporters. If Nimitz balked, Drake could explain he'd merely been following Austin's orders. Drake saw an opportunity to remain loyal to Nimitz yet still improve Fleet public relations.

On a large sheet of paper, he drew up a plan that included massive expansions of personnel at all levels: assistant public relations officers, press officers, assistant press officers, radio officers, administrative officers, photographic coordinators, photographic officers, assistant officers, and so on. Drake had neither proposed nor managed such a large organization in his life. Most of his career had been spent as a solo reporter and editor at the *Times* or as the head of a public relations duo in Los Angeles or Pearl Harbor. Nevertheless, the next day, he walked downstairs and handed Austin the plan.

Austin looked it over. He could see that Drake had taken the opportunity to propose a fantastical wish list. "This is fine, you've done exactly what I told you. Now let's sit down, roll up our sleeves, and get practical. We know that Admiral Nimitz would not be too happy to authorize this sort of organization," he said.[18] Drake pulled out a pencil from his shirt pocket and began lining out positions until Austin agreed it had been trimmed sufficiently. "I'll take this to the Admiral today," Austin told him. Tapping his pencil on his desk, Drake waited in his office, eyeing the door. Austin eventually appeared at the threshold, holding up the plan bearing Nimitz's stamp. "Approved!" Austin exclaimed. Relieved, Drake assured Austin he'd implement the plan right away.

But Drake's foot-dragging propensities had reemerged. In March 1942, Berry had pushed Drake to establish a Fleet press censor position, but the billet had taken four months to fill. Even with Ward sitting across from him, Drake continued to influence censorship decisions. Now Drake wanted to ensure that the massive expansion of Fleet public relations that Nimitz had just approved would allow him to maintain control. When Austin confronted Drake weeks later about his lack of progress on the plan, Drake reassured him he was working on it, but managing public relations activities for Operation Forager (Saipan) consumed most of his time, and he was soon out again with the Fleet. Drake nevertheless felt the pressure. He warned McArdle in a July 4, 1944, letter from Saipan, "Because we have been unable to add and train the key officers we needed, CINCPAC press relations is about to assume responsibility for a BB-sized job with PT-crew. We will need every experienced officer we can find for independent duty."[19]

Few could blame Drake for wanting to escape the personnel issues at the Cement Pot. A tenfold increase in CINCPAC staff required an upward expansion of the headquarters building. Air hammers pounded the third floor as the breastworks around the top of the building were taken off to add more stories. "All day long the hammering came down through the walls and shook our teeth," recalled McArdle, who was forced to stay at his desk.[20] The air was filled "with a din so palpable you could crack walnuts on it. At these times, even if you could hear the telephones ring, it didn't do any good to answer them—the conversation was strictly one-way."[21] The noise and commotion around the public relations office proved unbearable. "There was not an officer on the public relations staff who would not have preferred being out forward where the shooting was than back at headquarters where the headaches were."

Drake was dealing with his own headaches on board the *Rocky Mount* anchored off Saipan. Vice Admiral Turner, usually supportive of Drake's efforts to improve public relations, was cautious about taking steps to expand correspondents' transmission facilities for fear of "merely annoying Adm. Nimitz."[22] Moreover, Drake reported that Turner's aide, who also served as the Amphibious Force's photo officer, "hangs on to everything photographic like a bird dog hangs on to fleas. He runs the photo lab with an iron hand and . . . I have to practically kiss his fanny to get anything."[23]

Adding to Drake's struggles, his typewriter malfunctioned, forcing him to sneak into the Flag Office during mealtimes to use a staff typewriter to get his own stories and photo captions written.

Austin wasn't sympathetic. He scoffed at Drake's inability to expand the public relations unit as he'd promised to do. Oblivious to Austin's growing dissatisfaction, Drake thought he was doing a splendid job. Bassett had written him, "Congratulations to you and all hands on the continuing masterful handling of the CenPAC press situation. It's piling up notable milestones in our business, Waldo, and is certainly splendid vindication of the long years of preparation for this very thing—in the days when we were targets of such eloquent snipers as Genial Bob Casey and Bombarding Barney McQuaid."[24] But despite Bassett's bouquet, the *Chicago Daily News* still hurled its brickbats. When *Daily News* correspondent William McGaffin's stories arrived too late for publication, editor Carroll Binder admonished Drake, "Unlike a correspondent for, say, the Baltimore *Sun* or any other individual newspaper, McGaffin is a syndicate correspondent serving eighty-two major newspapers with a paid circulation in excess of 11,000,000. His dispatches and those of other Chicago Daily News Foreign Service correspondents are carried daily by leased wire from coast to coast from 7 to 11 A.M. E.W.T. They are judged by the editors in competition with those of the AP and UP. If his copy comes trailing in days late it not only is not used but the Service receives a bad rating in the eyes of its clients."[25] Drake offered Binder his usual reassurances about CINCPAC's effort to improve transmission speed.

Amid routine tensions with the *Daily News*, on August 9, 1944, the *Camp Lejeune Globe* published an article headlined, "American Newspaper Found in Jap Army Bivouac Area."[26] Drake's prewar work for ONI had resurfaced, specifically his April 1, 1940, article for the *Times*, "Fleet Ready for Maneuvers." In that article, Drake had described the Battle Force's composition and preparations for its upcoming wargame in the Pacific. His assertion that "complete secrecy enshrouds the war-game missions" had caught the attention of someone in the Japanese military who'd appreciated the disclosure of the Fleet's Order of Battle. The *Camp Lejeune Globe* article noted the surprise of the Marines on Saipan. "This is the last place in the world you would expect to find an American newspaper. Though it was more than two years old it was dug out of a Japanese Army bivouac area at Garapan when the Second Marine Division was pushing through that city. At the bottom of a box was a carefully folded copy of the Los Angeles Times." The writer teased Drake, explaining that his story had divulged "how the Navy planned to simulate warfare in all its intensity, even, said Captain Drake, down to the very important question of how 'to grab a sandwich in the heat of battle.'" Drake was being given the unearthed copy of the *Times* as a "Saipan souvenir." The story amused CINCPAC staff members, except for Austin. Toward the end of summer, Austin concluded Drake wasn't up to the task of expanding and improving Fleet public relations. He began telling other officers that Drake couldn't let go of control.

By late August 1944, with the end of the Pacific war on the horizon, Drake's press releases and speeches conveyed a strong sense of inevitable victory. On August 24, Drake drafted remarks for Nimitz on the thirty-first anniversary of naval aviation for NBC's popular *March of Time* radio program. The opening paragraph declared, "The first essential to victory in the Pacific is control of the sea approaches to the Japanese Empire. With that control established, we can curtail the flow of vital raw materials into Japan. We can sever the ocean routes over which Japan must send the men and machines of war to her conquered territories. Japan's so-called co-prosperity sphere would then become a no-prosperity sphere. At the same time, we seek safe passage for the quantities of supplies and manpower we will need to bring Japan to unconditional surrender."[27] He paid tribute to the men and women who'd created the powerful naval aviation force and concluded, "To all, our congratulations and best wishes for continued success in shaping our road to Tokyo." For Drake, the prospect of sailing triumphantly into Tokyo Bay with Nimitz and the Fleet was tantalizingly close.

As he'd done countless times before, Nimitz penciled out a few spare words and added a couple of new ones, tightening up Drake's draft remarks. Nimitz squeezed a bit more drama out of the sentence, "This area is not completely closed to the enemy, but he enters it at his peril," editing it to read, "Although this area is not completely closed to the enemy, he enters it only at his peril." To his many capabilities, we can add Nimitz's skill as a copy editor. Across thirty-two months, Nimitz had established a smooth rhythm with his PRO. The two men shared an understanding about how things should be said. In many ways, Drake had become an extension of Nimitz's voice. Once again, Nimitz signed off on Drake's draft remarks, "OK as amended. CWN." But unseen to Nimitz and his newsman, Fleet public relations were not okay, and Austin and others were determined to do something about it.

Drake and Nimitz's promotion of naval aviation didn't impress Forrestal's Assistant Secretary of the Navy for Air, Mr. Artemus Gates. A former director at Pan American Airways, Gates was a friend and ally of both Secretary Forrestal and Rear Admiral Towers, Deputy Commander-in-Chief, Pacific Fleet. Gates, Forrestal, and Towers has constantly pushed Nimitz to elevate public awareness of naval aviation. Towers, especially, had lobbied Nimitz the entire war to place naval aviators in senior command positions.[28] In March 1944, Forrestal had complained to Towers about the lack of publicity in the Pacific: "So far as public information is concerned it seemed to me that we had very inadequate coverage in the Marshalls. For example, so far as I know, there were no pictures taken of the fleet itself or any segments of it. In the film that was shown to the public here there were shots of only two vessels—one a battleship and one a cruiser offshore Kwajalein."[29] Forrestal's frustration was clear: "I can assure you with confidence that no one back here has the slightest conception of the scope or the magnitude of the power that we are now employing in the Pacific."[30]

Aware of Forrestal's dissatisfaction, in May 1944, Gates enlisted the help of Emmet Crozier, a reporter for the *New York Herald Tribune*, to assess how the Navy might improve its coverage and promotion of naval aviation. Crozier, a fifty-one-year-old New Englander, had gained notoriety for his wartime commentary. He served as the *Herald Tribune*'s leading authority on military affairs, and his word carried weight. Crozier's memorandum to Gates in May 1944 amounted to a seven-page indictment of Drake.

Crozier began with a confession: "I realize I have gone rather far afield from our original objective. . . . I also realize that some of the observations herein are blunt and undiplomatic."[31] Crozier declared, "The newspapermen returning from the Pacific tell of indifference, neglect, hostility from Navy officials charged with public relations functions. News dispatches and pictures have been subject to apparently needless delays, unwarranted interference and arbitrary editorial meddling and censorship in no way related to security. Incidents of misunderstanding and personal strife have been too numerous to be regarded as isolated clashes of temperament." As evidence for his claims, Crozier explained he'd gathered information from six correspondents, three editors, one civilian, and six naval officers. The memorandum continued,

> The consensus of opinion was that (1) through 1942 and most of 1943 Navy public relations in the Pacific were incredibly bad, with a continuous state of tension and bitterness between the press and the Navy public relations officer; (2) dispatches were needlessly held up from one week to two months, subjected to arbitrary and unreasonable censorship, pictures were delayed (3) conditions have improved somewhat since the fall of 1943 but are still bad; (4) all the persons interviewed said that the situation was due partly to Navy's indifference, more especially to the shortcomings, ill-suited personality and general incompetence of Captain Waldo Drake.

Crozier included comments from anonymous Navy officers. These were damning:

- WALDO DRAKE CinCPac Public Relations Officer: serves as principal bottleneck of all Navy news from the Pacific . . . He is absent-minded . . . unimaginative and anti-aviation. Refuses to permit stories of individual aviators to be released. Makes hasty decisions and frequently reverses them in 5 or 6 hour periods. Lacks the confidence of the correspondents. Recently they decided to boycott him (i.e. no Navy publicity at all) but their home offices said 'No'.
- Conducts press conferences like a Lord dealing with peasants, so that many press writers refuse to attend . . . [Drake] constantly decided on the news merit of stories, which isn't his function at all.
- At press conferences constantly interrupts newsmen, takes lead in the questioning, jumps around from one topic to another, never finishing any one. This gets both the newsmen and the fliers being interviewed hopelessly out of step.

- Insists on having all release times for communiques, despatches, press releases etc. based on West Coast Newspaper deadlines. Eastern and Midwestern sheets scream to no avail.
- Dislikes certain correspondents and makes things tough for them. One INS correspondent wanted to go to Midway, ComAirPac . . . had fixed it for him. Drake got it cancelled, told him he could go by surface ship if at all. Then tried—unsuccessfully—to get this INS's man's credentials cancelled.
- He [Drake] was, we understand, a mediocre waterfront reporter somewhere on the West Coast. Newspapermen, from the moment he took over, had trouble with him. His great talent, it seemed, was to turn down any request they might make and arbitrarily censor to death anything they might whip up about the Navy.
- Recently, in the South Pacific, when asked what qualification Drake has for this important job, an informant replied, "He was picked for the job because he knew how to say 'No.'"

Crozier fired another salvo.

From other sources I have been informed that Captain Drake has caused the credentials of several competent correspondents to be cancelled because of personal animus; that he once issued an order forbidding air transport to all correspondents in the South Pacific, regardless of urgency; that he has arbitrarily killed stories of moving human interest. . . . He is also reported to have killed other stories built around the exploits of a single carrier or destroyer on the ground that it might make crews of other carrier or destroyers jealous.

Crozier concluded, "From the evidence at hand it is obvious that Captain Drake is unfitted for his post and should be relieved."

On June 3, 1944, Gates forwarded Crozier's memorandum to Forrestal with his endorsement, adding,

Everything I have heard about him [Drake] over a period of time backs up what Crozier has found. I talked with Secretary Knox several times about this and he apparently had received similar reports. However, using the powers of persuasion, Mr. Knox had been unable to get Admiral Nimitz to make a change.[32]

Gathering Gates, Crozier, and others' reports about Fleet public relations was in keeping with Secretary Forrestal's managerial style. "His brisk impatience to learn, to resolve, was unceasing, and feeling the need for certain information in a hurry, he would send two or three assistants, unbeknownst to each other, to obtain it," his biographers noted.[33] After reading Crozier's memorandum, Forrestal committed himself to succeeding where his predecessor, Knox, had failed.

Drake now faced a double whammy. Unbeknownst to him, a journalist he'd never met had denigrated him among the leadership of the Navy Department, and the Secretary of the Navy, by concealing the attack, had denied him the chance to rebut the claims, some of which were demonstrably false.[34]

Adding to Forrestal's anxiety, the June 6, 1944, Allied invasion of Normandy had completely knocked the Pacific Fleet off newspaper front pages. Confronted with D-day, Crozier's memorandum, and Gates' endorsement, Forrestal ordered a contingent of OPR officials to Pearl Harbor to refashion Fleet public relations. Rear Admiral Merrill, director of OPR, led the group. Merrill was a South Pacific combat veteran who'd earned a Navy Cross and Legion of Merit, but he possessed no public relations experience. Merrill was unhappy about coming to Washington, D.C., but he'd been given no choice. Merrill's longtime friend, George Healy, deputy director of OWI's Domestic Branch, joined the coterie headed to Pearl Harbor. Merrill and Healy were tasked with figuring out how to remove Drake without provoking Nimitz's defenses.[35]

A thirty-nine-year-old Mississippian, Healy was a prominent journalist for the *New Orleans Times-Picayune*. He later recounted, "Tip Merrill had encouraged Jim Forrestal to call on me for this special mission for the navy. Ever since he had been made chief of navy public relations, he had been itching to get back to forward areas. My discussion with Jim Forrestal opened the door. The secretary, incidentally, was a frustrated newspaperman; he had been a cub reporter before entering the investment business and acknowledged that he'd like to be one again. I told the secretary that if he'd get Elmer Davis' approval, I'd undertake the job he proposed for me. Elmer approved immediately."[36]

Gates arranged air transport for the group, and when they arrived in Pearl Harbor, Healy wasted no time in confirming the situation. "To most of the correspondents, particularly Bob Casey of the *Chicago Daily News* [recently returned to the Pacific], Robert McCormick of NBC, and Frank Tremaine of UP, Capt. Waldo Drake, USNR, the censor-public relations officer, was a hindrance to prompt movement of news of the Pacific war. A few correspondents, including William H. Ewing of the *Honolulu Star-Bulletin*, spoke well of Captain Drake's work."[37] Healy arranged to meet Drake one-on-one at the Oahu Country Club.

Drake greeted Healy when he arrived at the club. He was eager to speak with Healy's boss at OWI, Elmer Davis, who was soon arriving in Pearl Harbor for briefings. After an exchange of pleasantries, the men sat at a table near a wall of windows overlooking the club's exquisite, jewel-like fairway. Watching Ray Mackland, a member of the still photo pool and later picture editor of *Life*, entering the club's lobby alone, Healy said to Drake, "There's Ray Mackland. Should we ask him to join us?"

"Whooo's Ray Mackland?" Drake asked, his speech impediment enhancing his air of superiority and disdain.[38] "He's nothing but a goddam photographer, is he?" Drake blurted.

Healy recoiled. Mackland had accompanied Healy and the OPR delegation to Oahu.

"With all your four stripes," Healy shot back, "you're not a good enough newspaperman to carry the film bags of some photographers I know."[39]

Drake apologized, but Healy now had the ammunition he needed:

After the Oahu Country Club experience, I determined . . . that Capt. Waldo Drake would have to be moved from Admiral Nimitz's staff. When I rejoined Admiral Merrill, I told him that I was going to recommend that Captain Drake be transferred. "That complicates our situation," Tip said. "I was told today by Admiral Nimitz that transfer of Captain Drake would not have his approval unless the captain received orders to a billet with as much authority and dignity as the one he has here." There was no such billet for a public relations officer in the United States Navy, unless Admiral Merrill wanted to move over and let Waldo become public relations director for the whole navy. This, I knew, Jim Forrestal would never approve.[40]

That night, Healy formulated a plan to reassign Drake to OWI as a deputy director, running the plan by several officers who supported the move but doubted Nimitz would agree to it. Back on the mainland, Healy wrote a recommendation for Forrestal's approval. The recommendation "commended Captain Drake for his service to Admirals Kimmel and Nimitz and recommended his transfer."[41] Forrestal too now had what he needed: the unequivocal support of OPR and OWI for Drake's reassignment. He suggested to Healy he draft a letter for Elmer Davis' signature formally requesting the Navy "assign to OWI a captain to serve as a deputy director of the agency."[42] Davis signed the formal request and returned it to Healy with a handwritten note indicating he was nervous that Nimitz might pull a bait-and-switch. "George, I signed the letter to Forrestal— hope you have arranged through Merrill or otherwise to see that we get Waldo and not some old rooster they merely want to get rid of."[43] Forrestal could now bring Davis' letter to the King-Nimitz conference in San Francisco in September.

The first prong of his dual attack on Drake now set, Forrestal turned to the second prong. In early August 1944, Forrestal called Capt. Min Miller into his office at the Main Navy building in Washington, D.C. Miller, forty-one years old, was an airman and Naval Academy graduate, a former assistant naval attaché in London, and director of training literature for the Bureau of Aeronautics. Miller had received his orders to report to Pearl Harbor but had been confused about them. He asked the secretary to explain them. "That's easy. We've got problems out in the Pacific," Forrestal told him.[44] He elaborated, "We see the end of the war. We know when we're going to close this war out. And MacArthur's winning the war. When this war is over, no one will know that the Navy was in it. It's been a Navy war the whole time; no one will ever know it. If we don't get something done about our public relations job in the Pacific, I can't go to Congress. We'll get no funding, no allocations, or anything. We've got to change the whole atmosphere." Forrestal continued, "Nimitz has got a [PRO] out there who is a disaster. I want you to go out there and get rid of him."

Miller asked, "Well, Mr. Secretary, why don't you just order him out?"

Forrestal said, "Nimitz likes him. He'd like to keep him out there, but something has got to be done. [. . .] you can do it, and it will take you about four minutes to get him out of there." Afterwards, Forrestal promised him, "Then I'll give you a big carrier." A carrier command was a real prize.

Miller responded, "Aye, aye, sir."[45]

Drake was in the forward area when Miller arrived in Pearl Harbor. He initially stayed out of the way, later claiming he did not know who to check in with or who to report to. That is unlikely. Austin later recalled, "To make a long story short—Waldo was moving a little slowly. I heard about a classmate of mine named Min Miller, who had done a very fine job on the picture side over in the European theater. So I requested that he be sent out to head up our picture section. I discussed it with Drake first."[46] According to Austin, Drake thought Miller would "be a man of the right background." Forrestal had pushed Miller to Pearl Harbor, but Austin had pulled him there.

Most of the correspondents Miller talked to confessed they "literally hated" Drake.[47] Hanson Baldwin of the *New York Times*, who'd returned to Pearl Harbor, told Miller that Drake kept a black book on them: so-and-so was not to be trusted, so-and-so was this and that, and so on. Miller never actually found the black book, but he entered Drake's York safe and discovered his personal papers, along with copies of correspondents' letters that District staff or Drake had censored. Miller showed the letters to Austin, who couldn't find much justification for them.[48] Drake's ONI indoctrination had caught up with him. Why the Fleet's PRO needed to keep copies of correspondents' censored letters wasn't easy to explain. Whether out of training, habit, or hubris, Drake's security proclivities had crossed a line. Austin wouldn't defend him.

Miller believed the inherent problem lay with the structure of the system: under no condition should a newsman oversee other newsmen because this inevitably introduced competition and jealousy, he thought. Miller presumed that when skilled reporters clashed with Drake, the PRO vowed to himself, "By golly, they're not going to tell me what to do."[49] If playing dirty was a fine art among Los Angeles newsmen, then having the goods on troublesome correspondents (i.e., personal letters) might have seemed to Drake like a good idea.

Miller had been in Pearl Harbor about three weeks, and since many of the reporters he encountered there were people he'd known in Washington, D.C., he was not without friends. He ate dinner with them and listened to their stories about how they were unable to do any work because of Drake. They argued they were just wasting their time. After several more days, Miller finally thought, "Something has got to be done. I've got orders from Forrestal here, and I'd better do something."[50] According to Austin, Miller "was not a shrinking violet, he was an aggressive type of individual."[51] Miller walked into the public relations office, grabbed the "Keep Out" sign on Drake's cubbyhole, and threw it in the trash. "I might as well make this my office," he declared. Cheers rang throughout the building as correspondents learned the news. But there was still a problem: Nimitz didn't know that Miller's assignment was to remove Drake. A group of correspondents devised a way to assist him. Frank Kelly of the *New York Herald Tribune* came to Miller and said, "Min, we want to see the admiral."[52] Miller called on Nimitz and said the correspondents wanted to see him.

"Fine, bring the boys in," Nimitz said.

Miller later reported he led twenty correspondents into Nimitz's office. According to Miller's memorandum to Nimitz, the number was six—the same number contained in Crozier's memorandum to Gates—and all of them had history with Drake.[53] The group included Frank Kelly, Crozier's colleague at the *Herald Tribune*, Robert Trumbull from the *New York Times*, who'd headed the Pacific War Correspondents Association, Robert McCormick from NBC, who also was a leader of the association and who'd complained to Healy about Drake, William McGaffin (Casey and McQuaid's colleague at the *Chicago Daily News*), John Beaufort from the *Christian Science Monitor*, and John Bishop from the *Saturday Evening Post*. Miller's memorandum to Nimitz framed the meeting as "a splendid opportunity to establish a complete understanding with the correspondents, and I recommend that you see them."[54] Miller later claimed he had no idea what the correspondents wanted to talk about; he assumed it was "something about an on-coming exercise or something."[55] That is unlikely. When the men sat down in Nimitz's office, the admiral asked, "Well, gentlemen, what can I do for you?"

Frank Kelly stood up, "Well, Admiral, I am the spokesman for this group, and we're here to tell you that we want Min Miller to be your new public relations man."[56]

Miller later stated he almost had a heart attack. "My God, if they'd just dig a hole here, that's where I'd go," he thought. Nimitz laughed it off. After some diplomatic exchanges between Nimitz and the correspondents, everyone went away mollified. As soon as Miller left the correspondents, he rushed back to Nimitz's office and said, "Admiral, all I can say is I had no idea what they were up to. I knew nothing about it."[57]

Nimitz said, "Oh, forget about it. No harm done."

Drake was on Saipan when he learned that Miller had usurped his PRO position. He'd gotten on the first plane back to Pearl Harbor. When he arrived at the public relations office, he found that Miller had commandeered his desk.[58] Drake immediately ordered a new desk in beside Miller's desk. Miller ordered the desk moved out. Drake ordered the desk moved in again. A comical "cold war" ensued. If someone called for the public relations officer and Drake answered the phone, he would say, "I am the public relations officer." If someone called for the public relations officer and Miller answered the phone, he would say, "Speaking." The callers became utterly "confused." After a few more instances of ill will between the two captains, Drake marched downstairs to talk to the admiral.

In his office, Nimitz showed Drake a letter signed by the six correspondents who'd met with him at Miller's request. The letter contained numerous charges and accusations against Drake.[59] Nimitz asked Drake to respond in writing, but no record of the specific charges or Drake's rebuttal has been found because they have been redacted in the memorandum mentioning them.[60] Nevertheless, based on the PRO and newsmen's previous clashes, one could assume the charges and accusations included invasions of privacy, favoritism and discrimination, aloofness, and excessive control. One could also presume Drake's rebuttal: denial, reassertion, and acquiescence when changes could be reasonably accommodated. The correspondents' letters aside, Nimitz told Drake he considered him the Fleet's PRO, but that Secretary Forrestal, who had power second only to the president, considered Miller held that title. Nimitz's hands were tied. Drake would need to travel to Washington, D.C., to try to sort things out with Forrestal.

█████████

With Drake on his way to Washington, D.C., Nimitz summoned Austin to his office. "Are you trying to get rid of Drake?"[61] he demanded to know. The admiral's blue-gray eyes stared icily at his chief of staff.

"No Admiral, I'm not trying to get rid of Drake. Waldo is a very fine man and a good newsman. He's certainly loyal, he works hard. But he's a one-man show type. I haven't found that he is as adept at delegating authority and holding people responsible for the use of that authority as he should be to head up an organization such as your public relations organization," Austin said.[62] Nimitz's stare eased. He couldn't dispute Austin's characterization of his PRO. He asked about Miller. Austin told him that Miller was "an aggressive type of chap" and that "he was one that would run a pretty smart operation."[63] Austin declined to mention that Miller had filched papers from Drake's safe.

Word spread among the journalists in Pearl Harbor that Drake was in trouble. His allies attempted to help him. Riley Allen, editor of the *Honolulu Star-Bulletin*, wrote to Nimitz on October 2,

As I understand that Captain W. W. Drake, Fleet Public Relations Officer, may shortly leave this area for an indefinite period, it seems appropriate to express the high esteem in which I hold him, both as an individual and as an officer of the United States Naval Reserve. We of the Star Bulletin have worked with Captain Drake since his first assignment to duty in this area not long before the outbreak of World War II in the Pacific. Consequently, we have seen his office and its duties develop during a most trying and difficult period. At times we have differed with Captain Drake on details of censorship, but we have never failed to recognize first, his complete devotion to duty; second, his unfailing desire to understand and to act intelligently upon the problems of news gathering, news writing and newspaper production and distribution we presented to him in connection with his assignment; and third, a spirit of courtesy and accommodation which we never found wanting even in the harassing days shortly after the outbreak of war, when his staff was undermanned and he and all of its members were overworked. On the occasions when we differed with him, we recognized that he was acting solely in accordance with his conception of the necessities of the case, and that he must necessarily put his duty before any personal preference or dislike.[64]

An October 2, 1944, letter addressed to Nimitz signed by journalists Richard Haller, William Ewing, Webley Edwards, B., Clayton, and Charles McMurtry also defended Drake:

We would like to go on record in support of Capt. W. W. Drake as Fleet Public Relations Officer. We do not pretend that we approve of all of Captain Drake's actions and policies. We do, however, recognize that many of his accomplishments on behalf of the press and radio have been achieved in the face of difficult obstacles. And we are convinced that no accurate evaluation of these accomplishments can be reached without a proper regard for such obstacles. We also believe the most difficult phase of Naval public relations in the Pacific war probably has passed, and that many of the obstacles of the trying early months of the war will automatically disappear. We would like to add that we are unanimously aware of Captain Drake's complete and selfless devotion to duty.[65]

Moved by letters of support for his newsman, Nimitz nevertheless could do little but wait for word on the outcome of Drake's meeting with Secretary Forrestal.

It took several days for Drake to reach Washington, D.C.,. He stopped in Los Angeles only long enough for a *Times* reporter to note the Fleet PRO "has been here on mysterious business."[66] The reporter reminded readers, "In case you don't remember, he was the demon harbor man for The Times for many years." The reporter hinted at Drake's state of mind. "Like most Navy people, he is pleased—and somewhat startled—to have public interest in the Pacific awakening after a long stretch of regarding it as bush league stuff by Europe-minded Easterners." Drake had already moved onward to Washington, D.C., by the time the article went to print.

When he arrived at the secretary's office on Monday morning October 9, 1944, Drake hoped to convince Forrestal that whatever public relations problems he'd heard about were just sour grapes from a handful of disgruntled correspondents in Pearl Harbor. Drake didn't know about Crozier's memorandum, nor did he know that some of his CINCPAC colleagues had provided its most damning content. But no amount of strategizing on what he might say to the secretary would matter. A letter Forrestal had received a few days before the meeting further convinced him not only that Drake needed to be reassigned to OWI but also that he could not be allowed to return to Pearl Harbor. The letter writer was Markey, Ghormley's former PRO, who'd been brought back into the public relations fold. Markey declared, "Up to his [Miller's] arrival Public Relations has been an unholy mess in the Pacific."[67] Markey warned the secretary,

> Waldo Drake's return to the States was made on a totally unsatisfactory basis. As it stands now, he will return here—and I can promise you that that will destroy all the good work that Captain Miller is able to do. Drake must be given a billet in the States in order to prevent his returning here. If he comes back even to pack his gear, the progress Captain Miller is making will be blown out of the water. When I took the matter up with Admiral Forrest Sherman he suggested that a suitable billet for Drake could be arranged in the States—possibly in Public Relations; but that until such a billet were arranged he doubted if the Admiral would release him. It is imperative—and I cannot sufficiently emphasize this point—that Drake does not return to Pearl Harbor.[68]

Forrestal got the message. Ushered into the secretary's well-appointed office, Drake found only Forrestal and his special assistant, Eugene Duffield, awaiting him.[69] There would be no broader audience to witness the exchange. Forrestal was too skilled an administrator to allow Drake a chance to plea for his PRO position. Instead, Forrestal praised Drake's service to the Navy, congratulated him on his success as Fleet PRO, and explained how OWI and the nation now urgently needed his exceptional services. Drake's sense of propriety ensured he'd yield to the secretary's blandishments. In less than ten minutes, an aide knocked on the door, telling the secretary he was needed elsewhere. The meeting was over.

Duffield told Drake he would not be returning to Pearl Harbor; instead, he was instructed to report to OWI. Needing to catch a breath of fresh air, Drake exited Main Navy. In Pearl Harbor, Nimitz had shielded his newsman, but the admiral's protection had vanished within the walls of Forrestal's office. Drake's allies—Lovette, Powell, Thacker, Howard, and sympathetic correspondents at CINCPAC—couldn't help him either. The Navy, an institution Drake had loved and cared for nearly his entire adult life, had rejected him. Worse, Forrestal seemingly had made him the scapegoat for all the public relations ills in the Pacific. Miller later admitted, "They hung it all on Waldo Drake."[70]

Drake was out. The Navy's configuration of actors, forces, and events—combined with Drake's personal limitations—had brought him to the end of his race. He would not be sailing into history; there would be no Tokyo Bay moment for him with Nimitz and the Fleet. His reassignment to OWI was presented to him as a win, a prestigious position that afforded him considerable influence. But Drake knew better. It was a face-saving move for the Navy. The upward trajectory that had marked his entire journalism career and service in the Naval Reserve had plateaued. Yet few people would scoff if Drake claimed his OWI position was consistent with that earlier ascendant arc. Drake consoled himself with the knowledge that as a man who'd spent his life protecting the Navy's image, at least his own image was well enough intact. Drake's loyalty and sense of duty ensured he would never write nor talk about his removal as Fleet PRO.

The day after their meeting, Forrestal wrote to Nimitz,

When I asked to have Captain Drake sent to Washington it was for the purpose of forming my own opinion as to his ability to handle the increasing public relations problems in the Pacific. I have seen enough of him since that time to be satisfied that he is not capable of prosecuting the kind of program that both you and I want the next six to eight months of the war. As you know, there have been many complaints about him from the newspaper people, but most of these I have discounted because I am fully aware that no man could be in the job he has occupied the last three years without incurring the displeasure of people who want to do unorthodox and impossible things, from a security standpoint.[71]

Forrestal relayed his decision:

> I suspect that from the latter point of view he has rendered good service to you in difficult times. Now, however, the situation has changed and we shall need positive and imaginative qualities along with professional knowledge of the Navy. Such positive qualities he obviously does not possess, and for that reason I am unwilling to have him continue in the Pacific theater.

The secretary tried to soften the blow:

> As I said above, I discount many of the so-called charges brought against him. He strikes me as a thoroughly honest and decent man, and I want to be sure that he gets full credit for the work he has done for you and we can find for him back here work which will afford him a satisfactory outlet for his energies. One such job which could be of considerable importance is the one that I mentioned in relation to OWI's request for us to assign someone to them who had a background in the Pacific operations. I am not sending this letter lightly or on an impulse. It is only because I am sure the decision is sound, both as far as the Navy is concerned and so far as you are concerned personally.

The next day, Duffield wrote to Markey. "If your dreams should come true, two extremes should be avoided. First, there should be no gloating, and, second, there should be no belated lionizing."[72] After receiving the secretary's letter, Nimitz privately lamented, "The publicity side of the war is getting so large, it almost overshadows the fighting side."[73] Yet Nimitz was unwilling to battle Forrestal any longer over his PRO. He authorized Drake's reassignment by dispatch on October 21, 1944: "While I regret to lose Capt. Drake who has served faithfully and well for so long and at times under very difficult conditions I am pleased he is going to such an important job and one of his liking. Capt. Miller is entirely satisfactory as his relief."[74]

* * * * * * * * * *

While Forrestal's plot to reassign Drake has been described as "Machiavellian,"[75] Drake also brought misfortune upon himself. He failed to perceive the necessity of ensuring Forrestal's satisfaction with his accomplishments as Fleet PRO. After Secretary Knox's death, the Navy's web of coalitions shifted, creating vulnerability. Drake believed that keeping Nimitz satisfied was good enough and that by doing so he could protect his PRO position. That logic had worked from 1942 through most of 1944. Drake's myopia concerning Forrestal's dissatisfaction ensured that once the secretary sought to remove him, Drake could do little to change Forrestal's mind.

Throughout the war, Drake's approach to public relations had been mostly reactive rather than proactive. Advancements typically came in response to accumulating complaints. His letters to Berry and Beecher reveal an inability to win favor with certain correspondents to neutralize their constant criticisms. Austin had invited Drake to expand the Fleet's public relations staff to help, but Drake couldn't do so quickly or effectively enough to earn Austin's trust. Drake's management of public relations ensured he'd earn the antipathy of correspondents who found themselves fighting with the Fleet PRO over task force assignments, censorship decisions, and transmission delays. When they finally perceived a clear opportunity, correspondents who loathed Drake rushed to oust him.

Drake's failure as Fleet PRO stemmed from his inability to develop a strategic-planning mindset. As Crozier's memorandum to Gates noted, "Its [read: Drake's] attitude consists of waiting for newspapermen, magazine writers and editors, radio agencies and others to ask questions, suggest ideas and make demands upon it. It meets these as they come; issues routine handouts; originates little."[76] By not collaborating with Nimitz, OPR officials, and journalists to establish concrete and measurable public relations objectives for the Fleet, there was little Drake could do to refute officials who asserted he'd failed to be "positive" or provide "fresh" news. By today's standards, Drake's inability to establish public relations objectives for the Fleet and supply his superiors with evidence of their attainment justified his removal. By professional standards circa 1944, however, justification for his removal is less clear-cut. Much of Miller's initial work as Fleet PRO either mirrored or amplified Drake's. The evidence of an immediate, profound, or enlightened shift in Fleet public relations is difficult to pinpoint in the archival record.

Nevertheless, Miller systematized the collection and analysis of public relations data in ways Drake failed to do. An important innovation involved distribution of a tracking sheet to Fleet units that required officials to identify public relations milestones and accomplishments. Miller also created a public relations newsletter, the *PACFLEET Public Information Bulletin*. Critically, Miller shifted the censoring of correspondents' personal mail out of the public relations unit. Where Drake failed to win Forrestal's favor, Miller earned it. For example, Forrestal praised Miller's effort to establish a hometown news service for the Navy. Miller also earned accolades from the *New York Times* for issuing a "model communique" in the aftermath of the Battle of Leyte Gulf.[77] Miller was able to increase the size of the Fleet public relations staff to handle the massive influx of correspondents in the last year of the war. For the Battle of Okinawa in April 1945, Miller and the Fleet PROs handled nearly 250 correspondents.[78]

Drake was unable to grow Fleet public relations quickly enough from the small, ancillary unit it had been in 1941 to the massive engine of publicity Forrestal wanted it to become by late 1944. It is difficult to see how Drake could have continued to survive as Fleet PRO without a profound transformation of his own mindset and administrative abilities. While he'd played a critical role in the rise of Navy public relations in the first thirty-four months of the war, toward the end of 1944, the Navy's public relations function had evolved faster than Drake could keep pace.

In addition to being warfighters, naval officers were managers in a large, bureaucratic organization characterized by "fealty with bosses and patrons, and alliances shaped through networks, coteries, cliques, and work groups that struggle through hard times together."[79] Within the labyrinth of the Navy's intersecting and rival managerial groups, the goal of each individual was survival and advancement. Drake was fortunate to have served for so long with the favored group in the Navy's hierarchy. Nimitz shielded his PRO from reassignment time after time. Among his many virtues was Nimitz's ability to maintain networks and alliances to ensure his subordinates survived and flourished.

But Forrestal's advancement created a new struggle for dominance. The newly appointed secretary needed to succeed in reassigning Drake to OWI not only for reasons of improved publicity as he saw them, but also for reasons of symbolic authority. "Real administrative effectiveness flows," Robert Jackall explains, "from the prestige that one establishes with other managers."[80] Such prestige is earned through the "socially recognized ability to work one's will, to get one's way, to have the say-so when one chooses in both the petty and large choices of organizational life."[81] Forrestal was willing to battle Nimitz for dominance in ways Knox wasn't in 1942 when he'd pushed for Berry to join the Fleet's public relations staff. In some ways, Drake's position was incidental to the larger struggle with the Navy's top brass that Forrestal had to provoke to assert his dominance.

That struggle began with King. Soon after his appointment as secretary, Forrestal established a twice-weekly staff meeting with the high-ranking civilians and admirals, but King failed to attend the first two meetings: "The following week, as the next meeting got under way, there was still no sign of the COMINCH, so Forrestal picked up the phone and called King. 'Admiral,' he said, in the presence of the entire navy hierarchy, 'I thought you might be interested in attending my staff meeting this morning, as I am about to issue operational orders to the fleet.' An irate but outmaneuvered King was there in five minutes, and thereafter attended the Secretary's staff meetings unless he was out of town."[82] Forrestal also pushed King to be more forthcoming with the press.

Nimitz was a shrewd manager, and he understood that even if capitulation to Forrestal was distasteful, there were benefits to be gained in acquiescing to Drake's reassignment. Trent Hone's 2022 volume, *Mastering the Art of Command*, depicts Nimitz's leadership of the Pacific Fleet in almost superhuman terms. Hone writes, "Nimitz was able to perform 'as close to perfection as human limitations permit' because of the collaborative environment he fostered, the trust he created, and the sense of unity he brought to the Pacific Fleet and Pacific Ocean Areas."[83] Drake's reassignment to OWI allows us to see the darker side of Nimitz's homespun persona. As Jackall explains, "Here the disarming grace that is a principal aspect of desirable managerial style can be particularly useful in making disingenuousness seem like 'straight arrow' behavior."[84] In other words, "Winning sometimes requires the willingness to move decisively against others, even though this might mean undermining their organizational careers."[85] For Nimitz to win in his larger struggle with Forrestal, he had to lose Drake. Nimitz's style of delegating authority and decision making ensured he'd be insulated from the taint of Drake's perceived mismanagement of public relations. Pushing authority downward provided Nimitz a wholly acceptable rationale "for not knowing about problems or for not trying to find out."[86]

Historians have emphasized Nimitz's statesmanlike demeanor, managerial skill, and "strategic artistry" in accounting for his success.[87] Unlike MacArthur, who was unabashedly political, Nimitz kept his focus on strategic objectives. To this day, the term "organizational politics" maintains an unpleasant connotation, but it is a primary vector of managerial power and influence. Politics is baked into the public relations function of the organization itself. Drake's story illustrates that Nimitz's ability to navigate the Navy's moral mazes was among his topmost skills: "The admiral was an expert in his own public relations; he never offended higher authority uselessly, and to him uselessly would mean going to bat for someone in serious personal trouble. That was the ancient Navy system."[88] When he saw Drake was in serious trouble with Forrestal, Nimitz stopped going to bat for his PRO.

The Fleet's public relations "problem" by mid-1944 was twofold: a perceived lack of fresh news, as Forrestal claimed, and that Drake was Nimitz's newsman. The need for a more "positive" and "imaginative" PRO offered a pretext for Forrestal to place his own newsman, Miller, at CINCPAC headquarters to better control and influence organizational politics. Organizational power is derived from one's position in the hierarchy as well as from one's control over knowledge, resources, and technical skill.[89] While Forrestal held legal authority over Nimitz by virtue of his position, he also needed more tangible control of the Fleet's public relations function to better wield his sources of power.

The scale and reputation of Fleet public relations clearly expanded and improved under Miller's stewardship, but could those outcomes have been attained had Nimitz fought more fervidly to retain Drake? Probably not. Old animosities lingered, and only a new Fleet PRO could truly sweep them away. Drake may have found a silver lining in the situation, however; he learned a few days after his reassignment that Miller and Nimitz had inexplicably released a prank communique that stated the Japanese Fleet had been defeated in 1592. The BBC, New York radio broadcasters, and other outlets mistook the prank as fact, disseminating the erroneous information. The *Times* reported, "Immediately the witch burners began looking for somebody to accuse but couldn't hang it on Capt. Waldo Drake, who usually gets the blame—he was here in Washington and got quite a bang out of the affair."[90] The ill-conceived joke was certainly not the type of "fresh" news Forrestal had had in mind. Indeed, the main reasons Forrestal claimed compelled Drake's reassignment—the possible creation of a separate Air Force and the Navy's subsumption into a larger Department of War (Defense)—eventually came to pass anyway. Forrestal himself had second thoughts about trying to control Fleet public relations shortly after reassigning Drake, finding his efforts had produced little immediate improvement. He considered asking King to take over the Navy's entire public relations function.[91] But Forrestal's reconsideration of the situation was far too late for Drake.

Nimitz wrote to his former PRO on October 24, 1944,

It is with deep regret that I am forced to lose your services as my Public Relations Officer, and I know that you will believe me when I tell you that I had little or no choice of action. I also want you to know that I greatly appreciate the splendid services you have rendered to me and to the Pacific Fleet during the period that I have been responsible for that fleet. It will give me great pleasure in a day or so to forward to you, through official channels, a Legion of Merit medal with appropriate citation covering your very fine work. I hope and believe that your new assignment is important to you and to the Navy, and I further hope that it will bring you into contact with us out here in the Pacific. I know that Elmer Davis could not make a more important and appropriate choice.[92]

The official Legion of Merit was later presented to Drake on behalf of the president. It stated,

> For exceptionally meritorious conduct in the performance of out-standing services to the Government of the United states as Public Relations Officer on the Staff of Commander in Chief, Pacific Fleet and Pacific Ocean Areas from December 31, 1941, to October 3, 1944. Working tirelessly and with intelligent application of superior professional knowledge throughout this prolonged period of vital operations, Captain Drake effectively facilitated the accurate and expeditious flow of important war news to the American Press, completely disregarding his personal safety to participate actively in the campaigns against the enemy Japanese-held Gilbert, Marshall, Marianas and Palau Islands. By his sound judgment and steadfast devotion to duty under difficult conditions, he contributed materially to the consistently efficient dissemination of the news from these highly strategic war areas for the American Public.[93]

But the honor was bittersweet; beneath the citation, on behalf of the president, appeared the signature of the Secretary of the Navy: James Forrestal.

❧❧❧❧❧❧❧❧❧❧❧

Back in Pearl Harbor, on the drizzly night of March 5, 1945, Bassett found himself staying late at the Cement Pot on Makalapa Hill. Six months earlier, Nimitz and his senior staff had decamped to their new headquarters on Guam. There, they would spend the remainder of the war. Bassett, finished with his PRO duties for both Halsey and the Twelfth Naval District, was serving as acting fleet photographic officer. Forlorn, he began typing a letter to Willie. He sat near where he and Drake once constituted the Fleet's entire public relations staff.

> It's a huge room, adjoining another and still another, that adjoin the one room Waldo and I had in the Old Days when we imagined we were some punkin's because we'd moved up from the SubBase to this

establishment overlooking the Harbor. I'm at some yeoman's desk; he's gone to his barracks, and it's late, and the last remaining hand has finished swabbing the floor, and most of the lights are out. Behind me, on the wall, is an array of photographs of all the correspondents out with the Fleet. Ernie Pyle, and J.P. Marquand (who says he's going to write a book about the Navy), and a lot of others. Even little Barbara Miller Finch [the first female correspondent accredited to the Fleet].[94]

Bassett's thoughts turned to his new boss, Pacific Fleet PRO Miller.

Time magazine this week tells all about the new Navy public relations and Min Miller, complete with a picture of him in flying togs. What it doesn't tell is about the sleepless nights we went through to get that "break"!—those photographs back to the States in 17 1/2 hours. With some pardonable pride, I can look back on all that, and reflect that at least one segment of the old discredited system, one small cog which was I, had a hand in it; and I can figure that maybe if I hadn't been there those remarkable pix wouldn't have flashed home so quickly.

Bassett's nostalgia reflected a certain truth: Miller's success was built upon public relations processes Drake had developed. Following the devastation at Pearl Harbor, through Midway, and during the grinding days of Guadalcanal, Tarawa, Kwajalein, Eniwetok, Saipan, and Peleliu, Drake struggled to develop those processes with colleagues including Bassett, Beecher, Berry, Lovette, McArdle, Markey, Mercer, Powell, and Ward. Victories were won, mostly through trial and error, but ultimately at a painful, personal cost. When the Fleet finally sailed into Tokyo Bay, Drake was nowhere to be found.

At OWI, Drake assisted officials in boosting the Fleet's public image. He remained at OWI until Japan's surrender. Bassett remained in Pearl Harbor, promoted to captain before returning to the *Times* after the war. Berry, returning from sea duty, would eventually become the public relations director for the nation's first secretary of defense: James Forrestal. Beecher would continue serving in senior public relations positions in the Navy and, later, the Department of Defense. In June 1945, OPR was renamed the

Office of Public Information (OPI), and Miller became its first director, serving until 1946. The structures and processes Miller and colleagues put in place helped ensure that publicity-averse admirals like Halsey, Kimmel, King, and Nimitz could never again so easily hamper Navy public relations. Those changes have reverberated in the Navy public affairs community to the present day in the form of OPI's successor organization: the Chief of Information and the Office of Information (CHINFO). How Miller and colleagues created those structures and processes is another story. All that mattered for Drake was that Miller was Fleet PRO; his own contributions to the rise of Navy public relations were soon forgotten.

10

Aftermath

Nothing is more noble, nothing more venerable, than loyalty.

—Cicero

JAPAN SIGNED THE instruments of surrender on board the USS *Missouri* (BB 63) in Tokyo Bay on September 2, 1945, but Drake's work for OWI did not immediately end. In October, the War Department appointed him as the sole press representative to the staff of Edwin Pauley, President Harry Truman's representative on the Allied Reparations Committee. The mission of the Allied Reparations Committee, Drake said, involved "ferreting out Japanese assets that can be used to foot the reparations bill."[1] Most of the fourteen members of the committee departed Washington, D.C., on November 1, 1945, bound for "Tokyo, Japan, Korea, Manchuria and China, via Manila, Philippines."[2] The headline in the *Times* announced Drake's return as Asiatic correspondent and press representative for the committee: " 'Times' Writer, Back from Navy, to Cover Orient."[3]

Nimitz arranged to meet his former PRO after learning Drake intended to stop in Pearl Harbor in advance of the committee's onward flight to Japan. It had been more than a year since Drake had set foot in the Cement Pot. He and Nimitz met in the admiral's office, their easy rapport returning. Nimitz explained to Drake he'd told Forrestal he wanted to become the new CNO (Chief of Naval Operations), the position King had held throughout most of the war and the highest uniformed position in the Navy. Consistent with the secretary's hostile attitude during the war, Forrestal had his own candidates for the job and opposed Nimitz's nomination: "I haven't got much enthusiasm out of the Secretary," Nimitz admitted, adding, "I'd like to know if you have any ideas that might help."[4] Drake saw a chance to show Nimitz he harbored no ill will about his reassignment to OWI.

The plan Drake had in mind offered the duo an opportunity for payback. "Just by chance, I do, Admiral," Drake said with a slight smirk. "My friend Ed Pauley is arriving to join the airplane that is taking us to Japan tomorrow, and he's the man who put Harry Truman in the White House. He succeeded in having him nominated at the Chicago convention and he later became Vice President. He's the only man, I think, who could help you." Nimitz grinned in the way the admiral always did when Drake presented him good news. "Well," said Nimitz, "bring him out."[5] The next day Drake introduced Pauley to Nimitz, and the two men talked privately about the possibility of Nimitz becoming CNO.

Pauley liked Nimitz immediately. In Nimitz's presence, Pauley called President Truman on the telephone, urging him to name Nimitz CNO. Exactly how much influence that call had is a matter of debate, but according to Nimitz's biographer, E. B. Potter, it "could not have hurt his chances."[6] Indeed, it may have paved the way for Nimitz's meeting with President Truman a few weeks later in Washington, D.C.,. After that meeting, on November 20, 1945, President Truman announced that Nimitz would succeed King as CNO. Forever loyal to Nimitz, Drake's final act as his newsman was to facilitate the admiral's promotion to the position above all others in the Navy he aspired to hold. Securing Nimitz's CNO appointment in the face of Forrestal's opposition must have tasted sweet and warranted a celebratory toast, if only in spirit.

⁂⁂⁂⁂⁂⁂⁂⁂⁂⁂⁂

Drake's postwar adventures for the *Times* took him through Asia, Europe, Africa, and the Middle East at pivotal moments in history. Those stories cannot be told here. In 1962, Drake returned to Southern California, and after more than forty years of combined service with the *Times*, he retired. He'd traveled the world several times over. The pages of his passports were black with ink. After retirement, Drake became involved in civic affairs and served on the boards of several Southern California community organizations. He kept active, playing tennis almost every day.

The *Santa Ana Register* published a profile of Drake on November 28, 1965, noting the sixty-eight-year-old retired reservist had been promoted in 1953 to rear admiral and had risen to the "highest naval rank achieved by a newspaperman."[7] Enjoying a resort-like atmosphere at their home in Three Arch Bay with Mary, Drake claimed he swam daily in the ocean "no matter how cold it is." He told his interviewers that his most cherished possessions were his memories of correspondents. He described Ernie Pyle "as a nice fellow" and Richard Tregaskis as a "courageous man—absolutely fearless in conduct." He also remembered Kimmel as "a great man" who was "crucified" in the press for the Navy's lack of preparedness for the Pearl Harbor attack. Nowhere did Drake or his interviewers hint at the struggles that characterized Drake's time on the CINCPAC staff.

On Christmas Day 1977, Drake spent the morning with Mary, and then, as usual, he grabbed his tennis racket and headed for the courts. Drake had started warming up when a sharp pain in his chest startled him. He realized he was having a heart attack. Always taking responsibility, Drake drove himself to the hospital, one hand squeezing his chest. He was administered care and a room at South Coast Hospital in Laguna Beach. His children were in different parts of the country, but Mary was at his side. South Coast Hospital was near the wide expanse of the Pacific Ocean. Much of the century's history—as well as Drake's own—had played out upon its shimmering surface. On December 27, 1977, a day of cloudless skies and a fair breeze, Waldo Drake died.

Three months later, on March 30, 1978, at 1400, the USS *Okinawa* (LPH 3) came to a full stop off the Southern California coast, the Port of Los Angeles in the distance. *Okinawa*'s flag at half-mast, her officers and enlisted men stood attentively on the hangar deck as the chaplain, Cdr. John Mowry, USN, solemnly performed the religious portion of the ceremony. A rifle squad of eight men, plus eight body and flag bearers, stood ready. The rifles fired their salute, and the ashes of Rear Adm. Waldo Drake, USNR (Ret.), were released into the Pacific Ocean.[8]

✦✦✦✦✦✦✦✦✦✦✦

In February 1948, *Life* photographer Jack Birns was on board a naval air transport flying from Shanghai to Tsingtao, China. Sitting across the aisle from Birns was a certain Commander Hawkins. When Hawkins noticed the gold-stamped *Life* on Birns' camera case, they began exchanging wartime tales. The tales eventually turned to Drake and his interactions with some of the more freewheeling correspondents he'd encountered in the Pacific. One correspondent had been CBS' Robert Landry. Landry did not think much of Drake and his "Navy rules." Drake told Landry he would cut his orders for home anytime he wanted them. Landry said that was fine with him as he never wanted to work anywhere near Drake again. Commander Hawkins relished the retelling of the tale. Birns then introduced Hawkins to the young man sitting next to him. It was John Drake, Waldo's twelve-year-old son. John was returning to the United States on board the USS *Bayfield* (APA 33), and Birns was escorting him from Shanghai to the ship as a favor to his father. John's disarming manner helped Hawkins hide his embarrassment.[9] This image of Drake—Nimitz's arrogant PRO "inclined to hot temper and sometimes injudicious use of language"—has endured for more than eighty years. In many ways, Drake deserved his reputation as CINCPAC's "meanest *hombre*." Yet the story remains complicated.

Drake's long affiliation with ONI led him to become the Pacific Fleet's first PRO, but his commitment to strict security provoked an adversarial relationship with the press that lasted his entire tenure at CINCPAC headquarters. When Drake learned in May of 1942 that he'd been transferred out of naval intelligence to public relations, he wrote to Berry, "This disturbs me greatly, Bob. I am glad to have the opportunity to work in public relations as long as you and Captain Lovette so desire. But I am disappointed at having had the door closed on my return to intelligence, on which I have worked for the past 16 years."[10] Berry tried to reassure him that he could return to ONI if needed.[11] Drake could never fully reconcile his commitment to security and his public relations duties.

Would Japan have gained any advantage by being aware of the public relations struggles Drake confronted in the aftermath of the Pearl Harbor attack? Commentators have argued that Japan missed a crucial opportunity to follow up the Pearl Harbor attack with an invasion of Oahu but the complicated logistics involved all but eliminated that possibility until after the completion of the Midway operation in June 1942. Japan's prewar plan was to strike Pearl Harbor to delay the Pacific Fleet's ability to intervene in operations elsewhere in the Western Pacific. Japanese officials hoped to expand, consolidate, and fortify their positions throughout the first half of 1942 to make territorial recapture so painful for U.S. forces that eventually war-weary Americans might consider ceding portions of the Pacific to the Japanese Empire. Japan mostly achieved its objectives and controlled nearly the entirety of the Western Pacific by mid-1942. It is doubtful that awareness of Drake's public relations struggles would have compelled different decisions or outcomes.

Japanese war plans did not specify how the American press might have been influenced to promote "war weariness" over the long term. Historian Sato Masaharu has acknowledged that Japan conducted propaganda campaigns aimed at American audiences, but there was no government-wide, systematic effort to influence U.S. public opinion.[12] Japanese officials likely assumed Americans would eventually gain an accurate picture of war losses despite whatever press censorship the U.S. military put in place. If Japan could simply accrue and maintain victories in the Pacific, U.S. press reporting of the situation might help speed negotiations, but such reporting was not *required* to ensure Japan's eventual success. In other words, military victories in the Pacific vastly exceeded the importance of U.S. press reporting. An analysis of the failure of Japanese propaganda conducted immediately after the war offered a similar conclusion that still resonates today:

> The war propagandist in dealing with enemy peoples must attempt to modify the behavior of a hostile audience which he but imperfectly understands and the current condition of which he can judge only from incomplete and inadequate sources. Moreover, he is generally working against a system of domestic propaganda or "information" whose perpetrators have every one of the advantages he lacks. It therefore seems to be a safe hypothesis that he is powerless to achieve his objectives until or unless continued military defeats, severe domestic privations, or other circumstances generally beyond his control undermine the enemy's morale, destroy confidence in enemy leadership, and thus create a receptive atmosphere for his suggestions.[13]

After the Pearl Harbor attack, American support for war with Japan was so overwhelming it is hard to imagine its widespread reconsideration in the absence of repetitive and decisive Japanese victories over U.S. forces. Drake's public relations and censorship decisions helped sustain the "surprise" framing of the Pearl Harbor attack, conceal the extent of the damage to the Pacific Fleet, and promote the image of America's inevitable triumph, but it would be an overstatement to claim that Drake's decisions, by themselves, somehow risked fundamentally altering the course of the war. American morale and resolve were not wholly dependent on Drake's red pencil.

If Drake and the Navy had permitted the full extent of the Pearl Harbor disaster to be known in the days and weeks following the attack, would it have influenced either Japanese war planning or American morale? Again, we cannot know for certain, but evidence suggests neither country would have much changed its view. Japanese broadcasts revealed that the IJN had a more accurate picture of the destruction at Pearl Harbor than what the U.S. Navy had publicly disclosed. Japan already knew most of what Drake and the censors were trying to conceal. Would releasing that information earlier to the American public have changed attitudes? Again, likely not. Soon after the attack, some commentators were already warning Americans that censorship was limiting what they were being told about Pearl Harbor. At what threshold Americans' resolve to avenge the Pearl Harbor attack would have been replaced by despair and a desire to negotiate is uncertain, but that threshold is undoubtedly higher than whatever information about the Fleet's actual losses Drake could have released.

Drake's difficulties as PRO were less externally driven and more internally generated; they can be reduced to his inability to consistently engage in what today is called strategic planning for public relations. Drake certainly displayed forethought and creativity, exemplified in efforts to establish a publicity campaign centered on "the typical enlisted man," ensure newsreel coverage of Fleet operations, place an award-winning Hollywood director on Midway Island before the battle, develop a Fleet newspaper, and so on. While some of his efforts did not pan out, others earned him accolades. Drake also advocated for clearer press policies and procedures, and he constantly urged top officials to "promulgate" public relations guidance for the Fleet and correspondents. But there is little evidence that

Drake consistently thought about his PRO duties *strategically*. He did not set concrete and measurable objectives for press coverage at the Fleet level, seek higher levels of correspondent support and satisfaction, work to ensure increased transmission speed, improve public opinion, and so on. Had he done so, it would have been more difficult for Secretary Forrestal and others to assert that Drake had failed to deliver "fresh" news or properly develop the Navy's public image. Such objective-setting and measurement activities were left for officials in OPR's Analysis Section in Washington, D.C., but it was in Drake's interest to define and conduct them at the Fleet level to ensure Forrestal and others (Towers, Gates, Austin, etc.) could not claim he lacked "positive" qualities.

Drake's childhood scars help explain why some of his "positive" qualities—especially his conflict-management skills—faltered. He'd experienced childhood abandonment and displayed aspects of trauma and narcissistic personality disorder. He lacked the emotional tools necessary to work effectively with those who most criticized him. Some readers may therefore conclude that the rise of Navy public relations occurred not because of Drake's efforts but despite them. There is evidence to support that conclusion. In his 1972 thesis, Robert Klinkerman argued, "Although the Navy began the war with the organization and directive to conduct an adequate information program, its efforts were mainly responsive rather than creative until circumstances dictated a more enlightened public relations stance in the later stages of the conflict."[14] One could read Klinkerman's claim as implicating Nimitz and Drake as the uncreative duo helming Fleet public relations, with Miller and his champion, Forrestal, representing the more "enlightened" view. Klinkerman avoided pinning blame for the Fleet's public relations shortcomings on Drake, but he acknowledged that the PRO "had a definite bearing on the operation."[15] Indeed, this book has underscored Drake's considerable influence.

But there is also evidence to support the conclusion that Drake significantly contributed to the rise of Navy public relations. In the prewar era, Drake leveraged his press connections to assist ONI in performing counterintelligence activities in Southern California. Given his extensive promotion of the Battle Force, it is reasonable to conclude that Drake was as much ONI's newsman during this era as the *Times*'. It is difficult to imagine anyone else being as well-positioned to serve as the first PRO for the Pacific Fleet. Even though Drake lacked strategic planning for public relations experience, his ability to muddle through the Pearl Harbor catastrophe without OPR guidance is commendable. Drake was able to steer a course through multiple, overlapping crises despite slow transmission processes and a convoluted censorship apparatus. Forrestal did not permit him to serve on Nimitz's staff for the duration of the war, but Drake provided a well-developed public relations unit to Miller and the scores of PROs who joined the Fleet for the final push to Tokyo Bay. If Drake hadn't put the foundational pieces in place, the massive expansion of Fleet public relations in the war's final year could not have occurred as it did.

In her 1946 analysis of the Fleet's wartime public relations, Irma Cunha concluded that Drake was reassigned to OWI not because he lacked public relations ability but because he lacked diplomacy. Likewise, in *The War Beat, Pacific*, Steven Casey writes, "Drake was never known for his diplomacy."[16] These are striking claims, for public relations has been defined as the art of creating and maintaining relationships with the people who matter most to your organization. Christopher Spicer (quoting public relations scholar W. P. Ehling) argues, "The primary purpose of public relations management is the 'resolution of conflict' between a specific organization and other organizations or stakeholders. . . . Hence, to have a 'public relations situation,' an organization must be placed in a situation that manifests actual or potential conflict."[17] The evidence of Drake's diplomacy is, in fact, the hundreds of letters he either drafted for Nimitz or sent himself to correspondents, editors, publishers, military officers, civic leaders, and ordinary Americans. Therefore, it is more precise to say that Drake lacked diplomacy with certain people he distrusted or who criticized him. Drake claimed in April 1943 that "90% of the trouble has been caused by a few newspapermen." That may have been true, but his professional responsibility was to manage those conflicts independently and expertly in ways that protected not only the Navy's security, but also its image and reputation.

But no matter how sincerely Drake sought to inform the American public, no matter how willing he was to push Navy officials to support correspondents, the fact remained that Drake was not trained as a strategic communicator: he was Nimitz's newsman. It was their relationship that most influenced the rise of Navy public relations in the Pacific. Drake was pleased with his responsibilities and the prestige and influence they brought him. He relished the war as the ultimate proving ground for his abilities. He could be forceful and frightening when ensuring that correspondents adhered to Navy rules. Drake was not content to simply allow correspondents to chronicle the Navy's war effort as they saw fit. He was personally too much involved with Nimitz for that, and it was almost inevitable that his impulse to protect his admiral, operational security, and the Navy's interests would collide with his duty to improve public understanding of the war and uphold the principles of a free press.

Drake's urge for active, daring participation in the war eventually led to his wounding from a Japanese mortar shell on Eniwetok. Although his actions endeared him to Nimitz, some officials in Pearl Harbor and Washington, D.C., did not approve of the way Drake handled Fleet public relations. These officials had agendas to be fulfilled, and the only way for that to occur, they believed, was to dramatically increase and improve press coverage of the Navy in the Pacific. After he became Navy Secretary, Forrestal orchestrated Drake's reassignment to OWI, ending Drake's tenure as Fleet PRO, installing Miller, and ushering in a transformation of public relations that would lead to organizational structures still found in the Navy public affairs community today.

In late January 1953, Miller, who'd retired from the Navy as a rear admiral, was serving as president of the Free Europe Committee, an anticommunist Central Intelligence Agency (CIA) front organization that operated thirteen high-power radio stations in Germany and Portugal known as "Radio Free Europe." Miller had traveled to Berlin to meet officials and prepare for the annual "Crusade for Freedom" fundraising drive. Waiting for a colleague in the lobby of his hotel, Miller saw a tall figure in a fine, navy-blue suit stride toward him. He looked vaguely familiar. Stopping in front of Miller, the gentleman said in an unusually raspy voice, "I bet you don't know who I am."

Miller, unable to place the gentleman, finally confessed, "No, I don't."

"I'm Waldo Drake," he said.

Miller's expression remained unchanged. Another moment passed, and the Pacific Fleet's first PRO walked away.[18]

When Nimitz wrote to Drake after his reassignment to OWI in October 1944, the admiral included a signed temporary citation. It stated: "His performance of duty was in keeping with the highest traditions of the naval service."[19] Drake's performance was imperfect, but he navigated treacherous waters and communication currents in ways that supported America's war against Japan. The Roman orator Marcus Tullius Cicero once declared, "Nothing is more noble, nothing more venerable, than loyalty." Drake was forever loyal to those he admired and respected. He was loyal to Nimitz and yearned for loyalty in return. From late December 1941 to October 1944, he received it in abundance; Nimitz fought time and again to protect his newsman. Nimitz's devotion to Drake provided the Fleet's PRO with reservoirs of emotional energy needed to loyally serve his country, his Navy, and his admiral. It makes perfect sense why Mary requested Drake's ashes be spread at sea, with only his beloved Navy family in attendance to honor him. It was a fitting end for Nimitz's newsman.

Notes

PREFACE

1. Irma Jeannette Cunha, "Problems of War Reporting in the Pacific" (MA thesis, Stanford University, 1946), i.
2. Ibid.

INTRODUCTION

1. The description of the Battle of Eniwetok is drawn from multiple sources: Associated Press, "All of Eniwetok Atoll Except Parry Isle Is Won," *New York Times*, February 21, 1944, 1; Associated Press, "American Navy Guns Killed 13 U.S. Troops at Eniwetok," *New York Times*, April 3, 1944, 1; George F. Horne, "U.S. Troops Take Eniwetok Island," *New York Times*, February 22, 1944, 1; Merle Miller, "Surprise Party at Eniwetok," *Yank*, March 31, 1944, 2–5; and "Battlefield scenes of US Marines combating Japanese forces on Eniwetok Island during World War II. HD Stock Footage," CriticalPast, May 2, 2014, accessed March 9, 2024, https://youtu.be/SQcE1urSgUE?si=7yTlPcrLggkXyANE. Drake's imagined disposition is assembled from letters and interviews.
2. The description of Drake's "grim visage" is drawn from various letters and interviews. His "brusque" manner is cited in "The Press: The Not-So-Silent Service," *Time*, December 6, 1943.
3. Frank Tremaine to Hamilton Bean, November 6, 1995.
4. Frank Knox to Hal O'Flaherty, April 7, 1941, Frank Knox Papers, 1898–1954, Box 4, Library of Congress, Washington, DC (hereafter Knox Papers).
5. Reports about Drake are found in Robert D. Klinkerman, "From Blackout at Pearl Harbor to Spotlight on Tokyo Bay: A Study of the Evolution in U.S. Navy Public Relations Policies and Practices" (MA thesis, University of Wisconsin, 1972), as well as in various letters and memoranda to Secretary Forrestal contained in Security Classified Correspondence (James Forrestal), Record Group 80 (hereafter Forrestal Correspondence), Box 119, National Archives and Records Administration II, College Park, MD (hereafter NARA II).
6. Miller, "Surprise Party at Eniwetok," 3.

7. Patsy Wagstaff in discussion with the author, September 2, 1995, Sunsites, AZ (hereafter Wagstaff interview).

8. Robert C. Miller to Hamilton Bean, February 29, 1996; Elliot Carlson, *Stanley Johnston's Blunder: The Reporter Who Spilled the Secret behind the US Navy's Victory at Midway* (Annapolis, MD: Naval Institute Press, 2017).

9. E. B. Potter, *Nimitz* (Annapolis, MD: Naval Institute Press, 2013), 32.

10. Frank Tremaine to Hamilton Bean, November 6, 1995.

11. Edwin Hoyt, *How They Won the War in the Pacific: Nimitz and His Admirals* (Lanham, MD: Rowman and Littlefield, 2011).

12. Charles P. Arnot, *Don't Kill the Messenger* (New York: Vantage Press, 1994), 96.

13. Klinkerman, "From Blackout at Pearl Harbor," 198.

14. This memorandum from Drake contains no title, date, nor distribution but is included with an enclosure dated October 12, 1943. Record Group 313, Naval Operating Forces, Commander-in-Chief, Pacific Fleet, Records Relating to Public Relations, ca. 1943–1946, Administrative Files, Public Relations General Policy to [PR Officer] Organization Material—General, Box 6 (hereafter Pacific Fleet PR Files, Box 6), NARA II.

15. Edward L. Bernays, *Propaganda* (New York: Horace Liveright, 1928), 10.

16. Waldo Drake, interview by Etta-Belle Kitchen, June 15, 1969, U.S. Naval Institute Oral History Collection, Annapolis, MD, 44 (hereafter Drake oral history).

17. "History of Navy Public Affairs," U.S. Navy Public Affairs Association, accessed May 25, 2023, https://www.usnpaa.org/history-of-navy-public-affairs.html.

18. Carlson, *Stanley Johnston's Blunder*; Steven Casey, *The War Beat, Pacific: The American Media at War against Japan* (Oxford: Oxford University Press, 2021); Klinkerman, "From Blackout at Pearl Harbor"; John McCallum, "US Censorship, Violence, and Moral Judgement in a Wartime Democracy, 1941–1945," *Diplomatic History* 41, no. 3 (2017): 543–66.

19. McCallum, "US Censorship," 544.

20. Klinkerman, "From Blackout at Pearl Harbor," 9.

21. Christopher Spicer, *Organizational Public Relations: A Political Perspective* (New York: Routledge, 2013), xiii.

22. Carlson, *Stanley Johnston's Blunder*, 104.

23. Discovering Casey's *The War Beat, Pacific* was a surprising but welcome coincidence after I had agreed in 2020 to revisit Drake's story for the Naval Institute Press.

24. Craig L. Symonds, *Nimitz at War: Command Leadership from Pearl Harbor to Tokyo Bay* (Oxford: Oxford University Press, 2022).

25. Trent Hone, *Mastering the Art of Command: Admiral Chester W. Nimitz and Victory* (Annapolis, MD: Naval Institute Press, 2022).

26. Robert Jackall, *Moral Mazes: The World of Corporate Managers* (Oxford: Oxford University Press, 1988).

27. Potter, *Nimitz*.

28. Michael W. Myers, *The Pacific War and Contingent Victory: Why Japanese Defeat Was Not Inevitable* (Lawrence: University Press of Kansas, 2015).

29. Brayton Harris, *Admiral Nimitz: The Commander of the Pacific Ocean Theater* (New York: St. Martin's Press, 2012).

30. Casey, *The War Beat, Pacific.*

31. Mary S. Mander, *Pen and Sword: American War Correspondents, 1898–1975* (Champaign: University of Illinois Press, 2010), 61.

32. "About Public Relations," Public Relations Society of America, accessed March 20, 2021, https://www.prsa.org/about/all-about-pr.

33. Spicer, *Organizational Public Relations*, 192.

34. Fredrick S. Siebert, "Federal Information Agencies – An Outline," *Journalism and Mass Communication Quarterly* 19, no. 1 (1942): 31.

35. Ryan Wadle, *Selling Sea Power: Public Relations and the U.S. Navy, 1917–1941* (Norman: University of Oklahoma Press, 2019), 229.

36. Harris, *Admiral Nimitz*, 73.

37. Casey, *The War Beat, Pacific*; Klinkerman, "From Blackout at Pearl Harbor."

38. Mander, *Pen and Sword.*

39. "PRSA Code of Ethics," Public Relations Society of America, accessed March 20, 2021, https://www.prsa.org/about/prsa-code-of-ethics.

40. Spicer, *Organizational Public Relations*, xi.

41. The author thanks Dr. Matthew Seeger for the insight that war significantly complicates some of the assumptions of contemporary public relations practice in terms of openness, transparency, and the public interest. Who determines the public interest in wartime is a fraught question.

42. On January 13, 2023, the director of the Office of the IRB, University of New Mexico (where the project first began), determined this project does not constitute human subjects research. The University of Colorado, Denver, concurred on January 23, 2023.

43. Regarding historical biography, see Bryan C. Taylor, "Organizing the 'Unknown Subject': Los Alamos, Espionage, and the Politics of Biography," *Quarterly Journal of Speech* 88, no. 1 (2002).

CHAPTER 1. THE DEAN OF THE SHIPPING NEWS REPORTERS

1. Material in this section is derived from two sources: Waldo Drake, interview by James Bassett, April 26, 1973, transcript, *Los Angeles Times* Records, Box 579, Huntington Library, Manuscript Collections, San Marino, CA (hereafter Drake-Bassett interview); and Scott Harrison, "From the Archives: A Look at the Los Angeles Times Newsroom in 1922," *Los Angeles Times*, July 20, 2018, accessed May 28, 2023, https://www.latimes.com/visuals/photography/la-me-fw-archives-los-angeles-times-newsroom-in-1922-htmlstory.html.

2. Drake-Bassett interview, 4.

3. Ibid.

4. Ibid., 3.

5. Mary Jane Brooks, "Drake Says Nazi Defeat Not to Alter Present Pacific Strategy," *Nashville Banner*, January 15, 1944, 1.

6. Information about Drake in this section is derived from discussions with family members, newspaper coverage, and Drake's military service records.

7. "Lost Umbrella: Owner Went to Get It and Found Lost Child," *Akron Times-Democrat*, November 28, 1901, 6.

8. "Rescue: Of a Little Boy Locked in a Church Basement at Springfield O., Was Timely," *Newark Advocate*, November 27, 1901, 8.

9. "Officers of High School Cadet Corps," *Press-Telegram*, October 14, 1919, 3.

10. "Co. B Winner of Rotary Cup in Contest," *Press-Telegram*, June 11, 1920, 11.

11. Material in this section is derived from various digitized Long Beach Polytechnic High School yearbooks from the period.

12. *Long Beach Daily Telegram*, April 7, 1920.

13. Waldo Drake, "City Library Use by Poly Students," *Long Beach Daily Telegram*, April 7, 1920, 17.

14. Rob Leicester Wagner, *Red Ink, White Lies: The Rise and Fall of Los Angeles Newspapers, 1920–1962* (Columbia, CA: Dragonflyer Press, 2000).

15. Ibid., 11.

16. "Over 1,000 Grammar School Pupils See 'Pinafore' Matinee," *Long Beach Daily Telegram*, May 19, 1920, 3.

17. This origin story for the field is sometimes disputed. Donald K. Wright, "History and Development of Public Relations Education in North America: A Critical Analysis," *Journal of Communication Management* 15, no. 3 (2011): 236–55.

18. Wadle, *Selling Sea Power*, 41.

19. Peter Karsten, *The Naval Aristocracy: The Golden Age of Annapolis and the Emergence of Modern American Navalism* (Annapolis, MD: Naval Institute Press, 1972), 25–26, 252.

20. Klinkerman, "From Blackout at Pearl Harbor," 6–7.

21. Naval District Manual, Record Group 181, Records of Naval Districts and Shore Establishments, Records of the 11th Naval District, District Communication Officer San Diego, Central Subject Files, 1916–47, Box 65, National Archives at Riverside, Riverside, CA (hereafter National Archives at Riverside).

22. Drake-Bassett interview.

23. *Los Angeles Times*, February 25, 1923, 101.

24. Wagner, *Red Ink, White Lies*.

25. "Twenty Years Ago," *San Pedro News-Pilot*, July 17, 1944, 5.

26. Wagner, *Red Ink, White Lies*, 50.

27. Wagstaff interview.

28. Ibid.

29. Ibid.

30. Ibid.

31. Ibid.

32. Items included "Action Near on Zone Bill" and "Shipping Board Shift to Port," *Los Angeles Times*, November 26, 1928, 14; *Los Angeles Times*, January 31, 1929, 21.

33. In July 2022, the author surveyed the area of the Drake home on Carolina Street to establish these claims.

34. Information about Barrymore, Lee, and Drake's yacht racing activities is found in numerous press reports from the era.

35. Drake-Bassett interview.

36. Ibid.

37. The quotations in this section are from "Navy's Axillary Needs Related to Rotarians," *News-Pilot*, October 21, 1935, 10.

38. "Waldo Drake to Washington," *News-Pilot*, April 29, 1931, 7.

39. Wagstaff interview. Whether Drake and Mary met his father, mother, or siblings at that time is unknown, but Ralph and Bertha would both die six years later in 1937, Ralph in Yellow Springs and Bertha in the State of Ohio Asylum for the Insane.

40. "Waldo Drake Hurt in East," *News-Pilot*, July 6, 1931, 1.

41. Memorandum from the Chief of the Bureau of Navigation to Commandants, December 3, 1937, Record Group 181, Records of Naval Districts and Shore Establishments, Eleventh Naval District, Office of the District Director of Naval Reserves, Central Subject Files, 1925–1954, Box 20, National Archives at Riverside.

42. Simon Bourgin, "Public Relations of Naval Expansion." *Public Opinion Quarterly* 3, no. 1 (January 1939): 113–17.

43. Waldo Drake, "Why Uncle Sam Is Worried about His Navy," *Los Angeles Times*, April 9, 1933, 100.

44. "Critical Plight of Uncle Sam's Navy," *San Bernardino Sun*, April 7, 1933, 19.

45. Waldo Drake, "Fleet Back from Cruise," *Los Angeles Times*, June 6, 1937, 15.

46. Ibid.

47. This description of the 1937 war game is drawn from page 164 of Arthur H. McCollum, interview by John T. Mason Jr., December 1970 through March 1971, Volume 1, U.S. Naval Institute Oral History Collection, Annapolis, MD (hereafter McCollum oral history).

48. *Los Angeles Times*, April 25, 1937, 1.

49. Waldo Drake, "The Fleet's Gone, Now Where's Our Coast Defense," *Los Angeles Times*, May 20, 1934, 94.

50. Waldo Drake, "Cotton Export Trade Periled," *Los Angeles Times*, March 21, 1937, 24.

51. Waldo Drake, "Japanese Oil Imports Soar," *Los Angeles Times*, May 9, 1938, 24; Waldo Drake, "Japan Move Confirmed: Action Taken toward Direct Government Control of Shipping," *Los Angeles Times*, October 30, 1938, 49.

52. McCollum oral history.

53. Wagner writes in *Red Ink, White Lies* that the city's largest newspaper, the *Examiner*, amplified stories of Japanese American disloyalty and "fifth columnists." Wagner gives credit to the *Times* for not mirroring the sentiments of Hearst-owned newspapers. While a few *Times* columnists expressed anti–Japanese American views, reporter Chester Hanson and columnists Lee Shipley and Bill Henry were critical of anti-Japanese movements in the area.

54. Wagstaff interview.

55. This letter from Drake to Mary provided by a family member is the only one discovered for this project. Others are assumed to no longer exist or are extremely difficult to find.

56. The information about Nimitz in this section is derived from the following sources: Hone, *Mastering the Art of Command*; Potter, *Nimitz*; and Symonds, *Nimitz at War*.

57. Wagstaff interview. Drake voiced this sentiment to his brother-in-law, a graduate of the Naval Academy, on only one known occasion.

58. See chapter 1 of Potter, *Nimitz*, for a discussion of Nimitz's views on reserve officers.

59. *Los Angeles Times*, September 18, 1938, 17.

60. *Los Angeles Times*, September 24, 1938, 21.

61. From the Chief of the Bureau of Navigation to All Ships and Stations, July 22, 1941, Record Group 181, Records of Naval Districts and Shore Establishments, Eleventh Naval District, Naval Base, Los Angeles–Long Beach California, Central Subject Files, 1940–1971, Box 80, National Archives at Riverside.

62. Jeffrey M. Dorwart, *Conflict of Duty: The U.S. Navy's Intelligence Dilemma, 1919–1945* (Annapolis, MD: Naval Institute Press, 1983).

CHAPTER 2. AN INTELLIGENCE DILEMMA

1. The descriptions of Admiral Kimmel and CINCPAC headquarters in this chapter are drawn from Paul Stillwell, ed., *Air Raid, Pearl Harbor! Recollections of a Day of Infamy* (Annapolis, MD: Naval Institute Press, 1981); Steve Twomey, *Countdown to Pearl Harbor: The Twelve Days to the Attack* (New York: Simon and Schuster, 2017); Frank Tremaine to Hamilton Bean, November 6, 1995.

2. Harold Stark to Kimmel [no date], Husband Edward Kimmel Papers, 1907–1999, Box 2, American Heritage Center, University of Wyoming, Laramie, WY (hereafter Kimmel Papers).

3. Klinkerman, "From Blackout at Pearl Harbor," 22.

4. Kimmel to Stark, April 22, 1941, Kimmel Papers.

5. Memorandum from Commandant to Director of Naval Intelligence, May 28, 1932, Record Group 181, Records of Naval Districts and Shore Establishments, Eleventh Naval District, Office of the District Director of Naval Reserves, Central Subject Files, 1925–1954, Box 20, National Archives at Riverside.

6. Dorwart, *Conflict of Duty*.

7. Material in this section is drawn from McCollum oral history.

8. McCollum oral history, 169.

9. Ibid.

10. Ibid., 186–87.

11. Ibid.

12. Ellis M. Zacharias, *Secret Missions: The Story of an Intelligence Officer* (New York: G. P. Putnam's Sons, 1946), 243.

13. Dorwart, *Conflict of Duty*, ix.

14. James Bassett Jr., interview by Etta-Belle Kitchen, May 28, 1969, U.S. Naval Institute Oral History Collection, Annapolis, MD, 26 (hereafter Bassett oral history).

15. Wadle, *Selling Sea Power*, 118.

16. Pedro A. Loureiro, "Japanese Espionage and American Countermeasures in Pre–Pearl Harbor California." *Journal of American-East Asian Relations* 3, no. 3 (1994): 197–210.

17. *Amending Merchant Marine Act, 1936: Hearings before the Committee on Merchant Marine and Fisheries, House of Representatives*, Seventy-fifth Congress, Second and Third Sessions on H.R. 8532 (1937) (statement of Waldo Drake, Chairman, National Defense, San Pedro Post of the American Legion of California), 400.

18. Ibid.

19. Ibid., 405.

20. Ibid.

21. Ibid.

22. Ibid.

23. Loureiro, "Japanese Espionage."

24. Rep. Charles J. Colden (D-CA), "Washington Notes," *Palos Verdes Peninsula News*, February 4, 1938, 4.

25. Dorwart, *Conflict of Duty*.

26. Waldo Drake, "Japan Navy Mission," *Los Angeles Times*, August 31, 1939, 17.

27. "Nippon Navy Men on Secret Tour," *Wilmington Daily Press Journal*, August 31, 1939, 6.

28. Dorwart, *Conflict of Duty*; McCollum oral history.

29. Waldo Drake, "Fleet Ready for Maneuvers," *Los Angeles Times*, April 1, 1940, 1.

30. Twomey, *Countdown to Pearl Harbor*.

31. "The Origins and Development of the Naval Operating Base Command," Commandant, Eleventh Naval District, Naval Operating Base, Terminal Island (San Pedro), California, United States Naval Administration in World War II, accessed May 30, 2023, https://www.ibiblio.org/hyperwar/USN/Admin-Hist/169-TI-NOB/169-TI-NOB-1.html.

32. Ibid.

33. Waldo Drake, "Alien Seamen Plans Revealed," *Los Angeles Times*, July 10, 1940, 19.

34. Ibid.

35. From Assistant Commandant to the Commandant, July 26, 1940, Record Group 181, Records of Naval Districts and Shore Establishments, Eleventh Naval District, Naval Base, Los Angeles—Long Beach California, Central Subject Files, 1940–1971, Box 73, National Archives at Riverside.

36. Ibid.

37. Ibid.

38. McCollum oral history, 78.

39. Studies conducted over the past hundred years have found 40 to 75 percent of media content is sourced from or influenced by public relations professionals. Jim Macnamara, "Journalism–PR Relations Revisited: The Good News, the Bad News, and Insights into Tomorrow's News," *Public Relations Review* 40, no. 5 (2014): 739–50.

40. The various press releases described in this section are included in Record Group 181, Records of Naval Districts and Shore Establishments, Eleventh Naval District, Naval Base, Los Angeles—Long Beach California, Central Subject Files, 1940–1971, Box 73, National Archives at Riverside.

41. The author conducted keyword searches via Newspapers.com to verify the publication of the related press release material.

42. Memorandum from the Secretary of the Navy to All Ships and Stations, September 30, 1940, Record Group 181, Records of Naval Districts and Shore Establishments, Eleventh Naval District, Naval Base, Los Angeles—Long Beach California, Central Subject Files, 1940–1971, Box 73, National Archives at Riverside.

43. Memorandum from the Commandant to District Activities, October 18, 1940, in ibid.

44. Memorandum from the Commander-in-Chief, United States Fleet to Commandant, Eleventh Naval District, October 19, 1940, in ibid.

45. "Counterintelligence in World War II," National Counterintelligence Center, accessed May 27, 2023, https://irp.fas.org/ops/ci/docs/ci2/2ch2_a.htm.

46. Ibid.

47. "Naval Intelligence Branch Opened in Federal Building," *Los Angeles Times*, January 18, 1941, 4.

48. Advertisements for these technologies are included in Record Group 181, Records of Naval Districts and Shore Establishments, Eleventh Naval District, Naval Base, Los Angeles—Long Beach California, Central Subject Files, 1940–1971, Box 80, National Archives at Riverside.

49. Memorandum from the Assistant Commandant to the Commandant, January 7, 1941, in ibid.

50. Memorandum from Branch District Intelligence Office, Los Angeles to District Intelligence Officer, January 2, 1941, in ibid.

51. Memorandum from Waldo Drake to the Federal Bureau of Investigation, Los Angeles, March 18, 1941, Robert H. Jackson Papers, 1816–1983, Box 93–94, Library of

Congress, Washington, DC (hereafter Jackson Papers). The author thanks Andy and Debbie McKane for supplying the memorandum.

52. Dr. Huettig would become a noted economist and activist after the war, but her daughter reported of those years in Southern California, "We had to move to Ojai, a valley directly east of Santa Barbara, when I was 11. We basically got run out of town." See Daniel Eagan, "Joan Churchill, ASC — An Evolving Eye," *American Cinematographer*, November 9, 2018, accessed May 27, 2023, https://theasc.com/articles/joan-churchill-asc-an-evolving-eye.

53. Dorwart, *Conflict of Duty*.

54. Memorandum from President Roosevelt to Attorney General, May 21, 1940, Box 93–94, Jackson Papers. The author thanks Andy and Debbie McKane for supplying the memorandum.

55. Memorandum from OPNAV to COMELEVEN, May 10, 1941, Record Group 181, Records of Naval Districts and Shore Establishments, Eleventh Naval District, Naval Base, Los Angeles—Long Beach California, Central Subject Files, 1940–1971, Box 80, National Archives at Riverside.

56. Memorandum from the Commandant to All Activities, March 10, 1941, Record Group 181, Records of Naval Districts and Shore Establishments, Eleventh Naval District, Naval Base, Los Angeles—Long Beach California, Central Subject Files, 1940–1971, Box 27, National Archives at Riverside.

57. James Bassett Files, 1936–1979, *Los Angeles Times* Records, Box 289, Huntington Library, Manuscript Collections, San Marino, CA (hereafter Bassett Files).

58. DIO-11ND Order No. 18, March 18, 1941, Record Group 181, Records of Naval Districts and Shore Establishments, Eleventh Naval District, Naval Base, Los Angeles—Long Beach California, Central Subject Files, 1940–1971, Box 27, National Archives at Riverside.

59. Ibid.

60. Kyle Palmer, "Shaw Confident He'll Win Re-election to Mayoralty," *Los Angeles Times*, March 5, 1941, 30.

61. Memorandum from the Chief of the Bureau of Navigation to the Commandant, Eleventh Naval District, March 14, 1941, Record Group 181, Records of Naval Districts and Shore Establishments, Eleventh Naval District, Naval Base, Los Angeles—Long Beach California, Central Subject Files, 1940–1971, Box 27, National Archives at Riverside.

62. Memorandum for Lt. Comdr. Ringle from the Commandant's Office, March 31, 1941, Record Group 181, Records of Naval Districts and Shore Establishments, Eleventh Naval District, Naval Base, Los Angeles—Long Beach California, Central Subject Files, 1940–1971, Box 27, National Archives at Riverside.

63. "Joe Shaw Declared Not Serving Navy," *Los Angeles Times*, April 3, 1941, 48.

64. This press release is untitled and numbered; it is included in Record Group 181, Records of Naval Districts and Shore Establishments, Eleventh Naval District, Naval

Base, Los Angeles—Long Beach California, Central Subject Files, 1940–1971, Box 73, National Archives at Riverside.

65. Loureiro, "Japanese Espionage," 209.

66. Ken Ringle, "What Did You Do Before The War, Dad?," *Washington Post*, December 6, 1981, accessed May 30, 2023, https://www.washingtonpost.com/archive/lifestyle/mag azine/1981/12/06/what-did-you-do-before-the-war-dad/a80178d5-82e6-4145-be4c -4e14691bdb6b/.

67. Information about the Tachibana spy ring is assembled from Ron Drabkin and Brad-ley W. Hart, "Agent Shinkawa Revisited: The Japanese Navy's Establishment of the Rut-land Intelligence Network in Southern California," *International Journal of Intelligence and Counter Intelligence* 35, no. 1 (2022): 31–56; and Pedro Loureiro, "The Imperial Japanese Navy and Espionage: The Itaru Tachibana Case," *International Journal of Intelligence and Counter Intelligence* 3, no. 1 (1989): 105–21.

68. Loureiro, "The Imperial Japanese Navy and Espionage," 115.

69. A.D.I.O. Order no. 3, Branch Intelligence Office, April 3, 1941, Records of Naval Dis-tricts and Shore Establishments, Eleventh Naval District, Naval Base, Los Angeles—Long Beach California, Central Subject Files, 1940–1971, Box 27, National Archives at Riverside.

70. Ibid.

71. Censorship Regulations, U.S. Navy, 1941, April 1941, Records Group 181, Record of Naval Districts and Shore Establishments, 11th Naval District, District Communica-tions Officer, San Diego, Central Subject Files, 1916–1947, Box 26, in ibid.

72. Ibid., 5.

73. *Los Angeles Times*, April 18, 1941, 33.

74. Memorandum from the Chief of Naval Operations to Commandants Naval Districts, May 9, 1941, Record Group 181, Records of Naval Districts and Shore Establishments, Eleventh Naval District, Office of the District Director of Naval Reserves, Central Sub-ject Files, 1925–1954, Box 20, National Archives at Riverside.

75. Investigation Report, May 21, 1941, Record Group 181, Records of Naval Districts and Shore Establishments, Eleventh Naval District, Naval Base, Los Angeles—Long Beach California, Central Subject Files, 1940–1971, Box 80, National Archives at Riverside.

76. Press Release No. 49, Record Group 181, Records of Naval Districts and Shore Estab-lishments, Eleventh Naval District, Naval Base, Los Angeles—Long Beach California, Central Subject Files, 1940–1971, Box 73, National Archives at Riverside.

77. Dorwart, *Conflict of Duty*.

CHAPTER 3. MUSTAFA'S MISFORTUNE

1. Herrick to Drake, November 7, 1941, Record Group 313, Records of Naval Oper-ating Forces, Commander-in-Chief, Pacific Fleet, Records Relating to Public Rela-tions, ca. 1943–1946, Administrative Files, Pre-war Semi-official PR Corresp. [1941]

to Public Relations General Policy, Box 5 (hereafter Pacific Fleet PR Files, Box 5), NARA II.

2. *LOOK*, November 18, 1941.

3. Stahlman to Drake, July 26, 1941, Pacific Fleet PR Files, Box 5, NARA II.

4. Drake to Herrick, August 16, 1941, Pacific Fleet PR Files, Box 5, NARA II.

5. Hallett Abend, *Ramparts of the Pacific* (Garden City, NY: Doubleday, Doran and Company, Inc., 1941).

6. Hallet Abend, "How the U.S. Navy Will Fight Japan," *LOOK*, November 18, 1941, 21.

7. See Twomey, *Countdown to Pearl Harbor*; Proceedings of Hewitt Inquiry, Hewitt Inquiry Exhibit No. 2, Narrative Statement of Record of Pearl Harbor Court of Inquiry, 450–61, accessed May 30, 2023, https://www.ibiblio.org/pha/pha/narrative/22.html.

8. "Waldo Drake, 'Times' Man, Gets Assignment with Fleet," *Los Angeles Times*, May 16, 1941, 39.

9. McCollum oral history.

10. The controversial "McCollum Memo" is described in Conrad Crane, review of *Day of Deceit: The Truth about FDR and Pearl Harbor*, by Robert B. Stinnett, *Parameters* 31, no. 1 (2001).

11. Stahlman reported to New Orleans as PRO for the Eighth Naval District a few months after the war commenced.

12. "An Autobiography by Robert Wallace Berry, Rear Admiral, United States Navy (Retired), 1978," unpublished manuscript, Box 1, Robert Wallace Berry Papers, Hoover Institution Library and Archives, Stanford University, Stanford, CA (hereafter Berry Papers), 2.

13. Ibid.

14. Leonard Lyons, "Broadway Medley," *Shamokin News-Dispatch*, June 13, 1941, 6.

15. Lee Van Atta, "L.A. Ship News Reporter Now Official Eyes, Ears of U.S. Fleet," *Honolulu Advertiser*, August 1, 1941, 3.

16. Quoted in Symonds, *Nimitz at War*, 16; Thomas B. Buell, *Master of Seapower: A Biography of Fleet Admiral Ernest J. King* (Annapolis, MD: Naval Institute Press, 2012).

17. Waldo Drake, "Naval Air Base Extension Seen," *Los Angeles Times*, December 11, 1936, 37.

18. Waldo Drake, "Fleet Will Sail Tomorrow to Hold Secret Maneuvers," *Los Angeles Times*, November 6, 1938, 42.

19. Buell, *Master of Seapower*.

20. Kimmel to Stark, April 22, 1941, Kimmel Papers.

21. Memorandum from the Chief of the Bureau of Navigation to All Ships and Stations, July 22, 1941, Record Group 181, Records of Naval Districts and Shore Establishments, Eleventh Naval District, Naval Base, Los Angeles—Long Beach California, Central Subject Files, 1940–1971, Box 80, National Archives at Riverside.

22. "Secretary of Navy Inspects New Base Site," *Long Beach Sun*, September 18, 1940, 14.

23. Waldo Drake, "Adams Arrives on Coast Tour," *Los Angeles Times*, May 11, 1931, 19.

24. King replaced Stark as CNO soon after the war commenced.

25. "An Autobiography by Robert Wallace Berry," 180.

26. Ibid.

27. Hoopes Townsend and Douglas Brinkley, *Driven Patriot: The Life and Times of James Forrestal* (Annapolis, MD: Naval Institute Press, 2012).

28. Van Atta, "L.A. Ship News Reporter," 1.

29. Memorandum from Assistant District Public Relations Officer to District Public Relations Officer, June 24, 1941, Record Group 181, Records of Naval Districts and Shore Establishments, Eleventh Naval District, Naval Base, Los Angeles—Long Beach California, Central Subject Files, 1940–1971, Box 73, National Archives at Riverside.

30. "Waldo Drake Is Coming as Press Man for Fleet," *Honolulu Star-Bulletin*, June 5, 1941, 7.

31. Van Atta, "L.A. Ship News Reporter." The race, first held in 1907, is still conducted today and known as "Transpac."

32. Van Atta, "L.A. Ship News Reporter," 3

33. Waldo Drake, "I Don't Think They'd Be Such Damned Fools," in *Air Raid: Pearl Harbor! Recollections of a Day of Infamy*, ed. Paul Stillwell (Annapolis, MD: Naval Institute Press, 1981), 269.

34. This description is assembled from Potter, *Nimitz*; Frank Tremaine to Hamilton Bean, November 6, 1995; and Twomey, *Countdown to Pearl Harbor*.

35. Drake to Stahlman, July 24, 1941, Pacific Fleet PR Files, Box 5, NARA II.

36. Information about Riddick's attitude toward Drake is included in Robert W. Berry, "Report of an Investigation of Navy Public Relations, Hawaii Area," February 22, 1942, to March 19, 1942 (hereafter Berry Report), Box 2, Berry Papers.

37. Memorandum from Waldo Drake to Public Relations Officers, August 5, 1941, RG 313, S370 R33 C14 S3 CinCUS Files 1941, Box 1. CinCUS 1941, Admiral Kimmel's Personal File, NARA II (courtesy of Andy and Debbie McKane).

38. Anderson to Kimmel, August 10, 1941, RG 313, S370 R33 C14 S3 CinCUS Files 1941, Box 1. CinCUS 1941, Admiral Kimmel's Personal File, NARA II (courtesy of Andy and Debbie McKane).

39. Kimmel to Anderson, August 12, 1941, RG 313, S370 R33 C14 S3 CinCUS Files 1941, Box 1. CinCUS 1941, Admiral Kimmel's Personal File, NARA II (courtesy of Andy and Debbie McKane).

40. The press release is included in the Bassett Files. A search for newspaper articles mentioning "Henry Harlan Blake" shows nationwide coverage in November 1941.

41. Kimmel to Hepburn, August 8, 1941, Pacific Fleet PR Files, Box 5, NARA II.

42. Ibid.

43. Kimmel to Nimitz, August 8, 1941, Pacific Fleet PR Files, Box 5, NARA II.

44. Drake to Stahlman, August 7, 1941, Pacific Fleet PR Files, Box 5, NARA II.

45. Ibid.

46. Lee Van Atta, "Noted Aviation Writer Is Public Relations Aid for US Fleet Here," *Honolulu Advertiser*, September 21, 1941, 3.

47. Drake to Stahlman, July 9, 1941, Pacific Fleet PR Files, Box 5, NARA II. Drake included the expression "busier than a brace of bird dogs" in several letters from the period.

48. James Bassett to Willie Bassett, August 11, 1940, Box 1, James E. Bassett Jr. Papers, 1929–1977, George J. Mitchell Department of Special Collections and Archives, Bowdoin College Library, Brunswick, ME (hereafter Bassett Papers).

49. "Mrs. Cromwell Heads China Relief Festival," *Honolulu Advertiser*, August 18, 1941, 1.

50. Ibid.

51. "Leland Lovette, Admiral, 69, Dies," *New York Times*, July 12, 1967, 43.

52. Kimmel to Stark, October 29, 1941, Kimmel Papers.

53. Kimmel to Stark, November 7, 1941, Kimmel Papers.

54. Stark to Kimmel, November 14, 1941, Kimmel Papers.

55. Memorandum to Commander Berry, November 13, 1941, Kimmel Papers.

56. Statement of Rear Admiral Husband E. Kimmel, U.S. Navy Retired, May 1942, Kimmel Papers.

57. Memorandum from the Assistant District Intelligence Officer to the Commandant, October 6, 1941, Record Group 181, Records of Naval Districts and Shore Establishments, Eleventh Naval District, Naval Base, Los Angeles—Long Beach California, Central Subject Files, 1940–1971, Box 75, National Archives at Riverside.

58. Memorandum from the District Intelligence Officer to the Commandant, October 13, 1941, Record Group 181, Records of Naval Districts and Shore Establishments, Eleventh Naval District, Naval Base, Los Angeles—Long Beach California, Central Subject Files, 1940–1971, Box 75, National Archives at Riverside.

59. Potter, *Nimitz*, 5.

60. Ibid., 6.

61. Drake, "I Don't Think They'd Be Such Damned Fools," 269; the scene with Kimmel is also described in Joseph C. Harsch, "A War Correspondent's Story," in *Air Raid: Pearl Harbor! Recollections of a Day of Infamy*, ed. Paul Stillwell (Annapolis, MD: Naval Institute Press, 1981), 263–68; and Joseph C. Harsch, *At The Hinge of History: A Reporter's Story* (Athens: University of Georgia Press, 1993).

62. Harsch, "A War Correspondent's Story," 264.

63. Ibid.

64. Ibid.

65. Ibid.

66. Drake, "I Don't Think They'd Be Such Damned Fools," 269.

Chapter 4. Pearl Harbor

1. The account provided in this section is derived from: Wagstaff interview; and John Drake discussion with author, Lilburn, GA, December 30, 1995 (hereafter John Drake interview).

2. Robert S. La Forte and Ronald E. Marcello, eds., *Remembering Pearl Harbor: Eyewitness Accounts by U.S. Military Men and Women* (Wilmington, DE: SR Books, 1991), 231.

3. John Drake interview.

4. Ibid.

5. Errol Drake in discussion with the author, Albuquerque, NM, March 15, 1996 (hereafter Errol Drake interview).

6. Twomey, *Countdown to Pearl Harbor*, 279.

7. Frank Tremaine and Kay Tremaine, *The Attack on Pearl Harbor: By Two Who Were There* (Fredericksburg, TX: Admiral Nimitz Foundation, 1997).

8. Accounts of the morning of the Pearl Harbor attack reveal contradictory information regarding Drake's whereabouts. Drake's son, John, claims the attack was underway when Drake was at home in Haleiwa. An account by Ruth "Woofie" Parker also places Drake in Haleiwa. Al Brick, however, claims that he and Drake were getting into a motor launch to film the *Arizona* "when she blew up." Brick's statement is nonsensical because the *Arizona* was one of the first casualties of the attack, and there would have been no obvious reason to film her prior to the massive explosion that occurred at approximately 0810, when eyewitnesses place Drake in Haleiwa. See Techla Murphy, "A Pearl Harbor Survivor: Henry S. Parker," *OutLook*, November 18, 2011, accessed May 31, 2023, https://outlookbythebay.com/military/2011/11/749/; Greg Wilsbacher, "Now It Can Be Shown! Fox Movietone Newsreel Footage from Pearl Harbor," December 5, 2016, Moving Image Research Collections (MIRC), accessed May 31, 2023, https://digital.library.sc.edu/blogs/mirc/2016/12/05/now-it-can-be-shown/. The most detailed analysis of Al Brick's film and activities is Greg Wilsbacher, "Al Brick: The Forgotten Newsreel Man at Pearl Harbor," *Moving Image* 10, no. 2 (Fall 2010), link.gale.com/apps/doc/A247740418/AONE?u=googlescholar&sid=sitemap&xid=529e75bb.

9. Potter, *Nimitz*.

10. Wilsbacher, "Now It Can Be Shown!"; Wilsbacher, "Al Brick."

11. It would be a year before a highly sanitized version of the footage was released.

12. Casey, *The War Beat, Pacific*. 14.

13. Klinkerman, "From Blackout at Pearl Harbor."

14. "S.F. Marine Editor Is Harbor Visitor," *News-Pilot*, April 18, 1928, 11.

15. Lee Van Atta, "Uncle Sam's Bluejackets Are Ready!," *Honolulu Advertiser*, October 5, 1941, 49.

16. "Navy Is Ready, Knox Declares," *Honolulu Advertiser*, December 1, 1941, 1.

17. "Only Powerful Two-Ocean Fleet Can Defend U.S., Knox Asserts," *Honolulu Advertiser*, December 7, 1941, 1.

18. "Navy Day Finds Navy Prepared for Its Duty," *Honolulu Advertiser*, October 27, 1941, 13.

19. Twomey, *Countdown to Pearl Harbor*.

20. McCollum oral history, 395.

21. Ibid., 396.

22. "War! Oahu Bombed by Japanese Planes," *Honolulu Star-Bulletin*, December 7, 1941, 1.

23. The number of correspondents in Pearl Harbor comes from Memorandum from Waldo Drake to 05, December 13, 1941, Pacific Fleet PR Files, Box 6, NARA II.

24. Memorandum from Waldo Drake to 05, December 12, 1941, Pacific Fleet PR Files, Box 6, NARA II.

25. Ibid.

26. Memorandum from Waldo Drake to 05, December 13, 1941, Pacific Fleet PR Files, Box 6, NARA II.

27. Jonas H. Ingram to Admiral E. J. King, December 13, 1941, Official Papers of Fleet Admiral Ernest J. King, microfilm, Wilmington, DE (hereafter King microfilm).

28. Potter, *Nimitz*.

29. Theodore Roosevelt Jr. to Frank Knox, December 11, 1941, Knox Papers.

30. These reactions are drawn from interviews contained in the Berry Report.

31. Brian Masaru Hayashi, "Frank Knox's Fifth Column in Hawai'i: The U.S. Navy, the Japanese, and the Pearl Harbor Attack," *Journal of American-East Asian Relations* 7, no. 2 (2020): 142–68.

32. "Naval Group Wants 2 Men to Tell Story," *Honolulu Star-Bulletin*, January 28, 1942, 1.

33. "Japanese Americans and the Wartime Experience in Hawaii," National WWII Museum, October 15, 2021, https://www.nationalww2museum.org/war/articles/japanese-americans-wartime-experience-hawaii.

34. Elizabeth P. McIntosh to Hamilton Bean, February 3, 1996.

35. McIntosh would later work for the Office of Strategic Services (OSS).

36. No evidence was found during this project that Drake had a direct line to the White House.

37. Elizabeth P. McIntosh to Hamilton Bean, February 3, 1996.

38. Ibid.

39. Cunha, "Problems of War Reporting"; Tremaine and Tremaine, *The Attack on Pearl Harbor*, 100.

40. Memorandum from Waldo Drake to 05, 20, January 3, 1942, Pacific Fleet PR Files, Box 6, NARA II.

41. Ibid.

42. Ibid.

43. The Navy's communiques are collected in Navy Department Communiques 1–300 and Pertinent Press Releases, December 10, 1941, to March 5, 1943, https://www.history.navy.mil/research/library/online-reading-room/title-list-alphabetically/n/navy-depart-communiques-1-300-pertinent-press-releases.html.

44. Tremaine and Tremaine, *The Attack on Pearl Harbor*, 100.

45. Keith Wheeler, *The Pacific Is My Beat* (New York: E. P. Dutton and Company, Inc., 1944), 27.

46. Drake's memoranda suggest that approximately two dozen correspondents were in Honolulu by early spring 1942, but the exact number is difficult to pinpoint.

47. John Drake interview.

48. "Naval Officer's Wife Returns," *Los Angeles Times*, January 30, 1942, 2.

49. Errol Drake interview.

50. Memorandum from the Commandant to [various commanding officers], May 27, 1941, Record Group 181, Records of Naval Districts and Shore Establishments, Eleventh Naval District, Naval Base, Los Angeles—Long Beach California, Central Subject Files, 1940–1971, Box 73, National Archives at Riverside.

51. Stark to Kimmel [no date], Kimmel Papers.

52. Drake to Stahlman, July 9, 1941, Pacific Fleet PR Files, Box 5, NARA II.

53. Ibid.

54. Macnamara, "Journalism–PR Relations Revisited."

55. Quoted in Ian W. Toll, *Twilight of the Gods: War in the Western Pacific, 1944–1945* (New York: W. W. Norton and Company, 2020), 21.

56. Matthew W. Seeger, "Best Practices in Crisis Communication: An Expert Panel Process," *Journal of Applied Communication Research* 34, no. 3 (2006): 232–44.

57. Ibid.

58. Wadle, *Selling Sea Power*.

59. Drake to Stahlman, July 9, 1941, Pacific Fleet PR Files, Box 5, NARA II.

60. These three documents are located in the Pacific Fleet PR Files, Box 5, NARA II.

61. James E. Grunig and Larissa Schneider Grunig, "Toward a Theory of the Public Relations Behavior of Organizations: Review of a Program of Research," *Journal of Public Relations Research* 1, no. 1–4 (1989): 27–63.

62. Today, the Public Relations Society of the America (PRSA) offers specialized accreditation in military public affairs (APR-M) focused principally on research, planning, implementing, and evaluating programs.

Chapter 5. Bad Manor

1. Information about Nimitz's appointment as CINCPAC and his departure to Oahu is included in Potter, *Nimitz*.

2. Descriptions of Nimitz are drawn from Hoyt, *How They Won the War in the Pacific*, 28.

3. Drake oral history, 5.

4. Ibid., 32.

5. Bassett oral history, 10.

6. Potter, *Nimitz*.

7. Hone, *Mastering the Art of Command*, 344.

8. Hoyt, *How They Won the War in the Pacific*, 220.

9. This memorandum follows page 6 of the Berry Report.

10. Drake oral history, 38.

11. Nimitz's note is attached to Memorandum from Waldo Drake to 05, 96, 02, January 7, 1942, Pacific Fleet PR Files, Box 6, NARA II.

12. Memorandum for 02, 00, January 4, 1941, Pacific Fleet PR Files, Box 6, NARA II.

13. Berry Report.

14. Tremaine and Tremaine, *The Attack on Pearl Harbor*.

15. Ibid.

16. The same policy language is included in Enclosure B, Pacific Fleet Letter 2L-43, February 10, 1943, Pacific Fleet PR Files, Box 5, NARA II.

17. Pacific Fleet Press Release No. 13, accessed June 1, 2023, https://ussslcca25.com/mcmur-07.htm.

18. John Drake showed the author a copy of the draft press release with the lines redacted at his home in Lilburn, GA, December 30, 1995. Unfortunately, the document could not be located in 2021. John Drake died in 2004.

19. Quoted in Casey, *The War Beat, Pacific*, 49.

20. Jim W. Hughes, *Eugene Smith: Shadow and Substance: The Life and Work of an American Photographer* (New York: McGraw-Hill, 1989).

21. Drake oral history, 42.

22. Ibid., 14.

23. Ibid.

24. Ibid.

25. Robert C. Miller to Hamilton Bean, February 29, 1996. Photocopied portions of Miller's diary, including the quotation, were provided to the author with this letter. Miller's diary is available via the Robert C. Miller papers, 1938–2004, American Heritage Center, University of Wyoming, Laramie, WY.

26. Joe James Custer, *Through the Perilous Night: The Astoria's Last Battle* (New York: Macmillan Co., 1944), 30.

27. Memorandum from the Secretary of the Navy to All Ships and Stations, March 13, 1942, Record Group 181, Records of Naval Districts and Shore Establishments, Records of the 11th Naval District, District Communication Officer San Diego, Central Subject Files, 1916–47, Box 65, National Archives at Riverside, Riverside, CA (hereafter National Archives at Riverside).

28. Hoyt, *How They Won the War in the Pacific*, 131.

29. Ibid., 132.

30. Toll, *Twilight of the Gods*, 21.

31. Bassett oral history, 9.

32. Arnot, *Don't Kill the Messenger*, 96. Given Bassett's penchant for wordplay, the author cannot rule out that Bassett may have covertly composed these jibes.

33. Custer, *Through the Perilous Night*, 78.

34. Tremaine and Tremaine, *The Attack on Pearl Harbor*.

35. Ibid., 165.

36. Descriptions of Casey and his activities are found in Casey, *The War Beat, Pacific*; Robert J. Casey, *Torpedo Junction: With the Pacific Fleet from Pearl Harbor to Midway* (Indianapolis, IN: Bobbs-Merrill Company, 1942).

37. Casey, *Torpedo Junction*, 51.

38. Potter, *Nimitz*, 36.

39. Ibid.

40. Potter's account of Nimitz declining Casey's meeting request conflicts with Berry's account of the meeting, details of which are included in the Berry Report. The discrepancy can be resolved if one considers the meeting was not "private."

41. Berry Report, 9.

42. Harsch, *At The Hinge of History*.

43. Ibid., 77.

44. Ibid.

45. Copies of intercepted messages are included in the Berry Papers.

46. Harsch, *At The Hinge of History*, 79.

47. Ray E. Boomhower, *Richard Tregaskis: Reporting under Fire from Guadalcanal to Vietnam* (Albuquerque: University of New Mexico Press, 2021), 64–65.

48. The kerfuffle is alluded to throughout the Berry Papers and in the Berry Report.

49. Drake to Kitts, February 20, 1942, Record Group 313, Records of Naval Operating Forces, Commander-in-Chief, Pacific Fleet, Records Relating to Public Relations, ca. 1943–1946, Administrative Files, Letters to and from Forward Area 2—June 25 Aug 45 to Cdr Waldo Drake Corresp, July–Oct 1942, Box 4 (hereafter Pacific Fleet PR Files, Box 4), NARA II.

50. Ibid.

51. Ray E. Boomhower, *Dispatches from the Pacific: The World War II Reporting of Robert L. Sherrod* (Bloomington: Indiana University Press, 2017); Casey, *The War Beat, Pacific*.

52. Casey, *The War Beat, Pacific*, 11.

53. Ibid.

54. Ibid.

55. Drake to Kitts, February 20, 1942, Pacific Fleet PR Files, Box 4, NARA II.

56. Drake to Berry, March 20, 1942, Pacific Fleet PR Files, Box 4, NARA II.

57. "Francis Louden Black," U.S. Naval Academy Virtual Memorial Hall, accessed June 2, 2023, https://usnamemorialhall.org/index.php/FRANCIS_L._BLACK,_CDR,_USN.

58. These details are included in Narrative by Commander E. J. Long, USNR, Gilbert and Marshall Islands, Public Relations Photographic, May 9, 1944, Papers of E. John Long, Archives Branch, Naval History and Heritage Command, Washington, DC (hereafter Long Report).

59. The description of the icebox contents is assembled from items found in various letters contained in the Bassett Papers.

60. James Bassett to Willie Bassett, June 21, 1942, Bassett Papers.

61. James Bassett to Willie Bassett, September 26, 1942, Bassett Papers.

62. James Bassett to Willie Bassett, May 10, 1942, Bassett Papers.

63. James Bassett to Willie Bassett, February 2, 1945, Bassett Papers.

64. Memorandum from Waldo Drake to 05 20 02, February 23, 1942, Pacific Fleet PR Files, Box 6, NARA II.

65. Ibid.

66. Tremaine and Tremaine, *The Attack on Pearl Harbor*, 65.

67. Ibid., 2.

68. Spicer, *Organizational Public Relations*, 146.

69. The Berry Report provides background and a day-by-day summary of the situation.

70. Berry Report, 6.

71. These cards are included in the Berry Papers.

72. Berry Report, 20.

73. Ibid., 9.

74. Ibid., 5.

75. Ibid., 30.

76. Ibid., 6.

77. Ibid., 22.

78. Ibid., 30.

79. "The Great Pacific Scoop," *Newsweek*, March 16, 1942, 64.

80. Ibid.

81. "Writer Said 'Scuttled': U.S. Navy Censor 'Fired,'" *Calgary Albertan*, March 19, 1942, 8.

82. Knox to Nimitz, June 2, 1942, Record Group 313, Records of Naval Operating Forces, Commander-in-Chief, Pacific Fleet, Records Relating to Public Relations, ca. 1943–1946, Administrative Files, A3-1 Organization (Public Relations) to Adm. Nimitz's PR Statements to August 1944, Box 1 (hereafter Pacific Fleet PR Files, Box 1), NARA II.

83. "Letters," *Newsweek*, May 18, 1942, 2

84. James Bassett to Willie Bassett, April 16, 1942, Bassett Papers.

85. Drake to Berry, June 3, 1942, Pacific Fleet PR Files, Box 5, NARA II.

86. Long Report, 4.

87. Jackall, *Moral Mazes*.

Chapter 6. Father Neptune

1. The account of Drake's practical joke is included in Alec MacDonald to Hamilton Bean, February 16, 1996.

2. Telegram from John Ford to Waldo Drake, June 2, 1942, Pacific Fleet PR Files, Box 6, NARA II.

3. Berry Report, 22.

4. Drake to Bolten, March 20, 1942, Pacific Fleet PR Files, Box 5, NARA II.

5. Ford to Drake, August 12, 1942, Pacific Fleet PR Files, Box 5, NARA II.

6. Berry to Drake, June 17, 1942, Pacific Fleet PR Files, Box 5, NARA II.

7. Memorandum from Drake to 02, June 9, 1942, Pacific Fleet PR Files, Box 6, NARA II.

8. Memorandum from Commander-in-Chief to Wiltse - Drake, June 16, 1942, Box 6, NARA II.

9. The account of the incident is included in oral history interview with Frank Tremaine, March 18, 1995, National Museum of the Pacific War Oral History Collection. The account of the incident is also included in Frank Tremaine to Hamilton Bean, November 6, 1995.

10. Memorandum from Commander-in-Chief, U.S. Pacific Fleet to PACIFIC FLEET, April 12, 1942, Pacific Fleet PR Files, Box 5, NARA II.

11. Laura Hillenbrand, *Unbroken: A World War II Story of Survival, Resilience, and Redemption* (New York: Random House, 2010).

12. Frank Tremaine, "Midway Spurs Plans," *Ventura County Star*, June 9, 1942, 1.

13. Memorandum from the Chief of the Bureau of Navigation to All Ships and Stations, July 11, 1941, Record Group 181, Records of Naval Districts and Shore Establishments, Eleventh Naval District, Office of the District Director of Naval Reserves, Central Subject Files, 1925–1954, Box 20, National Archives at Riverside.

14. "America's Fleet Air Force Leads the World," *Los Angeles Times*, November 21, 1926, 38.

15. This portion of Miller's diary was included in Robert C. Miller to Hamilton Bean, February 29, 1996.

16. Ibid.

17. Drake to Berry, July 16, 1942, Pacific Fleet PR Files, Box 5, NARA II.

18. Robert C. Miller to Hamilton Bean, February 29, 1996.

19. The Doolittle raids on April 18, 1942, likewise produced good news for the allies, but Navy officials did not immediately confirm Japanese radio reports of the bombings due to security. Drake referred reporters to the Navy Department in Washington for further information.

20. Drake to Francis, July 9, 1942, Pacific Fleet PR Files, Box 5, NARA II.

21. Drake to Baldwin, July 12, 1942, Pacific Fleet PR Files, Box 5, NARA II.

22. Carlson, *Stanley Johnston's Blunder*.

23. Ibid.

24. Ibid.

25. Memorandum from Drake to Berry, June 18, 1942, Pacific Fleet PR Files, Box 5, NARA II.

26. Memorandum from Bassett to Drake, June 17, 1942, Pacific Fleet PR Files, Box 5, NARA II.

27. FBI Summary Memorandum, Record Group 65, FBI records, File 100-HQ-22351-181, NARA II, 9.

28. Drake to Berry, July 16, 1942, Pacific Fleet PR Files, Box 5, NARA II.

29. Carlson, *Stanley Johnston's Blunder*, 251n11.

30. Memorandum Re: Stanley Claude Samuel Johnston; Espionage – J, June 20, 1942, Record Group 65, FBI records, File 100-HQ-22351-181, NARA II.

31. Carlson, *Stanley Johnston's Blunder*.

32. James Bassett to Willie Bassett, June 21, 1942, Bassett Papers.

33. Drake to Johnston, September 30, 1942, Record Group 313, Records of Naval Operating Forces, Commander-in-Chief, Pacific Fleet, Records Relating to Public Relations, ca. 1943–1946, Administrative Files, Correspondents – Status of to Planning – Special Visitors to POA, Box 13 (hereafter Pacific Fleet PR Files, Box 13), NARA II.

34. Arnot, *Don't Kill the Messenger*, 95.

35. Ibid.

36. Ibid.

37. Richard Tregaskis, *Guadalcanal Diary* (Eau Claire, WI: E. M. Hale and Company, 1943), 11.

38. Ibid. Other descriptions of interactions between Tregaskis and Drake are found in Ray E. Boomhower, *Richard Tregaskis: Reporting under Fire from Guadalcanal to Vietnam* (Albuquerque: University of New Mexico Press, 2021).

39. James Bassett to Willie Bassett, July 14, 1942, Bassett Papers.

40. James Bassett to Willie Bassett, July 21, 1942, Bassett Papers.

41. Memorandum from Commander in Chief, United States Pacific Fleet to the Secretary of the Navy, July 18, 1942. The author did not locate this memorandum in the Pacific Fleet PR Files; a copy is included in a cache of documents and photographs provided by Drake's grandson, Scott Drake, to the author November 9, 2022 (hereafter Scott Drake materials).

42. Drake to Hotchkiss, July 22, 1942, Pacific Fleet PR Files, Box 5, NARA II.

43. Memorandum from Lovette to King, October 31, 1942, King microfilm.

44. Berry to Drake, July 19, 1942, Pacific Fleet PR Files, Box 5, NARA II.

45. Berry to Drake, July 23, 1942, Pacific Fleet PR Files, Box 5, NARA II.

46. Lillian Berson Frankel, ed., *Scrapbook of Real-Life Stories for Young People: The Best from the Newspapers* (New York: Sterling Publishing Co., Inc., 1958), 145.

47. Berry to Drake, July 23, 1942, Pacific Fleet PR Files, Box 5, NARA II.

48. Drake to Berry, July 29, 1942, Pacific Fleet PR Files, Box 5, NARA II.

49. Francis to Drake, July 28, 1942, Pacific Fleet PR Files, Box 5, NARA II.

50. Ford to Drake, August 12, 1942, Pacific Fleet PR Files, Box 5, NARA II.

51. Drake to Ford, August 21, 1942, Pacific Fleet PR Files, Box 5, NARA II.

52. The description is included in the Long Report.

53. "Purely Personal," *Los Angeles Times*, November 12, 1944, 51.

54. The description of the office is drawn from the photograph included herein courtesy of Jennifer Drake Schroeder.

55. Drake to Powell, September 5, 1942, Pacific Fleet PR Files, Box 5, NARA II.

56. Memorandum from Waldo Drake to 02, December 2, 1942, Pacific Fleet PR Files, Box 5, NARA II.

57. James Bassett to Willie Bassett, April 7, 1942, Bassett Papers.

58. Drake to Hotchkiss, September 5, 1942, Pacific Fleet PR Files, Box 5, NARA II.

59. Drake oral history. Collins served as chief of staff of the Army's Hawaiian Department. Smith, commander of the Army's 27th Infantry Division, would later gain notoriety for his relief at the hands of Lt. Gen. Holland Smith, USMC, during the Battle of Saipan in July 1944.

60. Ibid, 12.

61. James Bassett to Willie Bassett, May 15, 1942, Bassett Papers.

62. James Bassett to Willie Bassett, October 5, 1942, Bassett Papers.

63. James Bassett to Willie Bassett, April 11, 1942, Bassett Papers.

64. James Bassett to Willie Bassett, September 23, 1942, Bassett Papers.

65. Wagstaff interview.

66. James Bassett to Willie Bassett, September 23, 1942, Bassett Papers.

67. Lovette to Nimitz, September 17, 1942, Pacific Fleet PR Files, Box 5, NARA II.

68. Drake to Howard, July 27, 1942, Pacific Fleet PR Files, Box 5, NARA II.

69. The speeches and letters included in this section are found in Pacific Fleet PR Files, Box 1, NARA II.

70. Command Summary of Fleet Admiral Chester W. Nimitz (hereafter "Graybook") vol. 1, 380.

71. "Graybook," vol. 3, 23.

72. King-Nimitz Conference Notes, July 5, 1942, King microfilm.

73. Drake to Hotchkiss, September 5, 1942, Pacific Fleet PR Files, Box 5, NARA II.

74. Ibid.

75. King-Nimitz Conference Minutes, September 19, 1942, King microfilm.

76. James Bassett to Willie Bassett, September 19, 1942, Bassett Papers.

Chapter 7. Dog Team

1. "Admiral Nimitz Visits Custer, Correspondent Wounded in the Solomons," *Brooklyn Daily Eagle*, September 24, 1942, 2.

2. "INS Man Dies in Pacific; Missing AP Writer Found," *Editor and Publisher*, September 26, 1942, 7.

3. Jack Singer, "Writer Riding in Torpedo Plane Sees Hit Scored on Jap Carrier," *Scranton Times*, September 16, 1942, 13.

4. This surge is documented in Klinkerman, "From Blackout at Pearl Harbor."

5. "The Truth—100 Days Late," *Tulsa Tribune*, September 18, 1942, 30.

6. Hoyt, *How They Won the War in the Pacific*, 141.

7. Drake to Powell, September 5, 1942, Pacific Fleet PR Files, Box 5, NARA II.

8. Drake to Berry, August 29, 1942, Pacific Fleet PR Files, Box 5, NARA II.

9. Ibid.

10. Drake to Markey, September 11, 1942, Pacific Fleet PR Files, Box 5, NARA II.

11. Drake to Berry, July 16, 1942, Pacific Fleet PR Files, Box 5, NARA II.

12. Drake to Markey, July 16, 1942, Pacific Fleet PR Files, Box 5, NARA II.

13. Lytle to Drake, August 2, 1942, Pacific Fleet PR Files, Box 5, NARA II.

14. Drake to Berry, August 29, 1942, Pacific Fleet PR Files, Box 5, NARA II.

15. Markey to Drake, July 29, 1942, Pacific Fleet PR Files, Box 5, NARA II.

16. Drake to Hotchkiss, September 5, 1942, Pacific Fleet PR Files, Box 5, NARA II.

17. Drake to Markey, September 11, 1942, Pacific Fleet PR Files, Box 5, NARA II.

18. Berry to Drake, September 24, 1942, Pacific Fleet PR Files, Box 5, NARA II.

19. Drake to Lovette, September 17, 1942, Pacific Fleet PR Files, Box 5, NARA II.

20. Drake to Berry, September 17, 1942, Pacific Fleet PR Files, Box 5, NARA II.

21. Drake to Markey, October 1, 1942, Pacific Fleet PR Files, Box 5, NARA II.

22. Drake to Beecher, October 10, 1942, Pacific Fleet PR Files, Box 5, NARA II.

23. Tremaine to Nimitz, October 16, 1942, Pacific Fleet PR Files, Box 5, NARA II.

24. Drake to Beecher, October 24, 1942, Pacific Fleet PR Files, Box 5, NARA II.

25. Knox to Nimitz, October 24, 1942, Pacific Fleet PR Files, Box 5, NARA II.

26. Nimitz confirmed the change January 23, 1943, in a meeting with Halsey; "Graybook," vol. 3, 90.

27. Drake to Markey, October 26, 1942, Pacific Fleet PR Files, Box 5, NARA II.

28. Drake to Powell, September 5, 1942, Pacific Fleet PR Files, Box 5, NARA II.

29. Nimitz to Holcomb, August 29, 1942, Pacific Fleet PR Files, Box 5, NARA II.

30. Drake to Berry, July 16, 1942, Pacific Fleet PR Files, Box 5, NARA II.

31. Drake to Lovette, September 17, 1942, Pacific Fleet PR Files, Box 5, NARA II.

32. William F. Halsey III and J. Bryan, *Admiral Halsey's Story* (New York: McGraw-Hill, 1947), 168.

33. Memorandum from the Commander, South Pacific Area and South Pacific Force to the Secretary of the Navy, January 24, 1943, World War II Administrative Histories Appendices, Public Relations, 34(29) thru 34(34), Naval History and Heritage Command, Washington, DC (hereafter Public Relations Administrative Histories, NHHC).

34. Rice to Clausen, January 27, 1943, Public Relations Administrative Histories, NHHC.

35. Buell, *Master of Seapower*, 252.

36. Casey, *The War Beat, Pacific*.

37. Potter, *Nimitz*, 222.

38. "'A Cheerful Man of Confident Tomorrows' Leads U.S. Pacific Fleet, Now Facing Mightiest Task," *Press of Atlantic City*, May 10, 1942, 17.

39. Frank Tremaine, "Acclaim Nimitz for Naval Edge in Pacific War," *The Leader-Post*, August 19, 1942, 2.

40. Boomhower, *Dispatches from the Pacific*, 60.

41. James Bassett to Willie Bassett, January 26, 1943, Bassett Papers.

42. "U.S. Now Strong in the Aleutians, Says McQuaid," *Honolulu Star-Bulletin*, January 27, 1943, 9.

43. Drake's "Neptunus Rex" card was included in the Scott Drake materials.

44. James Bassett to Willie Bassett, March 31, 1943, Bassett Papers.

45. Memorandum from Waldo Drake to 05, 95, 02, 00, March 29, 1943, Pacific Fleet PR Files, Box 5, NARA II.

46. Ryan Wadle, "Straight Naval Information Is Our Function," *Naval History Magazine* 36, no. 1 (2022).

47. Joseph Driscoll, *Pacific Victory 1945* (Philadelphia, PA: J. B. Lippincott Company, 1944), 225.

48. Memorandum from Waldo Drake to 05, 95, 02, 00, March 29, 1943, Pacific Fleet PR Files, Box 5, NARA II.

49. Hoyt, *How They Won the War in the Pacific*, 222.

50. "'Cards-on-Table' Parley to Air Navy Censorship," *Editor and Publisher*, April 24, 1943, 16.

51. Photographs of the conference discussed in this section are included in the Berry Papers.

52. Walter Schneider, "Better War Coverage May Result from Meeting of Navy PR Staff," *Editor and Publisher*, May 1, 1943, 6.

53. A transcript of Drake's remarks is included in Public Relations Administrative Histories, NHHC, but it appears that Drake's speech impediment rendered the remarks mostly unintelligible. The transcriptionist finally gave up, writing "cannot understand."

54. Schneider, "Better War Coverage," 6.

55. Photographs of the reception noted in this section are included in the Berry Papers.

56. Photo included in the Berry Papers.

57. "Special to The New York Times," *New York Times*, April 27, 1943, 1.

58. Schneider, "Better War Coverage," 44.

59. Judi Marshall, "Viewing Organizational Communication from a Feminist Perspective: A Critique and Some Offerings," in *Communication Yearbook 16*, ed. Stanly A. Deetz (Newbury Park, CA: Sage 1993), 124.

60. Spicer, *Organizational Public Relations*.

CHAPTER 8. GAME, SET, MATCH

1. The description is drawn from Drake oral history and Hoyt, *How They Won the War in the Pacific*.

2. Memorandum from Tom Yarbrough to Admiral Nimitz, July 27, 1943, Pacific Fleet PR Files, Box 1, NARA II.

3. Memorandum from T. M. Lambert to Frank Rounds, June 30, 1943, Public Relations Administrative Histories, NHHC.

4. O'Keefe to Nimitz, July 10, 1943, Pacific Fleet PR Files, Box 5, NARA II.
5. Halsey and Bryan, *Admiral Halsey's Story*, 169.
6. Richardson to Nimitz, August 24, 1943, Public Relations Administrative Histories, NHHC.
7. This memorandum from Drake contains no title, date, nor distribution but is included with an enclosure dated October 12, 1943, Pacific Fleet PR Files, Box 6, NARA II.
8. Memorandum from Waldo Drake to F-02 F-00, October 25, 1943, Pacific Fleet PR Files, Box 5, NARA II.
9. Memorandum from COMINCH to Beecher [no date], Public Relations Administrative Histories, NHHC.
10. Memorandum from T. M. Lambert to Frank Rounds, July 10, 1943, Public Relations Administrative Histories, NHHC.
11. Klinkerman, "From Blackout at Pearl Harbor," 197.
12. Nimitz to Lovette, October 23, 1943, Pacific Fleet PR Files, Box 4, NARA II.
13. Drake to Bassett, November 1, 1943, Pacific Fleet PR Files, Box 4, NARA II.
14. Drake to Bassett, November 25, 1943, Pacific Fleet PR Files, Box 4, NARA II. The position eventually went to Bassett.
15. John Martin McCallum III, "Democratic Violence and the Transformation of American Moral Sentiments in the 'Good War'" (PhD diss., University of Chicago, 2017), 112–13.
16. Ibid., 112.
17. Potter, *Nimitz*, 257.
18. This communique is included in Navy Department Communiques 301–600 and Pacific Fleet Communiques, March 6, 1943 to May 24, 1945, accessed June 1, 2023, https://www.history.navy.mil/research/library/online-reading-room/title-list-alphabetically/n/navy-depart-communiques-301-600.html.
19. Klinkerman, "From Blackout at Pearl Harbor," 198.
20. McCallum, "Democratic Violence."
21. The situation is described in Cunha, "Problems of War Reporting."
22. The "snooper" scene is described in Hoyt, *How They Won the War in the Pacific*, 325.
23. B. J. McQuaid, "Troops Find Trip to Hawaii Pleasant; Have Good Times," *Cincinnati Post*, June 25, 1942, 14.
24. B. J. McQuaid, "Army and Navy Argue but Both Won Battle of Midway," *Pittsburgh Press*, June 29, 1942, 7.
25. Hoyt, *How They Won the War in the Pacific*, 325.
26. Ibid., 326.
27. Drake to Stahlman, December 12, 1943, Pacific Fleet PR Files, Box 4, NARA II.
28. McCallum, "Democratic Violence," 113.
29. Ibid.
30. "The Press: The Not-So-Silent Service," *Time*, December 6, 1943, https://content.time.com/time/subscriber/article/0,33009,850773,00.html.

31. In their letters and memoranda, Drake and Bassett referred to criticisms as "brickbats" and praise as "bouquets."

32. Bassett to Drake, December 16, 1944, Pacific Fleet PR Files, Box 4, NARA II.

33. Pacific War Correspondents Association to Admiral Nimitz, December 16, 1943, Pacific Fleet PR Files, Box 13, NARA II.

34. Memorandum from Waldo Drake to 02, December 25, 1943, Pacific Fleet PR Files, Box 13, NARA II.

35. "Replies to PWAC's 19 Recommendations," [no date], Pacific Fleet PR Files, Box 13, NARA II.

36. Drake to Bren, January 6, 1944, Pacific Fleet PR Files, Box 5, NARA II.

37. According to Symonds, *Nimitz at War.*

38. "Fellow Texans and Friends of Texans!" January 16, 1944, Pacific Fleet PR Files, Box 1.

39. Memorandum from Waldo Drake for Captain Wiltse, June 15, 1943, Pacific Fleet PR Files, Box 1. Nimitz's remarks are included in a handwritten note accompanying the memorandum.

40. Bassett to Drake, December 16, 1943, Pacific Fleet PR Files, Box 4, NARA II.

41. Margaret Sanders, "We've Just Begun to Fight in Pacific, Comdr. Drake Says," *Nashville Tennessean*, January 15, 1944, 2.

42. Drake oral history, 45.

43. Walter C. Cochrane, "Death and Carnage Rule as Americans Take Marshalls," *Lubbock Morning Avalanche*, February 10, 1944, 2.

44. Leif Erickson, "Correspondents Give On-the-Spot Radio Accounts of Invasion," *Washington, D.C., Evening Star*, February 2, 1944, 6.

45. Hoyt, *How They Won the War in the Pacific*, 342.

46. James Lane, "Bushemi Puts Gary on WWII Front Line - His Last Words: 'Be Sure to Get Those Pictures Back to the Office Right Away,'" *Post-Tribune*, May 28, 2006, 3.

47. Miller, "Surprise Party at Eniwetok."

48. Ray E. Boomhower, *One Shot: The World War II Photography of John A. Bushemi* (Indianapolis: Indiana Historical Society Press, 2004).

49. Lane, "Bushemi Puts Gary on WWII Front Line," 3.

50. The account of Drake refusing medical attention is drawn from Miller, "Surprise Party at Eniwetok."

51. Laselle Gilman, "Honolulu War Diary," *Honolulu Advertiser*, March 5, 1944, 16. Some censors used a "blue pencil." Drake appears to have used a red pencil.

52. Lane, "Bushemi Puts Gary on WWII Front Line."

53. Jack Birns to Craig Sinclair, July 3, 1991, Waldo Drake folder, *Los Angeles Times* Records, Box 618, Huntington Library, Manuscript Collections, San Marino, CA.

54. Wagstaff interview.

55. The photographs are found in the online *Life* Photo Collection, accessed June 3, 2023, https://artsandculture.google.com/asset/capt-waldo-drake/BAHhJFwEsRVQ4g?hl=en.

56. Letter from Waldo Drake to Bill and John Drake, March 10, 1944. The author was shown this letter during his interview with John Drake, Lilburn, Georgia, December 30, 1995.

57. Waldo Drake to "Whom It May Concern," March 7, 1944, Pacific Fleet PR Files, Box 5, NARA II.

58. "Organization and Duties, Public Relations Section, Staff, Commander in Chief, Pacific Fleet," October 1, 1944, Pacific Fleet PR Files, Box 1, NARA II.

59. Ibid.

60. Drake to Bassett, January 6, 1944, Pacific Fleet PR Files, Box 4, NARA II.

61. Memorandum from Waldo Drake for 6, June 3, 1944, Record Group 313, Records of Naval Operating Forces, Commander-in-Chief, Pacific Fleet, Records Relating to Public Relations, ca. 1943–1946, Administrative Files, Correspondents - Status of Planning – Special Visitors to POA General, Box 13 (hereafter Pacific Fleet PR Files, Box 13), NARA II.

62. These activities are noted across the Pacific Fleet PR Files. Drake's activities related to Saipan are discussed in Casey, *The War Beat, Pacific*; and Toll, *Twilight of the Gods*.

63. "We'll Beat Jap at Any Game—FDR, in Hawaii," *Atlanta Constitution*, August 11, 1944, 3.

64. Hoyt, *How They Won the War in the Pacific*, 70.

65. Drake oral history, 48.

Chapter 9. Forrestal's Crosshairs

1. The April 28, 1944, statement [untitled] is included in Pacific Fleet PR Files, Box 1 , NARA II.

2. Harold B. Miller, interviewed by John T. Mason Jr., April 1981 through September 1981, U.S. Naval Institute Oral History Collection, Annapolis, MD (hereafter Miller oral history), 139.

3. Ibid.

4. Forrestal to Hoyt, September 2, 1944, Forrestal Correspondence, Box 132, NARA II.

5. King-Nimitz Conference Notes, September 26, 1943, King microfilm.

6. Minutes of Pacific Conference, San Francisco, California, 29 September – 1 October, 1944, Part II - Future Operations, King microfilm.

7. Note appended to January 1944 summary, WD – July 25, 1944, Public Relations Administrative Histories, NHHC.

8. Memorandum from Commander in Chief, United States Fleet and Chief of Naval Operations, September 30, 1944, Forrestal Correspondence, Box 119, NARA II.

9. Minutes of Pacific Conference, San Francisco, California, 29 September – 1 October, 1944, Part II - Future Operations, King microfilm.

10. Preston V. Mercer, interviewed by John T. Mason Jr., October 18, 1969, U.S. Naval Institute Oral History Collection, Annapolis, MD (hereafter Mercer oral history), 6.

11. Minutes of Pacific Conference, San Francisco, California, 29 September – 1 October, 1944, Part II - Future Operations, King microfilm.

12. Ibid.

13. Townsend and Brinkley, *Driven Patriot*, 192.

14. Minutes of Pacific Conference, San Francisco, California, 29 September – 1 October, 1944, Part II - Future Operations, King microfilm.

15. Long Report, 1.

16. Memorandum from Forrestal to Merrill, June 15, 1944, Forrestal Correspondence, Box 119, NARA II.

17. The Reminiscences of Vice Adm. Bernard L. Austin, interview by Cdr. Paul L. Hooper, USNR (Ret.), 1971, U.S. Naval Institute, Annapolis, MD, 26 (hereafter Austin Reminiscences).

18. Ibid., 280.

19. Drake to McArdle, July 4, 1944, Pacific Fleet PR Files, Box 4, NARA II.

20. Hoyt, *How They Won the War in the Pacific*, 326.

21. Ibid.

22. The handwritten note from Turner to Drake is undated but attached to an undated draft memorandum likely composed by Drake in late June 1944, Pacific Fleet PR Files, Box 4, NARA II.

23. Drake to McArdle, June 27, 1944, Pacific Fleet PR Files, Box 4, NARA II.

24. Bassett to Drake, February 3, 1944, Pacific Fleet PR Files, Box 4, NARA II.

25. Binder to Drake, August 14, 1944, Pacific Fleet PR Files, Box 5, NARA II.

26. TSgt. Pete Zurlinder, "American Newspaper Found in Jap Army Bivouac Area," *Camp Lejeune Globe*, August 9, 1944, 3.

27. Proposed Remarks by Admiral on March of Time Program, August 24, 1944, Pacific Fleet PR Files, Box 1, NARA II.

28. Clark G. Reynolds, *Admiral John H. Towers: The Struggle for Naval Air Supremacy* (Annapolis, MD: Naval Institute Press, 2017).

29. Forrestal to Towers, March 10, 1944, RG 313, Records Relating to Public Relations, ca. 1943–1946, A7-2 Censorship and Security to Photos – Policy May 1942 to July 1944, Box 10, NARA II.

30. Ibid.

31. Memorandum from E. Crozier to Mr. Gates, May 26, 1944, Forrestal Correspondence, Box 119, NARA II.

32. Memorandum from ALQ to Secretary Forrestal, June 3, 1944, Forrestal Correspondence, Box 119, NARA II.

33. Townsend and Brinkley, *Driven Patriot*, 143.

34. The "double whammy" is an established maneuver among national security officials. Gordon R. Mitchell, "Team B Intelligence Coups." *Quarterly Journal of Speech* 92, no. 2 (2006): 144–73.

35. George William Healy, *A Lifetime on Deadline: Self-Portrait of a Southern Journalist* (New Orleans: Pelican Publishing, 1976).

36. Ibid., 140.

37. Ibid., 141.

38. Ibid., 142.

39. Ibid.

40. Ibid.

41. Ibid., 147.

42. Ibid.

43. Ibid.

44. Miller oral history, 138.

45. Ibid., 139.

46. Austin Reminiscences, 281.

47. Miller oral history, 140.

48. Austin Reminiscences.

49. Miller oral history, 140.

50. Ibid.

51. Austin Reminiscences, 281.

52. Miller oral history, 141.

53. Memorandum from H. B. Miller to 00, September 19, 1944, Pacific Fleet PR Files, Box 1, NARA II.

54. Ibid.

55. Miller oral history, 142.

56. Ibid.

57. Ibid.

58. The scene is included in Hoyt, *How They Won the War in the Pacific*, 417.

59. The letter is mentioned in a copy of an undated memorandum from Waldo Drake to Admiral Nimitz, Edward J. Long Papers, Box 3, NHHC (hereafter Long Papers).

60. The copy of Drake's memorandum to Nimitz included in Box 3, Long Papers omits the specific charges and responses. No copies of the full memorandum were found.

61. Austin Reminiscences, 282.

62. Ibid.

63. Ibid., 283.

64. Riley to Nimitz, October 2, 1944, Box 3, Long Papers.

65. Haller et al. to Nimitz, October 2, 1944, Box 3, Long Papers.

66. "Visitor," *Los Angeles Times*, October 9, 1944, 13.

67. Markey to Forrestal, October 3, 1944, Forrestal Correspondence, Box 119, NARA II.

68. Ibid.

69. The scene in Forrestal's office in this section is imagined and reconstructed by the author based on the subsequent letters from Forrestal and Duffield to Nimitz and

Markey as well as what is known about Forrestal's managerial style. Because there are no known records of this meeting, no quotations are used in this passage, but based on the documentary record, it is possible similar utterances were exchanged.

70. Miller oral history, 139.
71. Forrestal to Nimitz, October 10, 1944, Forrestal Correspondence, Box 119, NARA II.
72. Duffield to Markey, October 11, 1944, Forrestal Correspondence, Box 119, NARA II.
73. Townsend and Brinkley, *Driven Patriot*, 192.
74. From CINCPAC 202136 to SECNAV, October 21, 1944, Forrestal Correspondence, Box 119, NARA II.
75. Townsend and Brinkley, *Driven Patriot*, 192.
76. Memorandum from E. Crozier to Mr. Gates, May 26, 1944, Forrestal Correspondence, Box 119, NARA II.
77. "A Model Communique," *Tulsa World*, November 10, 1944, 8.
78. Klinkerman, "From Blackout at Pearl Harbor."
79. Jackall, *Moral Mazes*, 39.
80. Ibid., 195.
81. Ibid.
82. Townsend and Brinkley, *Driven Patriot*, 188.
83. Hone, *Mastering the Art of Command*, 354.
84. Jackall, *Moral Mazes*, 196.
85. Ibid.
86. Ibid., 194.
87. Hone, *Mastering the Art of Command*.
88. Hoyt, *How They Won the War in the Pacific*, 459.
89. Spicer, *Organizational Public Relations*.
90. Bill Henry, "By the Way," Report, *Los Angeles Times*, October 14, 1944, 9.
91. Duffield to Forrestal, December 23, 1944, Forrestal Correspondence, Box 119, NARA II.
92. The original letter from Nimitz to Drake, October 24, 1944, is included in the Scott Drake materials.
93. The citation is included in the Scott Drake materials.
94. James Bassett to Willie Bassett, March 2, 1945, Bassett Papers.

CHAPTER 10. AFTERMATH

1. "MacArthur Orders Ruthless Jap Prison Guards Arrested," *Greensboro Daily News*, November 9, 1945, 1.
2. Ibid.
3. "'Times' Writer, Back from Navy, to Cover Orient," *Los Angeles Times*, October 28, 1945, 15.
4. Potter, *Nimitz*, 407.
5. Ibid.

6. Ibid.

7. Dee Asher and David Asher, "Life Was Sometimes a Bit Frantic," *Santa Ana Register*, October 28, 1965, C7.

8. Letter from Capt. B. R. Boland to Mary Drake, April 6, 1978, Scott Drake materials.

9. The story is included in Jack Birns to Craig Sinclair, July 3, 1991.

10. Drake to Berry, May 11, 1942, Pacific Fleet PR Files, Box 5, NARA II.

11. Berry to Drake, May 21, 1942, Pacific Fleet PR Files, Box 5, NARA II.

12. Sato Masaharu, "'Negro Propaganda Operations': Japan's Short-Wave Radio Broadcasts for World War II Black Americans." *Historical Journal of Film, Radio and Television* 19, no. 1 (1999): 5–26.

13. Joel V. Berreman, "Assumptions About America in Japanese War Propaganda to the United States," *American Journal of Sociology* 54, no. 2 (1948): 117.

14. Klinkerman, "From Blackout at Pearl Harbor," 10.

15. Ibid., 11.

16. Casey, *The War Beat, Pacific*, 178.

17. Spicer, *Organizational Public Relations*, 140.

18. Miller oral history, 143.

19. The temporary citation is included in the Scott Drake materials.

Bibliography

Abend, Hallett. *Ramparts of the Pacific*. Garden City, NY: Doubleday, Doran and Company, Inc., 1941.

"About Public Relations." Public Relations Society of America. Accessed March 20, 2021. https://www.prsa.org/about/all-about-pr.

Arnot, Charles P. *Don't Kill the Messenger*. New York: Vantage Press, 1994.

Austin, Bernard L. Interview by Cdr. Paul L. Hooper, USNR (Ret.). 1971, U.S. Naval Institute, Annapolis, MD.

"An Autobiography by Robert Wallace Berry, Rear Admiral, United States Navy (Retired), 1978." Unpublished manuscript. Box 1, Robert Wallace Berry Papers, Hoover Institution Library and Archives, Stanford University, Stanford, CA.

Bassett, James Jr. Interview by Etta-Belle Kitchen. May 28, 1969. U.S. Naval Institute Oral History Collection. Annapolis, MD.

Bassett, James E., Jr. Papers, 1929–1977, George J. Mitchell Department of Special Collections and Archives, Bowdoin College Library, Brunswick, ME.

Bernays, Edward L. *Propaganda*. New York: Horace Liveright, 1928.

Berreman, Joel V. "Assumptions about America in Japanese War Propaganda to the United States." *American Journal of Sociology* 54, no. 2 (1948): 108–17.

Boomhower, Ray E. *Dispatches from the Pacific: The World War II Reporting of Robert L. Sherrod*. Bloomington: Indiana University Press, 2017.

Boomhower, Ray E. *One Shot: The World War II Photography of John A. Bushemi*. Indianapolis: Indiana Historical Society Press, 2004.

Boomhower, Ray E. *Richard Tregaskis: Reporting under Fire from Guadalcanal to Vietnam*. Albuquerque: University of New Mexico Press, 2021.

Bourgin, Simon. "Public Relations of Naval Expansion." *Public Opinion Quarterly* 3, no. 1 (January 1939): 113–17.

Buell, Thomas B. *Master of Seapower: A Biography of Fleet Admiral Ernest J. King*. Annapolis, MD: Naval Institute Press, 2012.

Carlson, Elliot. *Stanley Johnston's Blunder: The Reporter Who Spilled the Secret behind the US Navy's Victory at Midway*. Annapolis, MD: Naval Institute Press, 2017.

Casey, Robert J. *Torpedo Junction: With the Pacific Fleet from Pearl Harbor to Midway*. Indianapolis, IN: Bobbs-Merrill Company, 1942.

Casey, Steven. *The War Beat, Pacific: The American Media at War against Japan*. Oxford: Oxford University Press, 2021.

Command Summary of Fleet Admiral Chester W. Nimitz ("Graybook"). American Naval Records Society, 2012. https://www.ibiblio.org/anrs/graybook.html.

Crane, Conrad. Review of *Day of Deceit: The Truth about FDR and Pearl Harbor*, by Robert B. Stinnett. *Parameters* 31, no. 1 (2001).

Cunha, Irma Jeannette. "Problems of War Reporting in the Pacific." MA thesis, Stanford University, 1946.

Custer, Joe James. *Through the Perilous Night: The Astoria's Last Battle*. New York: Macmillan Co., 1944.

Dorwart, Jeffrey M. *Conflict of Duty: The U.S. Navy's Intelligence Dilemma, 1919–1945*. Annapolis, MD: Naval Institute Press, 1983.

Drabkin, Ron, and Bradley W. Hart. "Agent Shinkawa Revisited: The Japanese Navy's Establishment of the Rutland Intelligence Network in Southern California." *International Journal of Intelligence and Counter Intelligence* 35, no. 1 (2022): 31–56.

Drake, Waldo. "'I Don't Think They'd Be Such Damned Fools.'" In *Air Raid: Pearl Harbor! Recollections of a Day of Infamy*, edited by Paul Stillwell, 269. Annapolis, MD: Naval Institute Press, 1981.

———. Interview by James Bassett. April 26, 1973. Transcript. *Los Angeles Times* Records, Box 579. Huntington Library, Manuscript Collections. San Marino, CA.

———. Interview by Etta-Belle Kitchen. June 15, 1969. U.S. Naval Institute Oral History Collection. Annapolis, MD.

Driscoll, Joseph. *Pacific Victory 1945*. Philadelphia, PA: J. B. Lippincott Company, 1944.

Frankel, Lillian Berson, ed. *Scrapbook of Real-Life Stories for Young People: The Best from the Newspapers*. New York: Sterling Publishing Co., Inc., 1958.

Grant, David, Cynthia Hardy, Cliff Oswick, and Linda L. Putnam, eds. *The Sage Handbook of Organizational Discourse*. Thousand Oaks, CA: Sage, 2004.

Grunig, James E., and Larissa Schneider Grunig. "Toward a Theory of the Public Relations Behavior of Organizations: Review of a Program of Research." *Journal of Public Relations Research* 1, no. 1–4 (1989): 27–63.

Guard, Harold, and John Tring. *The Pacific War Uncensored: A War Correspondent's Unvarnished Account of the Fight against Japan*. Havertown, PA: Casemate, 2011.

Halsey, William F. III, and J. Bryan. *Admiral Halsey's Story*. New York: McGraw-Hill, 1947.

Harris, Brayton. *Admiral Nimitz: The Commander of the Pacific Ocean Theater*. New York: St. Martin's Press, 2012.

Harsch, Joseph C. *At the Hinge of History: A Reporter's Story*. Athens: University of Georgia Press, 1993.

———. "A War Correspondent's Story." In *Air Raid: Pearl Harbor! Recollections of a Day of Infamy*, edited by Paul Stillwell. Annapolis, MD: Naval Institute Press, 1981.

Hayashi, Brian Masaru. "Frank Knox's Fifth Column in Hawai'i: The U.S. Navy, the Japanese, and the Pearl Harbor Attack." *Journal of American-East Asian Relations* 7, no. 2 (2020): 142–68.

Healy, George William. *A Lifetime on Deadline: Self-Portrait of a Southern Journalist*. New Orleans: Pelican Publishing, 1976.

Hillenbrand, Laura. *Unbroken: A World War II Story of Survival, Resilience, and Redemption*. New York: Random House, 2010.

"History of Navy Public Affairs." U.S. Navy Public Affairs Association. Accessed May 25, 2023. https://www.usnpaa.org/history-of-navy-public-affairs.html.

Hone, Trent. *Mastering the Art of Command: Admiral Chester W. Nimitz and Victory*. Annapolis, MD: Naval Institute Press, 2022.

Hoyt, Edwin. *How They Won the War in the Pacific: Nimitz and His Admirals*. Lanham, MD: Rowman and Littlefield, 2011.

Hughes, Jim W. *Eugene Smith: Shadow and Substance: The Life and Work of an American Photographer*. New York: McGraw-Hill, 1989.

Jackall, Robert. *Moral Mazes: The World of Corporate Managers*. Oxford: Oxford University Press, 1988.

Jackson, Robert H. Papers, 1816–1983. Library of Congress, Manuscript Division, Washington, DC.

Jordan, Robert Smith. *A Newsman Remembered: Ralph Burdette Jordan and His Times 1896–1953*. iUniverse, 2011.

Karsten, Peter. *The Naval Aristocracy: The Golden Age of Annapolis and the Emergence of Modern American Navalism*. Annapolis, MD: Naval Institute Press, 1972.

King, Ernest J. Official Papers of Fleet Admiral Ernest J. King. Microfilm. Wilmington, DE.

Klinkerman, Robert D. "From Blackout at Pearl Harbor to Spotlight on Tokyo Bay: A Study of the Evolution in U.S. Navy Public Relations Policies and Practices." MA thesis, University of Wisconsin, 1972.

Knox, Frank. Papers, 1898–1954. Library of Congress, Manuscript Division, Washington, DC.

La Forte, Robert S., and Ronald E. Marcello, eds. *Remembering Pearl Harbor: Eyewitness Accounts by U.S. Military Men and Women*. Wilmington, DE: SR Books, 1991.

Loureiro, Pedro A. "Japanese Espionage and American Countermeasures in Pre–Pearl Harbor California." *Journal of American-East Asian Relations* 3, no. 3 (1994): 197–210.

———. "The Imperial Japanese Navy and Espionage: The Itaru Tachibana Case." *International Journal of Intelligence and CounterIntelligence* 3, no. 1 (1989): 105–21.

Macnamara, Jim. "Journalism–PR Relations Revisited: The Good News, the Bad News, and Insights into Tomorrow's News." *Public Relations Review* 40, no. 5 (2014): 739–50.

Mander, Mary S. *Pen and Sword: American War Correspondents, 1898–1975*. Urbana: University of Illinois Press, 2010.

Marshall, Judi. "Viewing Organizational Communication from a Feminist Perspective: A Critique and Some Offerings." In *Communication Yearbook 16*, edited by Stanley A. Deetz. Newbury Park, CA: Sage, 1993.

Masaharu, Sato. "'Negro Propaganda Operations': Japan's Short-Wave Radio Broadcasts for World War II Black Americans." *Historical Journal of Film, Radio and Television* 19, no. 1 (1999): 5–26.

McCallum, John Martin III. "Democratic Violence and the Transformation of American Moral Sentiments in the 'Good War.'" PhD dissertation, University of Chicago, 2017.

———. "US Censorship, Violence, and Moral Judgement in a Wartime Democracy, 1941–1945." *Diplomatic History* 41, no. 3 (2017): 543–66.

McCollum, Arthur H. Interview by John T. Mason Jr. December 1970 through March 1971. Volume 1, U.S. Naval Institute Oral History Collection. Annapolis, MD.

Mercer, Preston V. Interviewed by John T. Mason Jr. October 18, 1969. U.S. Naval Institute Oral History Collection. Annapolis, MD.

Miller, Harold B. Interviewed by John T. Mason Jr. April 1981 through September 1981. U.S. Naval Institute Oral History Collection. Annapolis, MD.

Mitchell, Gordon R. "Team B Intelligence Coups." *Quarterly Journal of Speech* 92, no. 2 (2006): 144–73.

Myers, Michael W. *The Pacific War and Contingent Victory: Why Japanese Defeat Was Not Inevitable*. Lawrence: University Press of Kansas, 2015.

Potter, Elmer Belmont. *Nimitz*. Annapolis, MD: Naval Institute Press, 2013.

"PRSA Code of Ethics." Public Relations Society of America. Accessed March 20, 2021. https://www.prsa.org/about/prsa-code-of-ethics.

Reynolds Clark G. *Admiral John H. Towers: The Struggle for Naval Air Supremacy*. Annapolis, MD: Naval Institute Press, 2017.

Seeger, Matthew W. "Best Practices in Crisis Communication: An Expert Panel Process." *Journal of Applied Communication Research* 34, no. 3 (2006): 232–44.

Siebert, Fredrick S. "Federal Information Agencies—An Outline." *Journalism and Mass Communication Quarterly* 19, no. 1 (1942): 28–33.

Spicer, Christopher. *Organizational Public Relations: A Political Perspective*. New York: Routledge, 2013.

Stillwell, Paul, ed. *Air Raid, Pearl Harbor! Recollections of a Day of Infamy*. Annapolis, MD: Naval Institute Press, 1981.

Symonds, Craig L. *Nimitz at War: Command Leadership from Pearl Harbor to Tokyo Bay*. Oxford: Oxford University Press, 2022.

Taylor, Bryan C. "Organizing the 'Unknown Subject': Los Alamos, Espionage, and the Politics of Biography." *Quarterly Journal of Speech* 88, no. 1 (2002): 33–49.

Toll, Ian W. *Twilight of the Gods: War in the Western Pacific, 1944–1945*. New York: W. W. Norton and Company: 2020.

Townsend, Hoopes, and Douglas Brinkley. *Driven Patriot: The Life and Times of James Forrestal*. Annapolis, MD: Naval Institute Press, 2012.

Tregaskis, Richard. *Guadalcanal Diary*. Eau Claire, WI: E. M. Hale and Company, 1943.

Tremaine, Frank. Interview by Richard Byrd, March 18, 1995. National Museum of the Pacific War Oral History Collection, Fredericksburg, TX.

Tremaine, Frank, and Kay Tremaine. *The Attack on Pearl Harbor: By Two Who Were There*. Fredericksburg, TX: Admiral Nimitz Foundation, 1997.

Twomey, Steve. *Countdown to Pearl Harbor: The Twelve Days to the Attack*. New York: Simon and Schuster, 2017.

Wadle, Ryan D. *Selling Sea Power: Public Relations and the US Navy, 1917–1941*. Norman: University of Oklahoma Press, 2019.

———. "Straight Naval Information Is Our Function." *Naval History Magazine* 36, no. 1 (2022).

Wagner, Rob Leicester. *Red Ink, White Lies: The Rise and Fall of Los Angeles Newspapers, 1920–1962*. Columbia, CA: Dragonflyer Press, 2000.

Wheeler, Keith, *The Pacific Is My Beat*. New York: E. P. Dutton and Company, Inc., 1944.

Wilsbacher, Greg. "Al Brick: The Forgotten Newsreel: Man at Pearl Harbor." *Moving Image* 10, no. 2, (Fall 2010). https://link.gale.com/apps/doc/A247740418/AONE?u=google scholar&sid=sitemap&xid=529e75bb.

Wright, Donald K. "History and Development of Public Relations Education in North America: A Critical Analysis." *Journal of Communication Management* 15, no. 3 (2011): 236–55.

Zacharias, Ellis M. *Secret Missions: The Story of an Intelligence Officer*. New York: G. P. Putnam's Sons, 1946.

Index

About the Author

Hamilton Bean, PhD, MBA, APR, is a professor in the Department of Communication at the University of Colorado Denver. He also serves as director of the University of Colorado Denver's International Studies Program. He specializes in the study of communication and security. He has applied communication theory to the study of extremism, counterterrorism, disinformation, intelligence, public diplomacy, and resilience. He has earned multiple awards for scholarship from the National Communication Association.